A TREATISE ON
MIND

VOLUME 5

An Esoteric Exposition of the

Bardo Thödol

PART B

The Natural State of Mind

Other Titles in the Series

The I Concept

Volume 1: The 'Self' or 'Non-Self' in Buddhism

Volume 2: Considerations of Mind - A Buddhist Enquiry

Volume 3: The Buddha-Womb and the Way to Liberation

Cellular Consciousness

Volume 4: Maṇḍalas - Their Nature and Development

Volume 5: An Esoteric Exposition of the Bardo Thödol (Part A)

The Way to Shambhala

Volume 6: Meditation and the Initiation Process

Volume 7: The Constitution of Shambhala

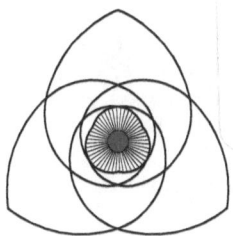

VOLUME FIVE

An Esoteric Exposition of the

Bardo Thödol

PART B

The Natural State of Mind

BODO BALSYS

UNIVERSAL DHARMA
PUBLICATIONS
SYDNEY, AUSTRALIA

ISBN 978-0-9923568-8-0

2nd Edition, 2025

Āḥ!

Homage to the Lord of Shambhala.
Inconceivable, inconceivable, beyond thought
Is the bejewelled crown of this most excelled Jina.
He whose Eye has taught many Buddhas.
And who will anoint the myriad,
that in the future lives will come.
As I bow to His Feet my Heart's afire.
Oh, this bliss, this love for my Lord
can barely be borne on my part.
It takes flight as the might of the Dove.
The flight of serene *nirvāṇic* embrace.
The flight of Light so bright.
The flight of Love so active tonight.
The flight of enlightenment for all to come to
their mind's Heart's attire.

Obeisance to the Gurus!
To the Buddhas of the three times.
To the Council of Bodhisattvas, *mahāsattvas*.
To them I pledge allegiance.

Oṁ Hūṁ! Hūṁ! Hūṁ!

Dedication

Thanks to my students, past, present and future, and in particular to those that have helped in the production of this Treatise.

Oṁ

Acknowledgments

Special thanks to Angie O'Sullivan, Kylie Smith,
and Ruth Fitzpatrick
for their tireless efforts in making this
series possible.

Oṁ

Contents

Preface....ix
1. The Bardo Thödol and the Natural State of Mind....
The Centres above the Diaphragm....1
Synonyms for Mind....1
Attributes of Mind and the Throat centre....19
The four major petals of the Throat centre....31
Attributes of Mind and the Heart centre....39
The forty-two Peaceful Deities....46
The cycles of 'seven days' of experience....55
2. The Bardo Thödol and the Natural State of Mind....
Major Influences below the Diaphragm....62
Mind and the seven Rays....62
The phenomena of Mind and the Jinas....67
The Mind and the Diaphragm centre....70
Mind and the *tathāgatagarbha*....76
Mind and Splenic centre I....86
The three times in one....98
3. Mind and the Īśvarī....103
Mind and the twenty-eight theriomorphic female deities....103
Mind and the Solar Plexus centre....113
Mind and the Sacral centre....121
The seven Rays and the centres below the diaphragm....129
Mind and the left Gonad centre....138
Mind and the right Gonad centre....147
4. Culmination of the Awakening of Mind....154
The natural liberation of mind....154
The twelve petals of the Head lotus....157
Summary of the petals of the Throat centre....170
Summary of the petals of the Heart centre....176
Conclusion....183
Bibliography....193
Index....195

Figures

Figure 1. The petals of the Throat centre....22
Figure 2. The four major petals of the Throat centre....32
Figure 3: Splenic centre I and Meditation....92

Preface

This treatise investigates Buddhist ideas concerning what mind is and how it relates to a concept of a 'self'. It is principally a study of the complex interrelationship between mind and phenomena, from the gross to the subtle—the physical, psychic, supersensory and supernal. This entails an explanation of how mind incorporates all phenomena in its *modus operandi,* and how eventually that mind is liberated from it, thereby becoming awakened. Thus the treatise explores the manner in which the corporeally orientated, concretised, intellectual mind eventually becomes transformed into the Clear Light of the abstracted Mind; a super-mind, a Buddha-Mind.

A Treatise on Mind is arranged in seven volumes, divided into three subsections. These are as follows:

The I Concept
Volume 1. *The 'Self' or 'Non-self' in Buddhism.*
Volume 2. *Considerations of Mind—A Buddhist Enquiry.*
Volume 3. *The Buddha-Womb and the Way to Liberation.*

Cellular Consciousness
Volume 4. *Maṇḍalas - Their Nature and Development.*
Volume 5. *An Esoteric Exposition of the Bardo Thödol.*
(This volume is published in two parts)

The Way to Shambhala
Volume 6. *Meditation and the Initiation Process.*
Volume 7. *The Constitution of Shambhala.*

The I Concept represents a necessary extensive revision[1] of a large work formerly published in one volume. Together the three volumes investigate the question of what a 'self' is and is not. This involves an analysis of the nature of consciousness, and the consciousness-stream of a human unit developing as a continuum through time. It will illustrate exactly what directs such a stream and how its *karma* is arranged so that enlightenment is the eventual outcome.

The first volume analyses Prāsaṅgika lines of reasoning, such as the 'Refutation of Partless Particles', and 'The Sevenfold Reasoning' in order to derive a clear deduction as to whether a 'self' exists, and if so what its limitations are, and if not, then what the alternative may be. The analysis resolves the historically vexing question of how—if there is no 'self'—can there be a continuity of mind that is coherently connected in an evolutionary manner through multiple rebirths.[2] In order to arrive at this explanation, many of the basic assumptions of Mahāyāna Buddhism, such as Dependent Origination and the Two Truths, are critically analysed.

The second volume provides an in-depth analysis of what mind is, how it relates to the concept of the Void *(śūnyatā),* and the evolution of consciousness. The analysis utilises Yogācāra-Vijñānavādin philosophy in order to comprehend the major attributes of mind, the *saṃskāras* that condition it, and the laws by means of which it operates.

The enquiry into the nature of what an 'I' is requires comprehension of the properties of the dual nature of mind, which consists of an empirical and abstract, enlightened part. As a means of doing this, the *ālayavijñāna* (the store of consciousness-attributes) is explored, alongside the entire philosophy of the 'eight consciousnesses' of this School.

Volume three focuses on the I-Consciousness and the subtle body, by first utilising a minor Tantra, *The Great Gates of Diamond Liberation,* to investigate the nature of the Heart centre and its functions, then the

---

1 The book was inadequately edited hence contains many errors and grammatical mistakes that have been corrected in this treatise.

2 My earlier work *Karma and the Rebirth of Consciousness* (Munshiram Manoharlal, Delhi, 2006) lays the background for this basic question.

chakras below the diaphragm. This is necessary to lay the foundation for the topics that will be the subject of the later volumes of this treatise concerning the nature of meditation, the construction of *maṇḍalas,* and the yoga of the *Bardo Thödol.*

The focus then shifts to investigate where the idea of a self-sustaining I-concept or 'Soul-form' may be found in Buddhist philosophy, given the denial of substantial self-existence prioritised in the philosophy of Emptiness. Following this, the pertinent chapters of the *Ratnagotravibhāga Śastra* are examined in detail so that a proper conclusion to the investigation can be obtained via the *buddhadharma.* This concerns an analysis of how the *ālayavijñāna* is organised, such that the rebirth process is possible for each human consciousness-stream, taking into account the *karma* that will eventually make each human unit a Buddha. In relation to this the ontological nature of the *tathāgatagarbha* (the Buddha-Womb) must be carefully analysed, as well as the organising principle of consciousness represented by the *chakras.* I thus establish that there is a form that appears upon the domain of the abstract Mind. I call this the Sambhogakāya Flower. The final two chapters of this volume principally define its characteristics.

The second subsection, *Cellular Consciousness,* is divided into two parts. Volume four deals with the question of what exactly constitutes a 'cell', metaphysically. The cell is viewed as a unit of consciousness that interrelates with other cells to form *maṇḍalas* of expression. Each such cell can be considered a form of 'self' that has a limited, though valid, body of expression. It is born, sustains a form of activity, and consequently dies when it outlives its usefulness. This mode of analysis is extended to include the myriad forms manifest in the world of phenomena known as *saṃsāra,* including the existence and functioning of *chakras.*

Volume five deals with the formative forces and evolutionary processes governing the prime cells (that is, *maṇḍalas* of expression), and the phenomenon that governs an entire world-sphere of evolutionary attainment. This is explored via an in-depth exposition of the *Bardo Thödol* and its 42 Peaceful and 58 Wrathful Deities. The text also incorporates a detailed exposition concerning the transformation of *saṃskāras* (consciousness-attributes developed through all past forms of activity) into enlightenment. The entire path of liberation enacted by a *yogin* via the principles of meditation, forms of concentration, and related techniques *(tapas, dhāraṇīs)* is explained. In doing so, the soteriological purpose of the various wrathful and theriomorphic deities is revealed. This volume is published in two parts. Part A explores chapter 5 of the *Bardo Thödol* concerning the transformation of *saṃskāras* via meditating upon the Peaceful and Wrathful Deities. This necessitates sound knowledge of the force centres (*chakras*) and the way their powers (*siddhis*) awaken. Part B deals with the gain of such transformations and the consequence of conversion of the attributes of the empirical mind into the liberated abstract Mind.

The third subsection, *The Way to Shambhala*, is also in two parts. They present an eclectic revelation of esoteric information integrating the main Eastern and Western religions. Volume six is a treatise on meditation and the Initiation process.[3] The meditation practice is directed towards the needs of individuals living within the context of our modern societies.

Volume six also includes a discussion of the path of Initiation as the means of gaining liberation from *saṃsāra*. The teaching in Volume five concerning the conversion of *saṃskāras* is supplementary to this path. The path of Initiation *is* the way to Shambhala. As many will choose to consciously undergo the precepts needed to undertake Initiation in the future, this invokes the necessity of providing much more revelatory information concerning this kingdom than has been provided hitherto.

How Shambhala is organised is the subject of Volume seven, which details the constitution of the Hierarchy of enlightened being[4] (the Council of Bodhisattvas). It illustrates how the presiding Lords who govern planetary evolution manifest. This detailed philosophy rests on the foundation of the information provided in all of the previous volumes, and necessitates a proper comprehension of the nature of the five Dhyāni Buddhas. To do so the awakening of the meditation-Mind, which is the objective of *A Treatise on Mind*, is essential.

---

3 The word Initiation is capitalised throughout the series of books to add emphasis to the fact that it is the process that makes one divine, liberated. It is the expression of divinity manifesting upon the planetary and cosmic landscape.

4 The word 'being' here is not pluralised because though this Hierarchy is constituted of a multiplicity of beings, together they represent one 'Being', one integral awakened Entity.

How to engage with this text

In this investigation many new ways of viewing conventional Buddhist arguments and rhetoric shall be pursued to develop the pure logic of the reader's mind, and to awaken revelations from their abstract Mind. New insights into the far-reaching light of the *dharma* will be revealed, which will form a basis for the illustration of an esoteric view that supersedes the bounds of conventionally accepted views. Readers should therefore analyse all arguments for themselves to discern the validity of what is presented. Such enquiry allows one to ascertain for oneself, what is logical and truthful, thus overcoming the blind acceptance of a certain dogma or line of reasoning that is otherwise universally accepted as correct. Only that which is discovered within each inquiring mind should be accepted. The remainder should, however, not be automatically discarded, but rather kept aside for later analysis when more data is available—unless the logic is obviously flawed, in which case it should be abandoned. There is no claim to infallibility in the information and arguments presented in this treatise, however, they are designed to offer scope for further meditation and enquiry by the earnest reader. If errors are found through impeccable logic, then the dialectical process may proceed. We can then accept or reject the new thesis and move forward, such that the evolution of human thought progresses, until we all stand enlightened.

This treatise hopes to assist that dialectical evolution by analysing major aspects of the *buddhadharma* as it exists and is taught today, to try to examine where errors may lie, or where the present modes of interpretation fall short of the true intended meaning. The aim is also to elaborate aspects of the *dharma* that could only be hinted at or cursorily explained by the wise ones of the past, because the basis for proper elaboration had not then been established. This analysis of *buddhadharma* will try to rectify some of the past inadequacies in order to explore and extend the *dharma* into arenas rarely investigated.

There will always be obstinate and dogmatic ones that staunchly cling to established views. This produces a reactive malaise in current Buddhist ontological and metaphysical thought. However, amongst the many practitioners of the *dharma* there are also those who have clarified their minds sufficiently to verify truth in whatever form it is presented, and will follow it at all costs to enlightenment. The Council of Bodhisattvas heartily seek such worthy ones. The signposts or guides upon the way to enlightenment have changed through the centuries, and contemporary practitioners of the *dharma* have yet to learn to clearly interpret the new directions. The guide books are now being written and many must come forth to understand and practice correctly.

If full comprehension of such guide books is achieved, those *dharma* practitioners yearning to become Bodhisattvas would rapidly become spiritually enlightened. Here is a rhyme and reason *for* Buddhism. The actual present dearth of enlightened beings informs us that little that is read is properly understood. The esoteric view presented in this treatise hopes to rectify this problem, so as to create better thinkers along the Bodhisattva way.

The numbers of Buddhists are growing in the world, thus Buddhism needs a true restorative flowering to rival that of the renaissance of debate and innovative thinkers of the early post-Nāgārjunian era. In order to achieve this it must synthesise the present wealth of scientific knowledge, alongside the best of the Western world's philosophical output.

Currently the *buddhadharma* is presented as an external body of knowledge held by the Buddha, Rinpoches, monks and lay teachers. This encourages practitioners to hero worship these figures and to heed many unenlightened utterances from such teachers, based on a belief system that encourages people to *uncritically* listen to them and adopt their views. When enlightened teachers *do appear* and find consolidated reasons for firing spiritual bullets for the cause of the enlightenment of humanity, then all truth can and will be known. The present lack of inwardly perceived knowledge from the fount of the *dharmakāya* on the part of many teachers blocks the production of an arsenal of weapons for solving the problems of suffering in the world. Few see little beyond the scope of vision in what they have been indoctrinated to believe, allowing for only rudimentary truths to be understood. While for the great majority this suffices, it is woefully inadequate for those genuinely seeking Bodhisattvahood and enlightenment. The cost to humanity in not being given an enlightened answer as to the nature of awakening, is profound.

We must go to the awakening of the Head lotus to find the most established reasoning powers. Without the 1,000 petals of the *sahasrāra padma* ablaze then there is little substance for proper understanding, little ability to hold the mind steady in the dynamic field of revelation that the *dharmakāya* represents. How can the unenlightened properly understand Buddhist scriptures, when there is little (revelation) coming from the Head centres of such beings? Much still needs to be taught concerning the way of awakening this lotus, and to help fill the lack is a major purpose of *A Treatise on Mind.*

Those who intend to reach enlightenment must go beyond the narrow sectarian allegiances promoted by many strands of contemporary Buddhism. Buddhism itself unfolded in a dialectical context with other heterodox Indian (and Chinese, etc.) traditions, and prospered on account of those engagements. When one sees the unfolding of enlightened wisdom in such a fashion, the particular information from specific schools of thought may be synthesised into a greater whole. Each school has various qualities and types of argument to resolve weaknesses in the opposing stream of thought. This highlights that there are particular aspects in each that may be right or wrong, or neither wholly right or wrong. Through this process we can find better answers, or if need be, create a new lineage or religion which is expressive of a synthesis of the various schools of thought.

The Buddha did not categorically reject the orthodox Indian religio-philosophical ideas of his time, nor did he simply accept them—he reformed them. He preserved the elements that he found to be true, and rejected those 'wrong views' which lead to moral and spiritual impairment. If the existing system needs reformation it becomes part of a Bodhisattva's meditation. The way a reforming Buddha incarnates is dependent on how he must fit into such a system. Thus he is essentially an outsider incarnating into it to demonstrate the new type of ideas he chooses to elaborate. If there is a lot of dogmatic resistance to the presented doctrine of truth, then a new religion is founded. If there is some acceptance then we see reformation. There is always room for improvement, to march forward closer to enlightenment's goal, be it for an individual or for a wisdom-religion as a whole. There is a need for reform throughout the religious world today.

By way of a hermeneutical strategy fit for this task, we ought look no further than the Buddha himself. The Buddha proposed that all students of the *dharma* should make their investigations through the *Four Points of Refuge*. These are:

1. The doctrine is one's point of refuge, not a person.
2. The meaning is one's point of refuge, not the letter.
3. The sacred texts whose meaning is defined are one's point of refuge, to those whose meaning needs definition.
4. Direct awareness is one's point of refuge, not discursive awareness.[5]

These four points can be summarised or rephrased as: the doctrine (*dharma*), true or esoteric meaning, right definition, and direct awareness are one's point of refuge, not adherence to sectarian bias, semantics, the dialectics of non-fully enlightened commentaries, or to illogical assertions. What may be long held to be truthful, but is not, upon proper analytical dissection, needs rectifying. Also, in other cases, a doctrine or teaching may indeed be correct, but the current interpretation leaves much to be desired, and hence should be reinterpreted from the position of a more embracive or esoteric view.

Hopefully this presentation finds welcoming minds that will carefully analyse it in line with their own understandings of the issues, and as a consequence build up a better understanding of the nature of what constitutes the path to enlightenment. Their way of walking as Bodhisattvas should be enriched as a consequence.

For a guide to understanding the pronunciation of Sanskrit words, please visit our website.

http://universaldharma.com/resources/pronounce-sanskrit/

Our online esoteric glossary also provides definitions for most of the terms used in this treatise.

http://universaldharma.com/resources/esoteric-glossary/

---

5 Griffith, P.J., *On Being Buddha, The Classical Doctrine of Buddhahood*, (Sri Satguru Publications, New Delhi, 1995), 52.

My eyes do weep as I stare into this troubled world,
For I dare not place my Heart in my brother's keep.
He would grapple that Heart with hands so rough
So as to destroy the fabric of its delicate stuff.
Oh to give, to give, my Heart does yearn,
But humanity must its embracive,
Humbling, pervasive scene yet to learn.
To destroy and tear with avarice they know,
But little care to sensitive rapture they show.
How to give its blood is my constant fare,
For that Love to bestow upon their Hearts I bemoan.
But they hide their Hearts behind mental-emotional walls.
No matter how one prods these walls won't fall,
So much belittling emotional self-concern prop their bastions.
Oh, how my eyes do weep as I stare.
I stare at their fearsome malls and halls.
That lock Love out from all their abodes
And do keep them trapped in realms of woe.

Oṁ Maṇi Padme Hūṁ

Guru Rinpoche as the King of Sahor

1

The Bardo Thödol and the Natural State of Mind

The Centres above the Diaphragm

Synonyms for Mind

The fourth chapter of the *Bardo Thödol* provides an integral component to the teachings regarding the Peaceful and Wrathful Deities, allowing practitioners to comprehend the natural state of Mind, of which these deities are an expression. Full quotations from the relevant texts shall be provided, allowing a proper hermeneutic elucidation. The version of *The Book of the Dead* translated by Gyurme Dorje entitled 'The Introduction to Awareness: Natural Liberation through Naked Perception'[1] shall be used and correlated when necessary with the translation from W.Y. Evans-Wentz's memorial pioneering work from a section entitled: 'Here follows the [yoga] of knowing the mind, the seeing of Reality, from "The Profound Doctrine of Self-Liberation by Meditating upon the Peaceful and Wrathful Deities"'.[2] Being a yoga, the objective of the practice is to develop the 'naked perception' of Mind, where theoretical comprehension is the first step. This text is part of the Nyingma tradition that is said to be originally written by Padmasambhava, and as such falls under the auspices of the Yogācāra-Mādhyamika philosophy.

The text in Gyurme's translation starts with:

1 Gyurme Dorje, Trans., *The Tibetan Book of the Dead: The Great Liberation by Hearing in the Intermediate States*, (Penguin Books, London, 2005), 35.

2 Evans-Wentz, W.Y. *The Tibetan Book of the Great Liberation*, (Oxford University Press, London, 1954), 193-240.

> Homage to the deities [embodying] the three buddha-bodies, who are the natural radiance of awareness.
>
> [Here], I shall present the teaching [known as] *The Introduction to Awareness: Natural Liberation through Naked Perception,* [which is an extract] from the *Peaceful and Wrathful Deities: A Profound Sacred Teaching, [entitled] Natural Liberation through [Recognition of] Enlightened Intention.* Thus, shall I introduce [to you the nature of] intrinsic awareness. So contemplate it well, O Fortunate Child of Buddha nature.
> SAMAYA *rgya rgya rgya*[3]

We begin with an homage to the victorious Ones that manifest via a *dharmakāya, sambhogakāya* and *nirmāṇakāya* of a Buddha. Such Ones embody the one all-pervasive Mind, which is the objective of this text to explain. In referring to the *nirmāṇakāya* there is a veiled reference for the serious practitioner to seek out such a One (the incarnation of a qualified enlightened teacher) for instruction. The complete *maṇḍala* of Peaceful and Wrathful deities can then be revealed in consciousness. The 'profound sacred teaching' shall henceforth follow.

The Buddha nature referred to is the *tathāgatagarbha,* which I have explained in terms of the Sambhogakāya Flower in Volume 3 of this treatise. The implication therefore is that these teachings are principally for Initiates who are yet to gain Buddhahood by mastering the attributes rayed down into the meditating one by this Flower via the Head lotus and *nāḍī* system. (As explained later in this volume.)

The meaning of the concluding mantra is explained by Evans-Wentz:

> This *mantra* indicates that the teachings about to be given are too profound and esoteric to be taught to, or comprehended by, any save *yogically* purified and disciplined disciples. The reference to the disciples as being blessed, or *karmically* fortunate, confirms this. The treatise before us may, therefore, be regarded as appertaining to the Secret Lore of the *Gurus.* In the eyes of initiated Tibetans of this School, the *mantra* itself is equivalent to a seal of secrecy placed upon these teachings. Sometimes, in some of the esoteric manuscripts, the seal of secrecy takes the form of a carefully drawn double *dorje,* perhaps in colour, such as appears on the cover of this volume...The Sanskrit

3 Gyurme, 38.

> *Samayā* of our text corresponds to the Tibetan form *Tog-pa (Rtogs-pa),* meaning 'thorough perception', 'infallible knowledge', 'complete realization of Truth'. It also means 'self-realization', or 'self-knowledge'. *Tog-pa* cannot be thoroughly comprehended without practice of *yoga.* The first step consists in comprehending *Tog-pa* intellectually; the second, in deepening or expanding this comprehension by study; the third, in meditating upon *Tog-pa;* and the fourth, in fully comprehending it, such complete comprehension being equivalent to the realization of Buddhahood, or *Nirvāṇa.* The thrice-repeated *gya (rgya)* is a Tibetan expression literally translated as 'vast'. The *mantra* may, therefore, be rendered as 'Vast, vast, vast is Divine Wisdom'.[4]

The term *samaya* (Tib. dam tshig) is also a sacred commitment or pledge in Tantricism. It means literally, 'coming together', thus *samaya* pledges the coming together of the divinity with the (traditional) representative image, the sacrificial offering embodying the divinity, or with the *yogin* or faithful worshipper who is one-pointedly focussed upon deity.

We begin with the section entitled 'The Importance of the Introduction to Awareness'. The associated text is:

EMAHO!

1. Though the single [nature of] mind, which completely pervades both cyclic existence and nirvāṇa,

   Has been naturally present from the beginning, you have not recognised it.

2. Even though its radiance and awareness have never been interrupted,

   You have not yet encountered its true face.

3. Even though it arises unimpededly in every facet [of existence],

   You have not as yet recognised [this single nature of mind].

4. In order that this [single] nature might be recognised by you,

   The Conquerors of the three times have taught an inconceivably [vast number of practices],

   Including the eighty-four thousand aspects of the [sacred] teachings.

---

4 Evans-Wentz, footnote, 202-203.

5. Yet, [despite this diversity], not even one of these [teachings] has been given by the Conquerors,

   Outside the context of an understanding of this nature!

6. [And even] though there are inestimable volumes of sacred writings, equally vast as the limits of space,

   Actually, [these teachings can be succinctly expressed in] a few words, which are the introduction to awareness.

7. Here [is] the direct [face to face] introduction

   To the enlightened intention of the Conquerors.

8. Here is the method for entering [into actual reality],

   [In this very moment], without reference to past or future [events].[5]

These general introductory statements concerning the single nature of Mind have a direct reference to the eight arms of the cross of direction in space. They present an overview of the mode of deliverance of this teaching of Mind via these directions, presenting the past, present and future methods as outlined below.

We start with the mantra *e-ma-ho,* which Evans-Wentz states is an 'interjection, commonly occurring in the religious literature of Tibet, expressive of compassion for all living creatures. In this context, it is to be regarded as being the *guru's* invocation addressed to the Buddhas and *Bodhisattvas* in super-human realms that They may telepathically bestow upon the disciples Their divine grace and guidance'.[6] All serious well-endowed practitioners receive such ear-whispered instructions to guide them esoterically upon the meditation path to liberation.

1. The *northeast* direction is that of 'unity'. It integrates the incoming factors which are to play a role in the *maṇḍalic* expression. In this case it is the *dharmakāyic* Mind that pervades all of space, incorporating the *śūnyatā-saṃsāra* integration. The first phrase also refers to the beginning of things, thus of the establishment of universal *karma,* as was explained in Volume 4, chapter 3 of this series ('Examination of Chaos and the Void'). We are told that this Mind has always existed, it only needs to be recognised.

5 Gyurme, 38-39. I have added the numbers to facilitate explanation.

6 Evans-Wentz, 203, footnote 5.

2. The *eastern* direction refers to the way inwards to the Heart of Life. It therefore refers to when the Heart centre is established and that which can be considered the Life's Blood of the *maṇḍala* can circulate. Such would normally be interpreted in terms of the *prāṇas* that produce liberation. Here they signify the natural emanation of this Mind, viewed in terms of its luminosity or radiance and lucid awareness as expressed throughout the *maṇḍala*.

   The reference to the 'true face' is not just a figure of speech, but literally refers to the seven facial orifices: two eyes, two ears, two nostrils and a mouth. They signify the septenaric nature of the conveyance of Mind into manifestation. This is signified also by the cycles of seven days of the *Bardo Thödol*, the seven main *chakras*, and the seven planes of perception. Quite an extensive philosophy could be elaborated here if one wished.

3. Next we have the *southeast* direction of 'expression', where the needed characteristics are seeded into the matrix of the *maṇḍala (saṃsāra)*. It thus arises 'unimpededly in every facet [of existence]'. The entire gamut of evolutionary development of mind and its eventual conversion into Mind must now be accomplished (associated with the rest of the arms of this cross) so that this single nature of Mind can be recognised.

4. The direction that now confronts us is *south*, wherein the deepest immersion into *saṃsāra* is manifest. We thus have the sum of the interrelations that incarnation brings. Here is found the activity of the Buddhas of 'the three times', of the past (Dīpaṅkara), present (Gautama) and future (Maitreya). They are the conquerors of *saṃsāra*, the Buddhas that come to educate us all with the symbolic 'eighty-four thousand' doctrines, thereby guiding us away from bondage. When analysing a large number such as eighty-four thousand, the zeros simply imply a vast proportion, literally that which awakens the 1,000 petalled lotus. The real implication is veiled in the number 84 = 7 x 12. Here (again) we have the septenaries of life implied, ordered according to the way the twelve petals of the Heart centre (with their zodiacal implications) unfold. These seven Ray attributes are multiplied by the way of activity of the

Heart centre, so that inevitably the twelve major petals of the Head centre are awakened. Literally this is the 'Door of the *Dharma*'.[7] Within this unfoldment is veiled the development of the sum of the *saṃskāras* and attributes of mind; and the way they are transformed into enlightenment-attributes.

5. We now move to the *southwest* arm of this cross, entitled 'understanding'. This relates to what is gained through experiencing *saṃsāra*. The text simply informs us that no matter what these Buddhas have taught, all such teachings are within the context of the transformation of the attributes developed by mind into those of Mind. The understanding then concerns what constitutes the naturalness of Mind.
6. In the *western* direction the understanding gained is utilised in the outward field of service that is humanity. This has produced many volumes of sacred writings generated by wise philosophers and the enlightened. Effectively these teachings fill all directions of space. Nevertheless the esoteric doctrine, though existentially vast, can be simplified in a few symbols, or mantric utterances. Literally it needs but a few words to explain the essence of what is implicated. This vast output of wisdom, and its distilled essence, is but the introductory background to the revelations attainable through knowing the Mind.
7. We proceed to the crux of the matter in the final two statements. The *northwest* direction constitutes the outward expression of the emanatory Will-of-Love *(bodhicitta)*, projecting thereby the gain of the entire evolutionary procession. This allows the liberated ones to meet 'face to face' with the Buddhas. Esoterically this statement refers to attaining the same level or dimension of perception where the Jinas can be found. From Eye to Eye can information now be directly transmitted. No veils (of substance or ignorance) exist between the victors. The luminous expression of all seven *chakras* ablaze speak volumes to them. Enlightened purpose can then be projected to where needed.
8. The *northern* direction of upwards to the Divine refers to the

7 Evans-Wentz, 204, footnote 1.

complete attainment of the *dharmakāyic* Mind, and the lucid pristine awareness of its Clear Light. One then resides in the eternal Now, with no need to revert to past habits or to anxiously anticipate the future. All is comprehended in one timeless embrace of Revelation.

We now proceed to 'The Actual Introduction to Awareness'. This section shall only be dealt with cursorily because it mainly concerns the differences between various philosophical systems. These differences have been provided by many authors to which I could add but little of a substantive nature. The first part of this section according to Gyurme:

> KYE HO!
> O fortunate children, listen to these words!
> The term 'mind' is commonplace and widely used,
> Yet there are those who do not understand [its meaning],
> Those who falsely understand it, those who partially understand it,
> And those who have not quite understood its genuine reality,
> Thus there has arisen an inconceivably vast number of assertions [as to the nature of mind],
> Posited by [the various] philosophical systems.
> Further, since ordinary persons do not understand [the meaning of the term 'mind'],
> And do not intuitively recognise its nature,
> They continue to roam through the six classes of sentient [rebirth] within the three world-systems,
> And consequently experience suffering.
> This is the fault of not understanding this intrinsic nature of mind.[8]

The section begins with the mantra *kye ho*, which is simply an invocation exhorting one to be attentive. 'Fortunate children' are the disciples, students of the great Ones, who consequently have auspicious *karma,* thus are fortunate indeed to be in a position to learn these teachings. They are yet at the beginning of their path to liberation, hence 'children'.

The remaining statements are clear enough for ordinary intellects to comprehend. There are two groups of five statements. They relate to the nature and progress of the five Jina wisdoms in each group. One

---

8 Gyurme, 39-40.

list is for the philosophers developing a critical analysis of mind/Mind. The second list concerns the development of mind in ordinary people. Paraphrasing therefore, the first list is:

a. Those who are plainly ignorant.
b. Those who speculate falsely, hence making ignorant assertions, because of the vicissitudes of the desire-mind utilised. Because they come from an emotional bias they do not understand the nature of the mind.
c. Those who have partially comprehended the nature of mind, as theirs is a fundamentally intellectual approach. However the subtleties of the dual nature of mind/Mind eludes them.
d. Those who 'have not quite understood its genuine reality'. They have awakened meditative abilities, and gained certain keen insights through the yogic methods of the various Buddhist schools of thought, but are not yet fully awakened.
e. The consequence of all the above is that there are a vast number of philosophical systems and texts that abound via which various avenues of truth can be found.

With respect to ordinary people we have:

a. It is taken for granted that the average person is ignorant of the nature of mind.
b. The next step concerns the intelligentsia, who are strongly intellectual but have not yet developed the intuition to listen to the voice of the Heart, which can speak in a timeless flash of revelation.
c. Consequently they need to continuously incarnate until such ability is developed.
d. This produces the educative process of suffering that *saṃsāra* provides. Inevitably comprehension of the Four Noble Truths is developed that necessitates following the Eightfold Path.
e. They can then gain comprehension of the intrinsic nature of Mind and become liberated from suffering.

The 'six classes of sentient beings' that seek rebirth are the denizens of the Six Realms. (Gods, *asuras,* humans, animals, *pretas,* and those suffering in the hell states.) They are all aspects of human consciousness undergoing experiences in various Bardo realms.

'The three world systems' are viewed in terms of the attributes of consciousness. They refer to the world governed by desire *(kāmadhātu)*, which produces all of the urges and *karma* causing one to perpetually seek rebirth in the Six Realms. Next is the world of form *(rūpadhātu)*, which refers to the concreted thought-forms generated by the empirical mind. Finally we have the formless realms *(arūpadhātu)* associated with the sub-planes of the higher Mind.

The next section deals with the differences between the various yoga systems of attainment in Buddhism.

1. Even though pious attendants and hermit buddhas claim that they understand [this single nature of mind] as the partial absence of self,

   They do not understand it exactly as it is.
2. Furthermore, being fettered by opinions held in accordance with their respective literatures and philosophical systems,

   There are those who do not perceive the inner radiance [directly]:
3. The pious attendants and hermit buddhas are obscured [in this respect] by their attachment to the subject-object dichotomy.
4. The adherents of Madhyamaka are obscured by their attachment to the extremes of the two truths.
5. The practitioners of Kriyātantra and Yogatantra are obscured by their attachment to the extremes of ritual service and attainment.
6. The practitioners of Mahāyoga and Anuyoga are obscured by their attachment to [the extremes of] space and awareness.
7. All these [practitioners] stray from the point because they polarise the non-dual reality,
8. And since they fail to unify [these extremes] in non-duality, they do not attain buddhahood.
9. Thus, all of those beings continue to roam in cyclic existence,
10. Because they persistently engage in [forms of] renunciation,
11. And in acts of rejection and acceptance with regard to their own minds,
12. Where [in reality] cyclic existence and nirvāṇa are inseparable.[9]

---

9 Ibid., 40.

I shall not explain here the attributes of the various schools of Buddhist thought and yoga traditions. Nor shall I further elucidate the associated shortcomings of the various forms of yoga. Gyurme's footnotes to them provide adequate background and point the reader to the texts wherein the arguments are supplied. Dudjom Rinpoche provides an excellent analysis.[10]

One should note that there are twelve main statements, which I have numbered, each dealing with a topic. This implies the general turning of the wheel of the Heart centre of the *buddhadharma* from its foundations in the pious attendants of the Buddha to the development of the subtle teachings of the supreme Ati yoga. Also implied is the development of the three types of enlightenment via the process of the evolution of these schools of thought.

Concerning Ati yoga, which is by deduction the doctrine espoused in the *Bardo Thödol*,[11] Dudjom Rinpoche states:

> As to the verbal definition of Atiyoga: [The Sanskrit] *ati* [Tib. *shin-tu*] means utmost, and also conveys the sense of supreme, best, perfect, climax and quintessence. [The Sanskrit] *yoga* [Tib. *rnal-'byor*] means union. Since it is the culmination of all yogas, it is the utmost or highest yoga, and since it is the nucleus of all aspects of the perfection stage, there is nothing else to be reached higher than Atiyoga. It is qualified by the word "great" [Tib. *chen-po*] because through it the reality unborn like the sky, which is most profound and difficult to analyse, is directly revealed[12]...with reference to the ultimate truth, objects of ideas, scrutiny and inference are utterly contradictory because it is a quiescence of conceptual elaboration, and an absence of symbolic doctrines. It does not abide in the path of verbalisation and conventions and it is not felt to pursue the imagination. For these reasons, if the occasions when meditative absorption in this pristine cognition or abiding mode of reality occurs are not recognised to be this same absorption in the spiritual and philosophical goal [of Atiyoga], which is effortless with respect to fundamental reality, then all that is studied

10 See Gyurme, 409. Dudjom Rinpoche in *The Nyingma School of Tibetan Buddhism*, 295-7, quotes from the Tantra of the *All-Accomplishing King*, in his explanation of the differences between these schools of thought.

11 I have modernised the concepts of Ati yoga in this series under the rubric of the Dharmakāya Way.

12 Dudjom Rinpoche, *The Nyingma School of Tibetan Buddhism*, 312.

> pertaining to ideas and scrutiny becomes verbal chaff; thought and understanding become waves of conceptualisation; meditation becomes apprehension of that; and experience the appraisal of it. It becomes extremely difficult even to approach the profound meaning of the abiding nature no matter how correctly it seems to arise in the face of the intellect[13]...in the general path of the Great Perfection, all conceptual elaborations become quiescent in the intrinsic expanse through meditative equipoise, without wavering from this disposition in which the presence of fundamental reality, the abiding nature without bondage or liberation is established.
>
> Other than that, nothing is contrived save that one abides constantly and naturally in the disposition of the supreme transcendence of intellect, which is free from all activities. All the suddenly arisen stains which appear through expressive power just become naturally pure, naturally clear and naturally liberated, without renunciation or antidote being applied, in the unchanging space of intrinsic awareness, the primal emptiness, in the manner of water and waves. Other than that, "meditation" and "meditative equipoise" are the labels conventionally applied to simple absorption in the intrinsic nature, just as it naturally occurs, without looking elsewhere, without purposefully meditating, without being fixed on one [point], without intellectualising, without conceptualising, without apprehending faults, without external clarifications and without internal attainment. Therefore the essence is emptiness, in that it is without thought or expression; signlessness, in that it is without conceptualisation; and aspirationlessness, in that it is without acceptance, rejection, hope or doubt. The three spheres naturally abide therein in an utterly pure character because there is no objective reference to the three times.[14]

This long quote has been provided because it elucidates the meaning of the natural state of Mind and its intrinsic awareness found in the text of the *Bardo Thödol*. The 'three spheres' of the quote refer to *kāmadhātu, rūpadhātu,* and *arūpadhātu* (the desire, form, and formless realms). With conception of the fundamentals of the Great Perfection *(rDzogs-Chen)* in one's mind we can proceed with the further analysis of the text.

---

13 Ibid., 314-315.

14 Ibid., 315-316.

The remaining portion of this section:

> Therefore, one should abandon all constructed teachings,
> And all [unnatural] states free from activity,
> And, by virtue of this *[Introduction to] Awareness: Natural Liberation through Naked Perception,* which is presented here,
> One should realise all things in the context of this great natural liberation.
> So it is that all [enlightened attributes] are brought to completion within the Great Perfection.
> SAMAYA *rgya rgya rgya*[15]

These five statements hint at the attributes of the five Dhyāni Buddhas that summarise the qualities of Ati yoga.

First we have Amoghasiddhi's All-accomplishing Wisdom, which is developed by abandoning 'all constructed teachings'. The hint here is that these teachings are representative of the above mentioned philosophies and yogas, leaving one to solely focus upon developing the Great Perfection (Ati yoga).

Along this line is found the expression of Ratnasambhava's Equalising Wisdom, wherein all unnatural states (desire-mind *saṃskāras)* are to be 'freed from activity'. Evans-Wentz's rendering here is: 'Therefore, practising the *Dharma,* freed from every attachment, grasp the whole essence of these teachings expounded in this Yoga of Self-Liberation by Knowing the Mind in its Real Nature'.[16] The desire-emotions that produce attachments to phenomena must be mastered and completely stilled to generate the harmonising qualities that equalise all attributes of mind into one universal flux of Mind.

We come now to the development of the discriminative abilities of the mind, and of the process of its transformation, so that the 'naked perception' of the one Mind can be gained. Amitābha's Discriminative Inner Wisdom thereby unfolds to produce its corresponding enlightenment.

The attributes of Akṣobhya's Mirror-like Wisdom follow in the development of 'this great natural liberation'. Here Mind is reflected into mind via the *śūnyatā* mirror.

---

15 Gyurme, 40-41.

16 Evans-Wentz, 207.

Finally we have the Great Perfection wherein everything is 'brought to completion' in Vairocana's Dharmadhātu wisdom. The entire process and vastness *(rgya)* of this ocean of virtuous Mind is then sealed by the Tantric pledge to master the demonstration of this wisdom, thus the use of the mantra *samaya rgya rgya rgya.*

The analysis proper starts with the section entitled 'Synonyms for Mind'. The text begins:

> As for this apparent and distinct [phenomenon] which is called 'mind':
> In terms of existence, it has no [inherent] existence whatsoever.
> In terms of origination, it is the source of the diverse joys and sorrows of cyclic existence and nirvāṇa,
> In terms of [philosophical] opinion, it is subject to opinions in accordance with the eleven vehicles,
> In terms of designation, it has an inconceivable number of distinct names:
> Some call it 'the nature of mind', the 'nature of mind itself',
> Some eternalists give it the name 'self',
> Pious attendants call it 'selflessness of the individual',[17]
> Cittamātrins call it 'mind',
> Some call it the 'Perfection of Discriminative Awareness',
> Some call it the 'Nucleus of the Sugata',
> Some call it the 'Great Seal',
> Some call it the 'Unique Seminal point',
> Some call it the 'Expanse of Reality',
> Some call it the 'Ground-of-all',
> And some call it 'ordinary [unfabricated consciousness]'[18]

The structure of this entire passage must be analysed to derive proper meaning. First there is the opening passage plus four sentences that start with the phrase 'In terms of'. This is of significance because the five phrases refer to the originating sources of all that can be considered Mind in Nature, namely the five Dhyāni Buddhas.

The first statement presented is 'As for this apparent and distinct [phenomenon] which is called "mind"'. Evans-Wentz provides here 'That which is commonly called mind is of intuitive Wisdom. (Literally "quick knowing", *prajña.*)'[19] As this analysis concerns the sum total

17 Evans-Wentz calls it 'The Essentiality of Doctrines', 209.

18 Gyurme, 41.

19 Evans-Wentz, *The Tibetan Book of the Great Liberation,* 208.

of the phenomena called 'mind', our focus is upon the emanational quality (wisdom) of the Jina that embodies this totality. This is 'the One Mind that embraces the whole of *Sangsāra* and *Nirvāṇa*',[20] namely Vairocana (and the Dharmadhātu Wisdom) who sits at the centre of the *maṇḍala* of the Jinas. Those who can emulate Vairocana therefore, also come to embody this 'quick knowing' (thus instantaneous) *prajña*. The term *prajña* (Tib. shes rab) means enlightened knowledge, analytical wisdom, and discriminative awareness. This wisdom is an expression of the universal Mind. A liberated one, who resides in the *dharmadhātu,* utilises this wisdom to organise the *ālayavijñāna* via which those ensnared in *saṃsāra* can be awakened.

The second statement presented is: 'In terms of existence, it has no [inherent] existence whatsoever'. This perspective is from the *eastern* direction of the *maṇḍala* of the Dhyāni Buddhas, where we find Akṣobhya's Mirror-like Wisdom. Existence and non-existence are thereby reflections that mirror each other. The meditative insight gained by comprehending the true nature of phenomena derives from the mind containing everything considered 'existence' by those ensnared by the wiles of *saṃsāra*. Because everything in *saṃsāra* is transient, fleeting, therefore things have no inherent existence or lasting permanence that such an existence would convey. From this statement then would be derived the doctrine of the two truths, which was analysed in the chapter on the two truths in Volume 1 of this *Treatise on Mind*. There is the relative truth concerning the nature of phenomena, and also the absolute Truth of the ultimate reality of *śūnyatā*. Here the focus is upon the absolute Truth, gained through meditative insight by the Mind's Eye resting in the Void that is the Heart's embrace. The egoistic pursuit of mindful endeavours is extinguished in the Void that is the truth of all that is and is not. All permutations of mind have no existence here. This is the goal of the generalised Buddhist meditation system.

Next we have the phrase 'In terms of origination', which refers to the *northern* direction of Amoghasiddhi's All-accomplishing Wisdom. Here (in *dharmakāya*) we have 'the source of the diverse joys and sorrows of cyclic existence and nirvāṇa', of all things associated with Mind and of its relation to mind. All of the related cycles, of the zodiac, *karma*, and

20 See Evans-Wentz, *The Tibetan Book of the Great Liberation,* 203.

of cosmic journeying, are mastered by means of the methodology of Amoghasiddhi's Wisdom. The term 'origination' refers to the philosophy of Dependent Origination (*pratītyasamutpāda*); the establishment of the twelve-fold cycle of interdependence stemming from ignorance.

Saṃsāra and *śūnyatā* are integrated by means of the expression of this Wisdom in terms of the nexus that incorporates both. The two truths are straddled by means of a third truth of relativity; that all things persist relative to something else. Even *śūnyatā* is relative with respect to *dharmakāya* and *saṃsāra*. *Saṃsāra* is an important part of this triad, and must persist so that enlightenment can evolve. The resultant *saṃsāra-śūnyatā* nexus is the bridge between phenomena and the universality of the *dharmakāya*.

The phrase 'In terms of [philosophic] opinion, it is subject to opinions in accordance with the eleven vehicles' relates to the Discriminating Inner Vision of Amitābha, and the *western* direction of outwards of service to humanity. The doctrines (opinions) of these 'eleven vehicles' include soteriological considerations, the methods of service for these Buddhist Schools. Their basic philosophic context ('discriminations') are explained in Volume 1 of this treatise, and involves the entire development of the corpus of Buddhism from the time of the Buddha to the present epoch. Specifically a deep analysis of the nature of mind and its relation to *śūnyatā* is emphasised, via the development of meditation techniques that allow one to overcome the factors of suffering. Liberation can thereby be gained from *saṃsāra*. Amitābha's Inner Vision involves a lucid methodical enquiry into the full spectrum of mind and its transformation into Mind. In the Mahāyāna stream the concourse of this development involved mainly the distinction between the Mādhyamika and the Yogācāra doctrines.

The phrase 'In terms of designation, it has an inconceivable number of distinct names' refers to the *southern* direction, of people's immersion in *saṃsāra*, to their proclivity to mentally name things they designate as 'real'. Thus there are all the categorisations of mind, which must become refined and integrated into unity by means of aspiration to the unifying attributes of Mind. This is effected by means of Ratnasambhava's Equalising Wisdom.

The text now observes the three categories or classes of philosophers, the Schools of reasoning (*nyāya*, rigs pa) that were historically concerned with analysing the attributes of mind. The term 'Eternalists' refers to the various Brahmaṇical philosophers. Evans-Wentz uses the term 'heretics' here.[21] They have a concept of eternal 'self' or Soul (*ātman*). Though errors may exist, the analysis of each school have something positive to contribute to the philosophical debate as to the nature of mind/Mind. For example, *The Yoga Sūtras of Patañjali* are concerned with the control of the vicissitudes of mind, which is very similar to the Yogācāra doctrines. In such a list one could also add the atheistic concepts of materialistic thinkers.

The phrase 'Pious attendants' refers to the adherents of the Theravādin Schools. Their outcome of the analysis of mind produces the *arhat's* contemplative absorption.

The next phrase ('Cittamātrins call it 'mind'') refers to the Yogācāra-Cittamātrin School, who describe it as it actually is, without philosophic distortion. This is the major teaching of the Mahayāna schools, and the foundation to the higher Tantric validation of Mind. Instead of 'mind' Evans-Wentz uses the term 'Wisdom'[22] (Tib. sems), to depict what the outcome of the evolution of mind is. He thus keeps the discourse in line with this dissertation, which is concerned with enlightenment-attributes.

Including the Cittamātrin view, we then have a list of eight qualifications associated with the Buddhist viewpoint, mostly beginning with the phrase 'Some call it'. This presentation also involves the higher correspondences of the eight consciousnesses of the Yogācāra philosophy. They can then be placed in the correct sequence upon the arms of the eight-spoked wheel *(aṣṭadiśas)* of direction in space.

The seven phrases containing the phrase 'some call it', after the reference to the Cittamātrins, can also refer to the seven Rays of Mind, whose qualities the serious student can integrate here. Also, the next chapter provides further detail, as this list is represented therein under the heading 'Synonyms for Awareness'.

1. For the *northern* direction we have the Cittamātrin view of 'the nature of mind itself' (Tib. sems-nyid). In its totality this is the *ālayavijñāna*, the vast expanse and store of *manasic* substance, contacted and

21 Evans-Wentz, *The Tibetan Book of the Great Liberation*, 208.

22 Ibid., 209.

experienced as the first level of gaining enlightenment.[23] It is the basis for the *arhat* form of absorption.

2. The 'Perfection of Discriminative Awareness', or what Evans-Wentz calls 'The Means of Attaining the Other Shore of Wisdom'[24] (*prajñāpāramitā*), relates to the *northeast* spoke of the wheel of direction in space, which has been designated 'unity' (of all companions in the *dharma).* The higher correspondence of the sense of *hearing* comes into play via this direction, for what is heard is the discourse of all the Buddhas—which emanates via the unity disseminated by enlightened beings. These teachings express the compendium of all wisdom (*prajñāpāramita*), and become the basis for attaining the *śūnyatā* enlightenment.
3. The 'Nucleus of the Sugata' (the *tathāgatagarbha*) refers to the *eastern* direction that produces the awakening of the innermost perceptions found at the Heart of Life. The potency of this Heart is the Buddha-Mind that is seeded into the qualities of the *tathāgatagarbha*-Sambhogakāya Flower. How it is the foundation of Buddhahood was explained in detail in Volume 3. Here exists the subtle correspondence of the sense of *taste,* which elevates consciousness with the highly refined experiences of the intrinsic nature of being/non-being. This then provides the background for the Initiation process that is the foundation for eventual liberation from *saṃsāra.*
4. The Great Seal is the *mahāmudrā* that comes as a consequence of the outward expression of one's perceptions (the *southeast* direction) of the myriad experiences *saṃsāra* offers. Inevitably this allows integration of all forms of dualities into unities. Eventually the attributes of *saṃsāra* can be fused with the Heart's perception of Buddhahood. Here the higher correspondence of the sense of *touch* is implicated, allowing the expression of the sense-perceptions to contact and thus experience the natural state of Mind that is the *mahāmudrā.* All aspects and attributes of enlightenment can then be gained through the incremental integrations of the various *iḍā-*

---

23 Earlier explained as the *ālayavijñāna* enlightenment.

24 Evans-Wentz, *The Tibetan Book of the Great Liberation,* 209.

piṅgalā dualities in the *nāḍīs*. The highest interpretation concerns the great fusion between members of the *deva* and human kingdoms at certain stages of the path to enlightenment. The *mahāmudrā* is the heart of the *dharmakāya* enlightenment.

5. The 'Unique Seminal point', or as Evans-Wentz describes it 'The Sole Seed'[25] (Thig-le, *bindu*), refers to the *southern* direction of this wheel of orientation in space, wherein the attributes of consciousness are expressed in the mind of the person. From this perspective the seminal point refers to the juncture between the Sambhogakāya Flower and the Head centre. The *bījas* that seed all attributes of consciousness can then flower. Another perspective relates to the anchoring of the Life-stream *(sūtrātmā)* in the Heart centre, which then becomes the basis for the generation of *bodhicitta*. Next we have the extension of this 'seed' as the jewel that is the heart of any *chakra*. From the relation between the *chakras* and the external environment the *saṃskāras* are generated. The defiled mind *(kliṣṭamanas)* then manifests as a natural outcome of the fusion of mind with the normal Watery environment of the individual. This *southern* direction is also a turning point in consciousness, where the Bodhisattva path awakens the need to master the Waters. A *yogin* emerges and consequently discovers a 'unique seminal point' at the juncture between the Base of Spine and Sacral centres (exoterically the tip of the penis). It allows the rising of *kuṇḍalinī* that dries up any remaining Waters and liberates consciousness.

6. The 'Expanse of Reality', or 'The Potentiality of Truth *(dharmadhātu)*',[26] relates to the *northwest* direction of (blissful) outward expression of the gain of one's experiences in the realms of being/non-being, the liberation of consciousness. The *dharmadhātu* then becomes the mantric expression of the awakened Bodhisattva engaged in his/her chosen field of service. Inevitably, it will denote the Sound of a new Jina travelling upon his newly found path in cosmos. The abstracted sense of *smell,* the subtlest of all perceptions, elevates mind into Mind via its highest possible state of intensity and expansiveness of perception.

---

25 Ibid.

26 Ibid.

7. The 'Ground of all' refers to the expansion of the sixth sense, the intellectual propensity of people relegated to the *western* direction of outwards towards human society. This propensity is the ground of all that later transpires in the field of consciousness, its many permutations and transformations as the sum of the *ālayavijñāna*. Here all of the ordinary Fires of mind are assimilated, integrated, directed into new enlightening arenas, and brought eventually to a natural conclusion. It is thereby the 'ground' of enlightenment.
8. We are all familiar with ordinary fabricated consciousness, wherein people speak to friends and others in society without properly structuring their thoughts. All elements of desire, glamour, emotions, and egoistical pursuits are thereby unthinkingly generated. This refers to the *southwest* direction of understanding in the field of application of *manasic* input. The sense developed and transformed is *sight*, which directly awakens the mind, and helps people to gauge their perspectives in life.

Attributes of Mind and the Throat centre

Having established the way that the sources of mind are directed and transformed in human consciousness, the nature of the *manasic prāṇas* as expressed by the various petals of the *chakras* and other considerations can now be analysed. This and the following chapters are a companion supplementary text to that previously presented on the Peaceful and Wrathful Deities. There our concern was with the processes of transformation from the normal states of emotional-mental interplay into enlightened attributes. All happens in the mind. In this present section we shall observe that all *prāṇas* are streams of *manasic* propensity, as they convey attributes of mind. These streams are processed by the various *chakras* that exist for this purpose. The Peaceful and Wrathful Deities are but force fields in the Clear Light of Mind.

Next follows a section entitled 'The Three Considerations':

> The following is the introduction [to the means of experiencing] this [single] nature [of mind]
> Through the application of three considerations:
> [First, recognise that] past thoughts are traceless, clear, and empty,

[Second, recognise that] future thoughts are unproduced and fresh,
And [third, recognise that] the present moment abides naturally and unconstructed.
When this ordinary, momentary consciousness is examined nakedly [and directly] by oneself,

1. Upon examination, it is a radiant awareness,
2. Which is free from the presence of an observer,
3. Manifestly stark and clear,
4. Completely empty and uncreated in all respects,
5. Lucid, without duality of radiance and emptiness,
6. Not permanent, for it is lacking inherent existence in all respects,
7. Not a mere nothingness, for it is radiant and clear,
8. Not a single entity, for it is clearly perceptible as a multiplicity,
9. Yet not existing inherently as a multiplicity, for it is indivisible and of a single savour.
10. This intrinsic awareness, which is not extraneously derived,
11. Is itself the genuine introduction to the abiding nature of [all] things.
12. For in this [intrinsic awareness], the three buddha-bodies are inseparable, and fully present as one:
13. Its emptiness and utter lack of inherent existence is the Buddha-body of Reality;
14. The natural resonance and radiance of this emptiness is the Buddha-body of Perfect Resource;
15. And its unimpeded arising in any form whatsoever is the Buddha-body of Emanation.
16. These three, fully present as one, are the very essence [of awareness] itself.[27]

These statements refer to the natural expression and unfoldment of the petals of the Throat centre (*viśuddha chakra*). This is the prime organ responsible for the conveyance of *manasic prāṇas.* All *saṃskāras* concerning mental propensity are thus controlled and directed from here. It is a sixteen-petalled lotus, with four major petals (conveying the *prāṇas* originally derived from the Base of Spine centre), plus twelve

27 Gyurme, 41-42. As usual I have added the numbers to each paragraph.

supporting petals (and twenty-four minor ones), which absorb the *prāṇas* from the Heart centre and from below the diaphragm coming via the twelve-petalled Splenic centre I. Because it is a direct expression of the emanation of mind, so also it is the organ of speech, esoterically therefore of mantric sound, which demonstrates the potency of mind/Mind.

With respect to recognising past thoughts as 'traceless, clear, and empty', Evans-Wentz's version is 'If one knows how to apply in a threefold manner this knowing of the mind, all past knowledge lost to memory becomes perfectly clear, and also knowledge of the future, thought of as unborn and unconceived'.[28] This yogic method of knowing Mind allows one to know 'how to apply in a threefold manner' a perception of the three times in one. The *past* therefore is not 'traceless', in the sense that one cannot find pathways to memory, as clearly we can all do so. Rather, the term 'traceless' refers to the fact that at this stage the associated *saṃskāras* have been cleansed of defilements that can leave karmic imprints traceable as future actions. In this natural state they are empty of *saṃsāric* affiliations. There are, however, *future* actions that will be made by the person, which have purpose, and residing in the *ālayavijñāna* or *dharmakāya* environment 'remain fresh'. With respect to *the present* one needs not to work to construct thoughts, but rather they will appear when needed and be instantaneously and appropriately utilised.

The *prāṇas* of the three times also flow in the form of the three major *nāḍīs,* where the *iḍā* stream conveying attributes of mind technically represents the past qualities developed. The *piṅgalā* stream (regulating the expression of *bodhicitta*) then represents the present flow of conscious expression, and the *suṣumṇā* continuously brings forth the future expression of being/non-being of such a one (who is actually liberated from mundane considerations of time). These *prāṇas* then vivify the major tiers of the *chakra* concerned, becoming the purifying and directing reservoir of energies for the activity of all its petals.

Having understood the nature of the three times from the perspective of Mind, we are now in a position to analyse the nature of *prāṇic* flow processed by the Throat centre of an accomplished one who has mastered the life process.

---

28 Evans-Wentz, 210.

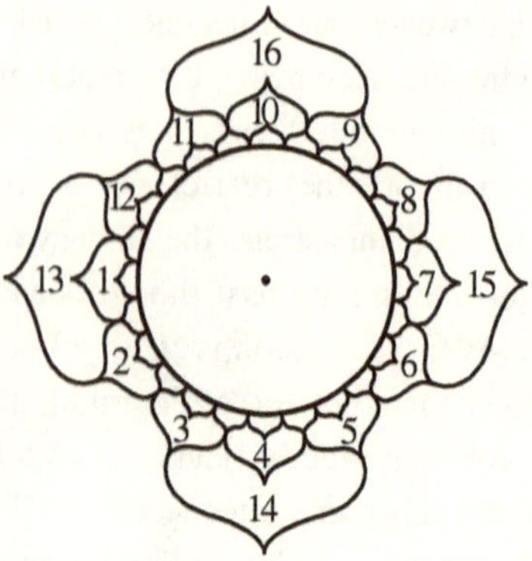

Figure 1. The petals of the Throat centre

In the analysis of these petals I shall provide the main points without delving into excessive detail. For each major lobe of this *chakra* there are 7 + 3 supporting petals, related to processing the seven Ray attributes and synthesised by the three major Rays. The decade of energies is then projected by a major petal either upwards towards the Ājñā centre, or downwards to the major centres below the diaphragm. The 7 + 3 petals can also be viewed in terms of the progress towards evolutionary perfection. When the major synthesising petal is counted and integrated with a major lobe of the Ājñā centre, then we essentially have the 7 + 5 combination of the sacred and non-sacred petals of a Heart centre. The emphasis of this combination is the development and projection of the five non-sacred *prāṇas* of mind. Eventually Mind is developed, which is sacred and divine.

The main focus of the 7 + 3 petals can be towards the ten petalled Solar Plexus centre to control the emotions, or upon the combined Sacral/Base of Spine centres to control desire and the lower creative forces, as well as the four Elements associated with the four petals of the Base centre. (Thus there are four main petals to each lobe of the Throat centre.) Also, there are three minor petals supporting one of the twelve numbered larger petals. When integrated by one major petal this combination allows the *prāṇas* of any of the five sense-consciousnesses to be projected via the associated direction that consciousness is focussed upon at any time. The four main petals organise the *prāṇas* into the attributes of the four Elements as associated with the *maṇḍala* of the five Dhyāni Buddhas, with Vairocana in the centre, Amoghasiddhi to the north, Akṣobhya to the east, Ratnasambhava to the south and Amitābha to the west. The fifth Element is conveyed through the centre of the *maṇḍala*.

The twelve main petals of the Throat are also affiliated with the twelve main petals of the Heart and Head centres, and are organised according to the conditioning influences of the signs of the zodiac. The four main lobes of the Throat centre make it a prime directing or focussing agent.

When viewing a north-south, east-west axis then there are eight major petals to consider, which allow the inception of the *prāṇas* of the eight consciousnesses, or to empower any of the eight petalled *chakras*.

Altogether there are 40 petals, but when working in conjunction with the two lobes of the Ājñā centre they make a symbiotic 42 petals capable of conveying all of the *prāṇas* of the 42 Peaceful Deities. The Ājñā centre is the directive Eye that projects the creative potencies of the mind/Mind in any of their combinations to empower the thoughts of the thinker. To do so the Ājñā and Throat centres must work with integrated purpose. When, therefore, we count the combined number of petals to the Ājñā and Throat centres, then there are 96 + 12 + 40 petals, plus we can add a virtual two petals (of the symbiotic relationship) making 150 (3 x 50) all told. They signify the complete mastery of all attributes of mind/Mind. Without the ability of the Eye to appropriately focus the mental attributes as signified by any of the combinations of these petals, *dhāraṇīs* and mantra would be ineffectual. Much is hinted at here for all true students of meditation, especially when correlations between groups of petals are analysed.

The meditative analysis of the natural state of Mind (the Clear Light) follows the pattern of the progression of the signs of the zodiac, which therefore condition this enquiry. Accordingly, these sixteen statements are found to be in the correct order for zodiacal analysis (as numbered in the figure) when applied to the *maṇḍala* of the Throat centre. At this stage of our analysis, the Wrathful Deities are no longer a concern, as all *saṃskāras* have been converted to their enlightened attributes. However, each of the sixteen statements hint at the processes that have produced enlightenment.

Though the description is presented in terms of fixed orientations, one must note that the wheels of petals turn, allowing the *prāṇas* of each of the petals associated with the zodiac to integrate with any of the four major petals. The statements presented are:

1. Upon examination, it is a radiant awareness.

One starts with the process of self-examination to comprehend what the true state of mind is by utilising one's own mind-structure to do so. Having found only radiant awareness, the fundamental nature or the natural state of the Mind, implies that the analyser is enlightened. He/she has already transmuted the base *saṃskāras* of mind into the Clear Light.

The beginning of procuring such enlightenment always necessitates travelling inwards to the Heart of Life (the eastern direction). This direction implicates the Arian petal, the start of the wheel of the inner twelve-petalled lotus of the Throat centre. It signifies the initial abstracted mental beginnings (upon the enlightenment-path).[29] Aries provides the instigating impetus to direct the entire course of this enquiry through to conclusion. Here the radiant awareness of the abstract Mind is awakened and utilised to observe and develop all of the other characteristics. The deep inner workings of the mind can then be comprehended from foundational attributes (first principles), and by extending the process of mental formations to enlightenment.

This eastern petal of the Throat centre therefore clarifies all *manasic prāṇas*. It strips bare the multifarious *saṃskāras* from complexities, leaving only the radiant lucidity of the Mind. The overall expression of the attributes of an enlightened Mind is specifically incorporated through processing and transmuting the *iḍā nāḍī* stream of the entire life process. Consciousness then resides at the nexus between *saṃsāra* and *śūnyatā*. This petal of the Throat centre therefore conveys the attributes of the *prāṇas* remaining after being purified from their defilements. These attributes (radiant awareness) also set the tone for the remainder of the petals.

---

29 The basic meanings of the signs of the zodiac with respect to the petals of the Heart lotus were explained in Volume 3 of this treatise, to which the reader must refer for detail. It is necessary to understand the properties of these signs if one wishes a sound comprehension of the nature of any twelve-petalled lotus, upon which the inner twelve petals of the Throat centre are based. The astrology utilised is that found in A.A. Bailey's *Esoteric Astrology*, (Lucis Press, London, 1968.)

2. Which is free from the presence of an observer.

The purpose of examining the nature of mind is to try to determine who or what is actually observing it. The next (Taurean) petal of the lotus rules the home environment, the evolution of the principle of desire focussed around the central concept of an 'I' or doer. It clothes the thought-form of whatever is to be. Therefore, upon the upward way it eliminates the comforting conscious environment of the thought of a 'self', an 'I' that is the actual observer. Wisdom is consequently wrought and the All-seeing Eye awakened. The central ego is found to be a thought construct conveniently expressed for any particular life around which thoughts can be attached, allowing a personal-I to manifest.[30] However, the reality is that there is a continuous series of such 'personal-I's' manifesting throughout time as each personality life comes and goes. Even within the context of one life there can be a series of personality shifts, signifying a new personal-I being constructed. (This is generally the effect of *saṃskāras* called forth from a past life when a similar happening occurs in the present life. They then pass through consciousness after being modified by the new life's considerations.) What is considered an 'I' is continuously 'coming and going', changing with each passing thought. It is a chimera of mind, attachment to which is therefore resolved properly via the expression of this second petal of the Throat centre.

3. Manifestly stark and clear.

Once the established concept of the 'I' as a construct of the mind is eliminated, the centre of one's existence then remains as 'manifestly stark and clear'. This 'remainder' thereby becomes the temple of Mind within which one continuously resides. These are the mysteries of which one is Initiated into as one travels through the wheel of the twelve petals of the Throat centre. The role of such a temple of Initiation into the mysteries of being/non-being is the function of the third petal to produce, as governed by Gemini the twins. Consequently, it is the first of the triad supporting the downwards focussed major petal, from whence upwards aspirational *prāṇas* proceed to the Heart centre.

30 The ability to vision the happenings of various past lives is a function of the Taurean petal, as it controls the opening of the Eye of vision, the Ājña centre.

Esoterically, this temple represents the entire *nāḍī* system, where the two pillars standing at its portals signify the *iḍā* and *piṇgalā nāḍīs*. The 'twins' symbolise the empirical mind (the mortal brother) and the abstract Mind (the immortal brother), who have learnt to join hands and together administer at the inner sanctum of the temple *(suṣumṇā)*. Its outer court is the expression of the normal sense-consciousness. All of the associated *saṃskāras* have to be purified and consecrated to enlightenment's quest before the individual can gain access to that which is revealed by Mind. Ritualistic oblations, devotion to concepts of deity, and finally yogic austerities, are all practiced in this temple before the natural state of Mind is revealed. Awareness then manifests 'stark and clear' within the rarefied energy field of the *suṣumṇā nāḍī* that can flow unimpeded and vitalise the central jewel of each *chakra*.

4. Completely empty and uncreated in all respects.

The Cancerian petal concerns the process of the incarnation of all thought constructs. It is the place of massed emotional consciousness, as it is the prime Watery sign of the zodiac. Emotions and desire are the main *karma*-producing propensities of individuals because they produce all forms of attachments to phenomena. By now, however, all attributes of such thoughts have been thoroughly cleansed of defilements through the yogic process that has completely dried up the Waters with the Fiery Element. Once properly processed, all *kāma-manasic saṃskāras* (emotional defilements) cannot form, thus are 'uncreated in all respects'. As the empirical mind no longer creates new karmic propensities, all that remains are enlightenment-attributes that are the natural state of Mind. Whatever *manasic* formations may manifest are energy patterns spontaneously forming and dissolving again in the Mind. Instead of *karma*-forming volitions (incarnations of thought) being created the processes that set one (and all others) free from attachment to *saṃsāra* manifest. Consequently, emptiness awakens and the clear luminosity of the Void is experienced as the natural foundation of Mind. Thus upon the material domain, the sphere of destiny, that which produces liberation, not enthrallment manifests.

5. Lucid, without duality of radiance and emptiness.

In this Leonine petal the nexus between *saṃsāra* and *śūnyatā* is found, wherein these two natural expressions of Mind are unified as one non dual expression. Leo the lion is the sign of the self-conscious individual, where the lion contentedly basks in the sunshine of its prowess. The sun represents the radiance of Mind in its complete glory. The transmuted correspondence of this 'self-ness' is here instigated in terms of the product that is the integration of all extremes. Residing here the enlightened Mind produces oneness, the lucid unity of all refined thoughts into one expressed *maṇḍala*. In this *saṃsāra-śūnyatā* bridge the Mind rests in its own natural state. It manifests the radiant aura of wisdom when needed, or is abstracted into *śūnyatā,* via deep meditation. Lucidity forms a triad with emptiness and radiance, where radiance is its emanation and emptiness its heart.

6. Not permanent, for it is lacking inherent existence in all respects.

Here the designations of mind that analyse and control all attributes of *saṃsāra*, of natural phenomena (conventionally viewed as 'existences') are established. These existences are embodied and governed by the feminine, *deva* kingdom, as consistent with the symbolism of Virgo the virgin. Virgo governs the entire material domain embodied by Nature *(saṃsāra).* All forms therein are organised by mind, but the vicissitudes of mind are impermanent. There is no inherent existence found there.[31] To find such an existence one must control all attributes of mind and strip from them the transience to reveal the real, which manifests a natural radiant luminosity. Such radiance is the emanation of Mind, which in itself veils the Void. *Śūnyatā* exists inherently, but is not an 'existence'. It mirrors the Real that is the *dharmakāya,* which manifests as Mind when *saṃsāra* is to be contacted. That which is inherently existing is the *dharmakāya* reflected into Mind via *śūnyatā.*

The *saṃskāras* utilised by mind to process phenomena are not permanent, they lack inherent existence, nevertheless they do have a relative permanence, according to the length of duration the phenomena persists. This sixth petal of the Throat centre thus regulates the projection of the *cittavṛtti* (modifications of mind) producing the actions whereby

31 The philosophy relating to the feminine *deva* kingdom could be analysed in terms of the concept of 'existence' (Life), but to do so one needs to incorporate consideration of the *dharmakāya* as Mind and the relation between Buddhas and their Consorts, as explained in part A.

one must interrelate with phenomena. The dual aspects of mind must here be considered. The mental vicissitudes are impermanent, illusory, however Mind is a natural extension of the *dharmakāya* at the *śūnyatā-saṃsāra* nexus. From this perspective Mind is real, but when relegated to *saṃsāra* the product lacks inherent existence.

7. Not a mere nothingness, for it is radiant and clear.

We now proceed to the judgement of all attributes of the great Wheel of Life (Libra the balances), the disseminator of the law (the *dharma*). The way the Mind works to express *dharma* is not a 'mere nothingness', its articulation is 'radiant and clear', no matter which direction the petals of the wheel manifest. This produces the absorption of the *prāṇas* from the Heart centre via the inner twelve petals of the Throat centre. Only this absorption can produce the Clear Light of the Mind. Thus is the nature of wisdom born of right contemplation. (Being the judge, the mediator between extremes, Libra governs the art of meditation.) The focus, therefore, of the dual aspect of mind of this verse is upon the Mind, whereas that of the previous statement was upon the mind. Libra arbitrates between the two, thus is able to discern between that which is 'not a mere nothingness' and that which is manifest.

8. Not a single entity, for it is clearly perceptible as a multiplicity.

Next we have the Scorpionic petal, which concerns the sum of testings preceding Initiation. The focus is upon transforming the major emotional-mental *saṃskāras* into their enlightened attributes. The process of transformation produces all major battlefields upon the path, as effected by the work of the Wrathful Deities. This is the major sign that governs the general gist of such activity. *Dhāraṇīs,* thoughts, mantras, and verbal instructions to be given during this process of transformation of *saṃskāras* are 'not a single entity', but must be 'clearly perceptible' in the minds of the receptive audience. This betokens the effects of the wisdom needing expression to assist the unenlightened to gain liberation. Words must be used to assist them cross the bridge to 'the other shore' and they are 'clearly a multiplicity'.

Taking all factors into account, this particular petal of the Throat centre generally possesses residual *karma* needing further refinement, as it is the main petal directing *prāṇic* transformation. Such *karma* manifests to instruct those still learning to convert *saṃskāras*. The development of correct enlightened speech (the effect of right organisation of mind, so that it emulates Mind) is the keynote here.

9. Yet not existing inherently as a multiplicity, for it is indivisible and of a single savour.

The Sagittarian petal of the archer fires the arrows of single-minded purpose outwards towards its target: enlightenment, the liberation of others, the development of the Bodhisattva *bhūmis*. All thoughts and attributes in the Mind of an enlightened one are parts of a *maṇḍala* of unified purpose. Enlightening all sentient beings is its goal. The way of thinking of the entire Council of Bodhisattvas is implied here. This Council, consisting of all enlightened beings, can be considered to exist 'inherently as a multiplicity', however, their collective Mind 'is indivisible and of a single savour'. To become enlightened therefore means to become an integrated part of the *maṇḍala* of the Hierarchy of enlightened ones. The Sagittarian petal fires the arrows of mind thereto, to play its role as part of the collective meditation to benefit the all. The disciple in this sign and petal of the Throat centre must therefore one-pointedly focus all thoughts towards the singularly minded purpose of enlightenment. Thus is developed the weaponry to defeat the multiplicity of foes seen specifically in the previous sign. In this petal the battle against unruly *saṃskāras* is won, and the gain directed to its right goal.

10. This intrinsic awareness, which is not extraneously derived.

The Capricornian petal (of the goat) governs the sum of the attributes of mind/Mind. Having mastered all previous tests to the summit of achievement, as symbolised by this sign, one's goal-fitted purpose has been achieved, thus this is the sign wherein Initiation finally takes place. This goal-fittedness is symbolised by the sure-footed goat climbing up the ragged crags of the mountain of mind to its summit. The Mind of the liberated one rightly organises all of the properties of the *maṇḍala* of activity derived from aeons of experiential observation and deduction from both *saṃsāra* and what *śūnyatā* veils. Once stripped of defilements the leftover is the awareness that is 'intrinsic', because when fused with love and wisdom it manifests as the *bodhicitta* that cannot be taught to one ('extraneously derived') but must be experienced. *Bodhicitta* is a completed *maṇḍala* of liberating power and is no longer an extraneous revelation, but comes from within. Nor is it interpolated into a person by a deity. The 'intrinsic awareness', the collective wisdom of what is contained in the Head lotus or of the entire Council of Bodhisattvas, is then completely known.

11. Is itself the genuine introduction to the abiding nature of [all] things.

Aquarius the water bearer, who pours out the Waters of Life to rightly succour all beings, governs the next petal. In this case the 'Waters' are analogous to the Airy or Aetheric Fires of the enlightened Mind. (An awakened consciousness-stream.) All things are sustained by Fire and directed by it's energy. Therefore the outpouring of wisdom from this petal presents 'the genuine introduction to the abiding nature of [all] things'. Aquarius governs the way of the Bodhisattva path, of the outpouring from the various stages of such a development by an individual. Once the *maṇḍala* of the collective Mind of the Hierarchy of enlightened being has been awakened in the meditating one then the 'nature of all things' is abided in. This relates to the various views of Bodhisattvas meditating via their respective Ray lines and how it is all incorporated into one unified meditation. The goal is to enlighten everyone, to reveal their inherent Buddha-nature. Divinity abides in all beings because it is the original emanation of the primordial Ray from the Ādi Buddha at the beginning of things, via his Consort. That which abides is symbolised by the two wavy lines of the glyph of this sign, denoting mutable streams of energy.

12. For in this [intrinsic awareness], the three buddha-bodies are inseparable, and fully present as one.

We come to the end of the wheel of Mind (in Pisces the fishes), thus to the nature of the abstraction into *dharmakāya*. Pisces terminates each cycle of activity in the Waters of *saṃsāra,* wherein the bonded fishes of the *tathāgatagarbha* (the *sambhogakāya* aspect) yoked to the personal-I (the *nirmaṇakāya)* swim. (The next sign, Aries the ram, begins the renewal process of a fresh *maṇḍala* of activity.) We therefore have one integral line of revelation from the *dharmakāya* to the Head lotus of the *yogin.* All lines (petals) of integration have been awakened and the complete *maṇḍala* spins in fourth dimensional motion to produce the *svabhāvikakāya* of fully awakened, naked radiance of Mind. Here at the ending of the cycles of Life the intrinsic awareness obtained is the primordial Mind of all the Buddhas, the *svabhāvikakāya,* the self-born body (the controversial 'fourth body of a Buddha'[32]). It is that self-existing fundamental expression from which all that is/is not emanated and is sustained by. The ineffable nature and organisation of the Mind that is cosmos is then experienced. The focussed, liberating purpose from the highest revelatory source is directed via the Clear Light through this petal of the Throat centre (signifying the unity of all the petals taken together) to the enthralled lives in *saṃsāra.* The purpose is to abstract all into the true fount or source of the intrinsic awareness known as *dharmakāya.* To do so the bonds of their links to *saṃsāra* must be broken.

The four major petals of the Throat centre

The four major petals of this *chakra* can be viewed to express attributes of the Buddha-body projected to the four directions of space. Effectively, they embody the functions and attributes of the Dhyāni Buddhas, viewed also as a manifest *vajra,* the adamantine 'diamond sceptre' wielded by the conquerors of the *prāṇas* of Mind in all of its permutations.

With respect to *prāṇic* circulation, the four major petals of the Throat centre allow receptivity to *kuṇḍalinī* from the Base of Spine centre. The twelve subsidiary petals can then experience all Fires capable of being expressed by the wheel of Life (the zodiac). The Throat centre thus becomes the organ of regulation of concreted as well as liberated Fires in their totality. Undue concretion, especially of the *kāma-manasic saṃskāras,* contributes to the many sicknesses associated with the Throat centre.[33] When the Waters are brought to the Throat it produces the powers of the orator that can sway the (emotional) masses. It can

---

32 *Svabhāvikakāya* (Tib. ngo bo nyid sku): nature body, body of absolute existence. The underlying indivisible essence of the three *kāyas* (*nirmaṇakāya, sambhogakāya,* and *dharmakāya*), the active and passive distinction of *dharmakāya. Svabhāvikakāya* can be considered the ocean of cosmic Mind to which the liberated one goes once earth ties have been severed.

33 Coughs, flus, speech impediments, thyroid problems.

also produce the projection of forceful, sometimes cruel and vicious forms of lying propaganda (via any of the eight directions of space), with their grave attendant *karma*.

The problems are exemplified when relatively refined energies are liberated from the lower centres, making it hard for the *yogin* or disciple to control the potency of the Fiery energies underlying speech. Wrathful Deities then appear manifesting their various protective guises. Forceful *prāṇas* of mind can also inadvertently be directed back to the lower centres of generation, and often hard to control physiological, psychic, and psychological perturbations are caused. The dangers of practical magic and the premature development of *siddhis* are all too obvious for those who have not made their speech harmless through the cultivation of *bodhicitta*. The prospective *yogin* must be well versed in the language of the Heart before attempts are made to use the Throat centre in Tantric application. The teaching concerning the nature of the Wrathful Protectors of the *dharma* exists for good reason in Buddhism. There are real forces at play in the premature awakening of the Fires that can cause serious problems for many lifetimes.

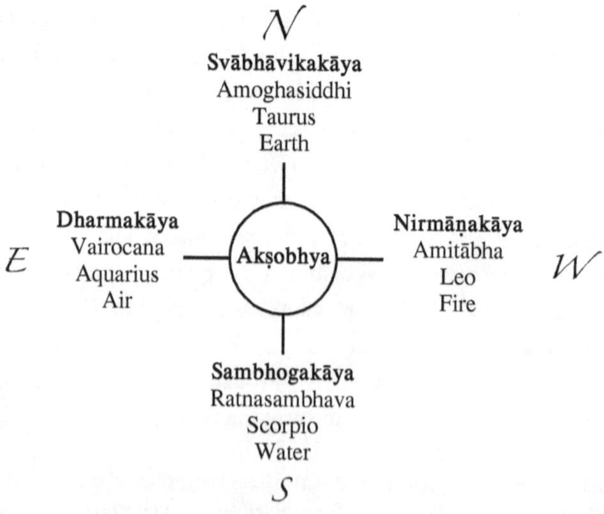

Figure 2. The four major petals of the Throat centre[34]

34 For a detailed explanation of why east and west are depicted opposite to the conventional orientation of a map, refer to page 197 in Volume 4 of this treatise.

Mind, *mantra* and *prāṇa,* the three being fixed as a *dhāraṇī* that organises substance to produce the ever-changing vicissitudes of the form. The Eye(s) direct and the hands manipulate the form. Here is veiled the secret of the appearance of all phenomena, and of its abstraction again into the natural lucidity of Mind. The *karma* of cause and effect applies at this level also. The motion that caused phenomena must also inevitably be countermanded by an equal and opposite motion.

Evans-Wentz provides a succinct, useful summary of the twelve attributes of Mind, under the heading 'Mind in its True State'.

> When one seeks one's mind in its true state, it is found to be quite intelligible, although invisible.
>
> In its true state, mind is naked, immaculate; not made of anything, being of the Voidness; clear, vacuous, without duality, transparent; timeless, uncompounded, unimpeded, colourless; not realizable as a separate thing, but as the unity of all things, yet not composed of them; of one taste, and transcendent over differentiation.
>
> Nor is one's own mind separable from other minds.[35]

The qualities of the four major petals of this *chakra* are summarised below with respect to the remaining four statements from the quote of Gyurme's. The focus is upon the Throat centre of an enlightened person.

13. Its emptiness and utter lack of inherent existence is the Buddha-body of Reality.

Emptiness refers to *śūnyatā,* whilst the *dharmakāya* can be considered the 'Buddha-body of Reality'. Normally *dharmakāya* would be viewed as an expression of the northernmost direction of a *maṇḍala.* However, taking the doctrine of the four Buddha bodies into account, the *svabhāvikakāya* would take the northern direction. The *dharmakāya,* therefore, is here relegated to the *eastern* direction, with the view that it manifests via *śūnyatā.* The *dharmakāyic* view via this petal of the Throat centre represents the Heart-doctrine that is the *dharma.*

Normally Akṣobhya would be ascribed to this eastern petal, drawing upon the most refined attribute possible of the developed *prāṇas* of the Heart in the head. However, because our view is upon the *dharmakāya,* Vairocana's Dharmadhātu Wisdom must be placed here. Akṣobhya's

35 Evans-Wentz, *The Tibetan Book of the Great Liberation*, 211-212.

Mirror-like Wisdom will then manifest at the centre of the *maṇḍala*. It thereby reflects the attributes of Love-Wisdom throughout the activities of this centre. It is essential for *bodhicitta* to empower the activities of every petal of this powerful directive centre if it is to not be a tool for active evil. The individual must express the inner developed potency for mantric speech, of which *śūnyatā* is the basis. The pure white *dharma* is consequently the outcome.

This means that the four major petals of this *chakra* take the attributes of the four arms of the cross of fixed, resolute affirmation of Bodhisattvic virtues. From this perspective, the northern petal is represented by the attributes of Taurus the bull, the eastern petal the qualities of Aquarius the water bearer, the southern petal the qualities of Scorpio the scorpion and the western petal those of Leo the lion. The western Fiery Leonine direction draws *bodhicitta* from Aquarius to ensure that Aetheric-Airy *dharmakāyic* energies of Life manifests through Bodhisattvic activity. The Aquarian disposition ensures a free flowing expression of pure liberating energy that floods the sum of Mind with compassionate wisdom. The Scorpionic petal, drawing from the Taurean field of wisdom, ensures the rapid awakening of all the petals of the flowers of Life as liberating energies. Scorpio esoterically stings the attributes of all these petals into action so that the 'essence of awareness' can reside in them. The nature of the tests mastered in this sign produced the background activity that caused the petals to awaken.

The attributes from the Throat tier of the Head centre are primarily directed to this eastern petal of the Throat centre, and processed by its subsidiary petals. The Throat centre governs the emanative Word, the mantric sound that stimulates awakening the panoply of myriad lives of experience and aspiration upwards to gain the Buddha-Mind. The *dharmakāya* integrates its purpose into the Heart centre, which then empowers this group of petals. This Heart's-Mind is the potency known as 'ultimate truth', and this major petal of the Throat centre governs any category of enlightened expression wherein the Word of Truth is to be used. The northern petal expresses the mantric power from the highest level of *dharmakāya* in terms of its Creativity. The western petal then draws the sustaining power from the *śūnyatā-saṃsāra* nexus for the mantric expression, and the southern petal wields the substance that builds the images of the real that are to be projected to fulfil their meditative purpose. The potency of the *dharmakāyic* Mind is therefore utilised when one goes inwards at this stage to speak words of wisdom. This *dharma* resonates to the needs of many.

14. The natural resonance and radiance of this emptiness is the Buddha-body of Perfect Resource.

This resonant radiance of emptiness manifests in the form of the *sambhogakāya* of the various Buddhas and Bodhisattvas, and is incorporated in the Sambhogakāya Flowers of humanity. Its activity is empowered in the *southern* direction of the Throat centre. Here we have the mode of expression of the Buddha-Mind in arenas other than just that associated with the physical domain. These include activity in the various Bardo fields (the subjective planes of perception) which must be brought into the domain of the *dharma*. The 'Perfect Resource' provided is that of the various sheaths of a Buddha body, the substance of the thoughts and images that are the veils of enlightenment. They are impressed by means of the awakening of the Eye of vision (Ājñā centre) whereby the generalised potency from the Head lotus can be directed to any part of the *nāḍī* system (the radiant jewel of the individual) so that the associated powers of the resources of the *chakras* can be utilised. Even though the created thought-forms or attributes of images are Watery, they inspire the devotional masses and are therefore liberating in nature. These images emanate from the Heart tier of the Head centre.

The Equalising potency of Ratnasambhava is developed and produces the forms that will produce enlightened realisations in the mind of the beholder. The qualities of Scorpio the scorpion, a Water sign, are utilised to energise the images of the real in such a way that the aspirants to the mysteries veiled by them are sufficiently tested to prove their worthiness for enlightenment.

15. And its unimpeded arising in any form whatsoever is the Buddha-body of Emanation.

The *nirmāṇakāya* of a Buddha or high grade Bodhisattva manifests via the *western* direction of outwards into the field of service, allowing the attributes of Mind to be broadcast via speech to be heard by people. Though considered an illusional emanation of a great one, the *nirmāṇakāya* represents the way each high grade Bodhisattva can serve humanity by expressing final conclusions of meditations upon the multifarious tasks regarding human liberation. All such illusional bodies of reality are born from Mind and are attributes of it, whilst the western direction is the natural conveyor of expressions of such *dharma* attributes to all human minds. The major *prāṇas* of any group of petals from the outer petals of the Solar Plexus in the head is directed through this particular petal of the Throat centre. The emblem of the lotus associated with the function of Amitābha who rules this western direction is thus portrayed.

Amitābha's Discriminating Inner Wisdom here draws the principle of compassion from the eastern direction (the *dharmakāya)* and is utilised to awaken the hearts of all who respond to the doctrine promulgated. Leo the lion governing this direction is the sign of the self-conscious individual, here the *nirmāṇakāya,* basking in the sun of accomplishment. Self-consciousness has been translated into the unique identity of Bodhisattvic purpose for each cycle of activity. Many can be liberated as they follow the laws of group evolution that the appearance of the heart of a *maṇḍala* of liberating, awakened ones provides. Mind thereby supplants mind upon a mass scale in the Fiery sun of revelatory light provided by such a one.

16. These three, fully present as one, are the very essence [of awareness] itself.

The *svābhāvikakāya* is represented by the northern synthesising petal of the Throat centre. It incorporates the collective Minds of all Buddhas that are engaged in their own intrinsic contemplations. It connotes the ability to convey Secret Mantra on all levels of expression, to bring about the causation of whatever is to be. There is thus an unbroken line of emanative Sound from the highest Buddha-field to the depths of *saṃsāra,* causing *māyā* to be organised by the Buddha *vacana* (Word). The Earthy Element is thereby exemplified, not in terms of an illusional field of expression, but in the form of a downward descent of a Buddha's Mind, clothing itself in ever-increasing density so that the minds of masses of individuals can comprehend the nature of what the Sounds reveal.

Through developing the Buddha-Mind this northern petal awakens its full creative potential in an individual, as it conveys the essentiality of the flowering activity of the entire Head lotus (*sahasrāra padma*) upon which it is focussed at any time. This petal draws *prāṇas* from any of the tiers of petals in the Head lotus, as projected via one or other of the four arms of the *viśvavajra* that governs the directions of the major *prāṇic* flow of this centre. The All-accomplishing Wisdom of Amoghasiddhi thus becomes the Jina expression developed. The All-seeing Eye associated with the sign Taurus the bull is fully awakened to vision in all directions and dimensions of space, and to project 'the very essence of Awareness' to wherever it is needed. The enlightenment-attributes gained from former incarnations are collectivised and directed upwards to become the *dharmakāya*. This is done in the form of the integrated body of expression *(trikāya)* of a Buddha. There is also a consequent natural downward flow of *dharma* from 'thus gone' ones of the past, the true essence *(svābhāvikakāya)* of all meditative impression.

So far the focus has been upon the way the petals of the Throat centre express the *saṃskāras* of enlightenment, this function, however, is a long way into the future for most people. Instead, the petals regulate *manasic saṃskāras* as categorised by the twelve signs of the zodiac analysed in a more mundane way. There is also a transition process from where an individual is primarily focused in terms of conventional (relative) truth, to when a *yogin* manifests the attributes of ultimate truth via the relative durations of any undertaking that *saṃskāras* present.

Regarding relative truth (concerning the major part of an individual's evolution), the four major petals are arranged in such a way that they collectivise the *saṃskāras* of a group of three petals each (signifying the *prāṇas* of 'body, speech, and mind'), and project them to one or other of the four cardinal directions for each of the four levels of *manasic* expression outlined below. Astrologically they relate to the four quadrants of the zodiac.

The four major petals of the Throat centre embody the qualities of one or other of the three major crosses at any time. The cardinal cross attributes manifest for Initiates, the fixed cross attributes for the loving types of individuals, or who are aspiring to tread the path to enlightenment, and the mutable cross for the average humanity engaged in the vicissitudes of *saṃsāra*. Taking the fixed cross as an example we see that the northern petal manifests the attributes of Taurus, which governs the entire field of the mind, directing *prāṇas* to and from the Ājñā and Head centres. The eastern petal embodies the group-conscious attributes of Aquarius, directing general *piṅgalā prāṇas* to and from the Heart centre. The southern petal takes the attributes of Scorpio, producing the many tests of life's processes as various *saṃskāras* are processed in the Splenic centres. As these obstacles are appropriately mastered, then petals of the associated *chakras* awaken. Finally, the western petal processes the entire Leonine field of expression of self-consciousness *(āhamkara),* and general *iḍā prāṇas* to and from the Solar Plexus centre producing caring, solicitous forms of emotions.

Each unit of four petals for each major direction is also receptive to one or other of the Fires that originate in the Base of Spine centre and then courses through the petals of the *chakras* of the rest of the system. In doing so the qualities of the associated centres are gained. The corresponding petal of the Throat centre directs developed *saṃskāras* of any of the four main Elements when a person is mentally active. Because the inner twelve petals revolve, so each petal moves in and out of the arena of expression of a major petal, according to the *saṃskāra* that is conveyed as a directive impulse *(manasic* Will).

When the four larger petals of any of the four directions are considered, then the seven Ray potencies that can be developed (associated with the seven minor petals they draw *prāṇas* from) are synthesised into the three large petals. They are then focussed via the largest petal that can project the image, idea, or word conveyed by the mind at any moment. Any one of the zodiacal petals (numbered from 1 to 12) incorporates the *prāṇas* from three minor petals. The three petals convey a *guṇa* of any attribute of a sense-consciousness experienced, or specifically *prāṇas* derived from the three worlds of human livingness. These energies are then focussed by the major synthesising petal and directed to the mind (the Head lotus). Generally one sense-impression at a time is experienced, but in reality all five sense-consciousnesses help to produce the *manasic saṃskāra* generated. Hence there are five petals of three different sizes to accommodate the process (garnering the *prāṇas* from the three worlds of human livingness).

With respect to the average person the northern petals are concerned with the abstraction of thoughts. The eastern group of petals direct the clarified *prāṇas* of thought gained through calm reflective pondering. They express loving, enlightening ideas. The southern petals recycle *prāṇas* from below the diaphragm. They repossess them to empower a person's normal thought life, and for converting into knowledgeable acquisitions of mind. These petals process the basic *kāma-manasic* thoughts derived from the Watery proclivity of the Solar Plexus. They employ the many selfish and desirous thoughts engendered. The western group of petals relegate the more mundane attributes of mind that are an expression of the world of ideas, the average intelligent thoughts and fields of investigation that are often reified and self-centred. Concepts of the 'I' reign supreme. Thus is outlined the arms of the mutable cross for this centre.

Attributes of Mind and the Heart centre

Having analysed the Throat centre's regulation of the (Fiery) *iḍā nāḍī prāṇas* in the body, we can now turn to the major organ regulating the flow of the *piṇgalā prāṇas;* the Heart centre. This centre has already been explained in some detail, therefore the reader must correlate the brief account presented below with the material presented earlier concerning the qualities of each petal. Both Gyurme's and Evans-Wentz's[36] translations shall be utilised.

The twelve statements are presented in the form of meditation instructions that may assist in comprehending the Heart centre's expression. We are informed that if we follow these twelve forms of insight (*śamatha*, calm abiding or tranquility meditation) then we are bound to succeed, because our meditation is upon the one reality of being/non-being. In contrast, *vipassanā,* the special penetrative or analytic insight, is meditation that draws impressions from the sixteen petals of the Throat centre.

Evans-Wentz uses the title 'Mind is Non-Created',[37] presenting us with a natural qualification of this 'one reality' of the Mind that is the Heart. The Heart's expanse simply is, it cannot be created, or found by means of the activity of mind, by anything related to the

36 Quotes from Evans-Wentz follow Gyurme's and are italicised.

37 Evans-Wentz, *The Tibetan Book of the Great Liberation,* 212.

modifications of the substance of mind (which are 'created' and thus continuously changing). To find this natural state of Mind one must therefore relinquish anything that is 'created' and simply reside in what remains, in the calm abiding.

[Consequence of the Introduction to Awareness]
When the introduction is powerfully applied in accordance with the [above] method of entering into this [reality]:

1. One's own immediate consciousness is this very [reality]!
   [Abiding] in this [reality], which is uncontrived and naturally radiant,
   How can one say that one does not understand the nature of mind?[38]

Mind in its true nature being non-created and self-radiant, how can one, without knowing the mind, assert that mind is created?[39]

We start with the easternmost (Arian) petal of the Heart centre, 'which is uncontrived and naturally radiant'. Such a consciousness is immediate, spontaneous because no effort is required to produce it, or bring it forth. It simply is (therefore is uncreated) and always will be. Once uncovered it will be understood to be the Mind's true essence. All *manasic saṃskāras* must inevitably be cleansed of defilements to reveal their natural uncreated self-radiant nature.

2. [Abiding] in this [reality], wherein there is nothing on which to meditate,
   How can one say that, by having entered into meditation, one was not successful?

There being in this yoga nothing objective upon which to meditate, how can one, without having ascertained the true nature of mind by meditation, assert that mind is created?

The precincts of the Taurean petal[40] are now entered, wherein the Eye of vision can be awakened through correct meditative approach to all of life's processes. Once the entire field of desire and attachment to things (governed by Taurus) has been eliminated, what then is there to

38 This and the remaining twelve statements in normal type are from Gyurme, 42-44. I have added the numbers to assist in the description of their meanings.

39 This and the remaining italicised statements are from Evens-Wentz, 212-214.

40 The zodiacal wheel is turning via Cancer in the southern position.

meditate upon (re the material domain)? The Heart's-Mind lies at ease, serene, visioning all things as they truly are, thus whatever query may have led one to meditate has been answered. How can one therefore say: 'one was not successful?'

3. [Abiding] in this [reality], which is one's actual awareness itself,
How can one say that one could not find one's own mind?

Mind in its true state being Reality, how can one, without having discovered one's own mind, assert that mind is created?

In the petal governed by Gemini the twins the temple of the Heart can be experienced, 'which is one's actual awareness itself'. Here the feminine and masculine *iḍā* and *piṅgalā nāḍīs* are blended in the inner sanctum of life's processes. This produces all that can be considered the Heart's true Mind. The *saṃskāras* of concepts of duality, of opposites, the one and the other, become merged into a fluid oneness that is pristine awareness wherein one abides.

4. [Abiding] in this [reality], the uninterrupted [union] of radiance and awareness.
How can one say that the [true] face of mind has not been seen?

Mind in its true state being undoubtedly ever-existing, how can one, without having seen the mind face to face, assert that mind is created?

Having united all opposites into the oneness, one then resides perpetually in the uninterrupted, ever-existing cosmic Waters of spaciousness (Love-Wisdom) governed by the Cancerian petal.[41] Love-Wisdom then is the shell or home perpetually carried by the crab. This petal also signifies the rebirthing process, wherein the true 'face' of reality is expressed into manifestation. It produces that phenomenal appearance that can see Mind 'face to face'.

We should note here that the face contains seven orifices, two eyes, two nostrils, two ears, and the mouth, which aptly symbolise the seven principles, Rays, attributes of incarnate life. The Reality or Truth that is 'the Face of the One' is reflected into the other face (the illusional 'self') allowing Mind to see 'face to face'. All happens in *śamatha*

41 The view here is the transmuted correspondence of the Water Element, rather than what is normally expressed in *saṃsāra*.

and experienced utilising *vipassanā* within the precincts of the Mind that is the Heart. Here the implication is that all *saṃskāras* of the life processes have been mastered, allowing perception of the true Face of the reality (the *tathāgatagarbha)* that emanated our existence.

> 5. [Abiding] in this [reality], which is itself the cogniser,
> How can one say that, though sought, this [cogniser] could not be found?

The thinking-principle being of the very essence of mind, how can one, without having sought and found it, assert that mind is created?

This (Leonine) petal represents the sign wherein self-consciousness (the I-concept) is developed. This 'cogniser' or thinking principle is transformed by means of the Heart's action into the self-organised principle that is 'the very essence of mind' that perceives the reality of whatever is and is not. This necessitates the *saṃskāras* that are concepts of a personal 'self' to be transmuted into a true perception that integrates the one into the many, the many into the multitude, and the multitude into the Universal All—all travelling together as One throughout the vast reaches of cosmos. The collective Mind of this Universal All is expressed and experienced as the Heart's Mind. It is non-created, it simply is, the true cogniser that is found.

> 6. [Abiding] in this [reality], where there is nothing at all to be done,
> How can one say that, whatever one did, one did not succeed?

Mind being transcendent over creation, and thus partaking of the Uncreated, how can one assert that mind is created?

The sixth petal governed by Virgo the virgin can now be analysed. Virgo rules the dissemination of Mind governing Nature, thus ruled by the creative potency of the *devas*. Integrating with this Mind produces a transcendence over creation. Because wherever one looks all one can see or perceive is but an expression or emanation of Mind, then there is nothing to be done but to abide in this natural state of Mind. This petal of the Heart centre culls and transforms the *saṃskāras* derived from one's interrelation with the external world. Here rests the foundation for experience of the externalised *karma* of *dharmakāya*.

> 7. Given that it is sufficient to leave [this awareness] as it is, uncontrived,
> How can one say that one could not continue to abide [in that state]?

Mind being in its primordial, unmodified naturalness non-created, as it should be taken to be, and without form, how can one assert that it is created?

The Libran petal of the Heart centre represents the interlude between extremes, the hub of the great wheel of Life turning. That 'uncontrived awareness', 'devoid of quality', therefore, represents the essence of what constitutes the Wheel in its totality. True impartiality allows the Libran to be the judge, integrating all via the wisdom of Love *(bodhicitta)* to establish the true centre between extremes. This petal thus brings all *saṃskāric* attributes to the Void, by stripping them bare of everything but the most essential intrinsic characteristics in which the meditating one continuously abides.

8. Given that it is sufficient to leave it as it is, without doing anything whatsoever,
How can one say that one could not do just that?

Inasmuch as mind can also be taken to be devoid of quality, how can one venture to assert that it is created?

We now come to the Scorpionic petal, which is the major petal dealing with transmuting the *saṃskāras* developed along the path of discipleship, such as strong desirous and often fanatical bias. Such *saṃskāras* must be eliminated or converted into the power to one-pointedly manifest yogic observations *(tapas)* and precepts *(samaya,* a sacred commitment). The *tapas* sets up its own rhythm of liberation, producing the enlightenment that the awakening of the Heart centre provides. One should therefore not change this rhythmic action, it should be left 'as it is' for the true nature of Mind to awaken. The phrase 'without doing anything whatsoever' therefore refers to the natural course of momentum that carries through the process of converting *saṃskāras,* once the *tapas* and *samaya* have become firmly established.

9. Given that, [within this reality], radiance, awareness, and emptiness are inseparable and spontaneously present,
How can one say that, by having practised, one attained nothing?

The self-born, qualityless mind, being like the Three Voids undifferentiated, unmodified, how can one assert that mind is created?

The Sagittarian petal of the Heart lotus fires the arrows of the unified 'three Voids', 'radiance, awareness, and emptiness' (symbolised by the two prongs and the point of the archer's arrow) towards whatever target in the far reaches of cosmos the meditator focuses. (Having liberated the *saṃskāras* that bind one to *saṃsāra,* the momentum achieved naturally drives one forward to the vastness of cosmic space.) This represents the gain of the accumulated experiences of aeons of *manasic* development, stripped bare of their unessential attributes. It becomes the *yogin's* keynote, via which others can perceive the projected intention.

The terms signifying the three Voids are the transformed essences of the three *guṇas,* the awakened expressions of the three main *nāḍīs.* The outpouring of the transmuted *iḍā* stream has revealed the emptiness that is the true nature of substance. The transformed *piṅgalā* stream has produced the natural lucidity of Mind ('awareness') when it is empty of phenomena. The *suṣumṇā* path has manifested the pervasive radiance of Mind. Radiance is an energy field that is integrated with all similar states of unbounded luminescence.

> 10. Given that [this reality] is naturally originating and spontaneously present, without causes and conditions,
> How can one say that, by having made the effort [to find it], one was incapable [of success]?

> *Mind being without objectivity and causation, self-originated, self-born, how can one, without having endeavoured to know mind, assert that mind is created?*

The Capricornian petal presents the vast expanse of Mind that comes from 'above' or beyond the conditions of this world sphere. This is the *dharmakāya,* which 'is naturally originating and spontaneously present, without causes and conditions'. We therefore have the nature of the expression that produces Buddhahood. The striving relegated to this petal is consequently towards cosmos, the 'self-originated, self-born' strata of being/non-being that spontaneously arises in those who are preparing to leave the conditionings of this earth sphere behind. In this petal, therefore, are eliminated the familiar *saṃskāras* that all Bodhisattvas utilise whilst they are actively engaged in their various forms of service work. The aggregate of associated *karma* they possess must eventually be eliminated so that when they become Buddhas they can altogether leave behind the spheres of activity concerning our earth.

> 11. Given that the arising and liberation of conceptual thoughts occur simultaneously,
> How can one say that, by having applied this antidote [to conceptual thoughts], one was not effective?

Inasmuch as Divine Wisdom dawns in accordance with its own time,[42] *and one is emancipated, how can opponents of these teachings assert that it is created?*

The eleventh, Aquarian petal of the great wheel of the Heart centre, exemplifies the attributes governing treading the Bodhisattva path. The generation of 'Divine Wisdom' is therefore exemplified, as well as all *saṃskāras* that produce the simultaneous arising and liberation of conceptual thoughts relegated as a service arena for humanity. All other types of *saṃskāras* are therefore eliminated or transformed. Enlightenment is the gain, *bodhicitta* is what remains after all has been said and done. *Bodhicitta* here becomes the Waters of the Heart's Life poured forth as the Wisdom needed to help enlighten all.

> 12. [Abiding] in this immediate consciousness itself,
> How can one say that one does not know this [reality]?

Mind being, as it is, of this nature, and thus unknowable,[43] *how can one assert that mind is created?*

Finally we have the Piscean petal, signifying the ending of any cycle of activity, of all forms of concretised empirical thinking and ratiocination, so that only that relegated to the abstract Mind ('this immediate consciousness itself') remains. The *saṃskāras* of the bounded finite expressions of mind are freed from their attachments, becoming therefore effortless, spontaneous, and desireless (self-less). Residing in the natural state of Mind, how then 'can one assert that it is created' or not know of its reality?

---

42 That is, the true state of timelessness.

43 That is, the finite mind cannot know the abstract mind.

The forty-two Peaceful Deities

The analysis so far has presented the forces of Mind that are expressed in the centres above the Diaphragm centre.[44] These centres synthesise the *iḍā* and *piṅgalā nāḍī* streams conveying the emanating *prāṇas* of the forty-two Peaceful Deities. These Deities are derived from the 'Synonyms for Mind', a permutation of the five Dhyāni Buddhas and Consorts, plus that of the overriding Ādi Buddha and their collective qualities; therefore of Primordial Mind. The permutations of Deities (the transformed attributes of mind) find expression via the twelve main petals of the Heart centre, plus the sixteen main petals of the Throat centre via the eight directions of space. Attributes of Mind permeate Space and govern recurring cycles of expression that drive forward the momentum of evolutionary change within the domains where form has meaning. These two *chakras* are needed for this expression. The Throat centre disseminates all the forces pertaining to the feminine (*iḍā nāḍī*), that inherently expresses the quality of wisdom. The Heart centre disseminates the masculine (*piṅgalā nāḍī*) aspect demonstrating the compassion of the Jinas. Together they manifest the attributes of the dual Ray of Love-Wisdom. This is the primal energy governing the force of conversion of dark matter (*citta*) into intensified luminosity. The third centre utilised by these permutations is the directive Eye (the Ājñā centre). It processes these two *nāḍīs* and conveys the integrating *suṣumṇā* energies, allowing the male-female forces to manifest in a non-dual form.

The six Buddhas of the *bhavacakra* find expression as the compassionate forces from above the diaphragm to transform the six consciousnesses below the diaphragm. (The domain of the Six Realms.) They logically work via any grouping of six theriomorphic female deities, however, the six petals of the Sacral centre, the energy distributer in the body, are controlled specifically via the agency of these force vectors. Thus the entire field of desire is processed with respect to the emanations of mind, and is eventually converted into Mind.

The Guardians similarly work to help transform the *prāṇas* guarded over by the animal-headed Gatekeepers. They work to extend the reach

44 Omitting the combined Head centres, which represent the integration of the entire *maṇḍala* of Life.

of the transformative forces from above the diaphragm right to the Base of Spine centre. The Consorts of the Guardians assist the normal working of this centre for average humans. This sets the tone for the types of *prāṇas* generated for the rest of the circulatory system. When a candidate appears that will tread the path of Initiation, with the consequent awakening of *kuṇḍalinī,* then the role of the Guardians comes into play to help protect candidates from the possible nefarious effects of awakening Fires. With them therefore the entire *maṇḍala* of the Wrathful Deities awaken to play their appointed roles.

The power of the Vidyādharas and Consorts plays the important role of helping to pacify and transform the *kāma-manasic* expression of the two pentads of the Solar Plexus centre into the higher *manasic* qualities that awaken the enlightened Mind. The reach of the eight Mahābodhisattvas manifests via the eight petals of the Diaphragm centre, whilst their Consorts work to help transform the *prāṇas* of Splenic centre II for humanity (where the major transformative battles in the body occur). Splenic centre I comes under the jurisdiction of the twelve Deities embodying the Heart centre at the appropriate time of transference of *saṃskāras* to the related petals of the Heart centre.

One can observe this process on the minute scale of an individual, wherein aspects of the above Deities manifest as intrinsic forces affecting consciousness. However, a more important view, from the perspective of an enlightened One, is to see them in terms of great transforming agents upon a planetary scale. In this light they manifest as various Lords occupying the kingdom of Shambhala (the planetary Head centre), assisting the evolutionary development of all lives upon our planet. All is then observed in terms of the progress of *prāṇic* forces (streams of lives) undergoing various trials of transformation upon an Initiation path that leads them from a lesser sphere of attainment of sentience or consciousness to a greater one. They finally travel out of a particular kingdom (represented by a specific *chakra)* into the next higher one.

Upon the attainment of yogic prowess the Ājñā centre specifically coordinates the activity of both groups from the Heart and Throat centres. The higher, supramundane *siddhis* then stand revealed in terms of the qualities of the Wisdoms of the five Dhyāni Buddhas, as expressions within the Womb of the Great Mother that is the Consort of the Ādi Buddha (Samantabhadra). *Saṃsāra* and *śūnyatā* are then integrated as one ineffable nexus of being/non-being that is the Buddha-Mind expressing the Dharmakāya Way. Thus the lowest and the highest spheres of mind/Mind are incorporated within cosmos.

The Throat, Heart and Ājñā centres consequently allow the sum of the attributes of Mind to be reflected in manifestation (*saṃsāra*) via the expression of various permutations of the Peaceful Deities. They fulfil the functions of the petals of each *chakra* as needed, according to the *prāṇas* manifesting at any time. Whenever these *prāṇic* forces manifest, then the functions of the eight directions of space *(aṣṭadiśas)* and their relation to the eight Mahābodhisattvas come into play. The Guardians can then demonstrate a role in guarding the cardinal directions of space via the four main petals of the Throat centre from any possible perturbation of mind, when *prāṇas* are flowing from below the diaphragm. They are also the main directive agents assisting in the transformation of the four major Elements into their Void aspects.

The Guardians normally regulate the main expression of Heart generated *manasic* input to the Throat centre. They are especially concerned with protecting against the unmerited effects of the *suṣumṇā* flow, which comes near the ending of the evolutionary process. Their influence is also demonstrated at the beginning of creative ventures for the instigation of all that must come to be via Mind. There are four main Elements that constitute the substratum of *saṃsāra,* whereby all consciousness transformations are undertaken. The fifth (Aether) is the substance of Space that carries it all. Therefore, when considering the Guardians, only four need to exist to manifest appropriate functions with respect to the Elements. Through their agency, empowering *prāṇas* flow via the four main petals of this centre to organise the attributes of mind and their transformation into Mind.

One can analyse the expression of the dynamic causative potency of Mind in its *own domain,* in terms of the empowerment of the forces of Love-Wisdom, rather than just in terms of Throat centre activity. The function of the Ādi Buddha, Dhyāni Buddhas and Consorts, plus that of the eight Mahābodhisattvas can then be observed. The Consorts of the Mahābodhisattvas are not counted here because they are responsible for the movement of these causative energies of Mind in *saṃsāra.* (The centres below the diaphragm.) They govern the substance to be moved, and therefore the appropriation of the *karma,* in order to express the vicissitudes and ramifications of Mind. This movement happens in terms of the eight consciousnesses (of the eight arms of the cross of direction in space). The Deities above the diaphragm govern the sum of emanative space.

This makes twenty (4 x 5) entities all told.[45] The 4 x 5 refers to the foundational energy substratum of space in terms of the geometry of pentagrams of energy oriented in the four cardinal directions endlessly repeated. When the protecting and focussing activities of the Guardians are added, then we get the number twenty-four (4 + 20). This number is important, as the *maṇḍala* of the underlying etheric grid of energies is based upon it. It signifies the 'blueprint' of whatever is to transpire as a space-time continuum, the consciousness-space of the awakening petals of a *chakra*. Upon this foundation arises the *maṇḍala* of all the patterns of petals of each *chakra*.[46] This number also constitutes a normal tier (or base number) of petals to a major *chakra*. They are based upon the powers of the number twelve. Double this number represents the needed *iḍā* and *piṅgalā* expression of the foundational energies. When the resultant twenty-four petals are doubled again then the *prāṇas* of these *nāḍīs* are further conveyed in terms of their inherent dualities. For this reason there are forty-eight petals to each lobe of the Ājñā centre. Also, twenty-four multiplied by the number four for the qualities of the four cardinal directions (or Elements) ruled by the Guardians provides us with the number 96, the number of inner petals to all major *chakras*.

The principle of active compassion (embodied by Avalokiteśvara) manifests via six liberating forces when the forces of Mind are expressed in the reflected, illusional world that is *saṃsāra*. These five sense consciousnesses plus the integrating intellect are the foundational idea behind the concept of the Six Realms of the *bhavacakra* (wheel of birth and death). Being the mechanism to distribute the energy of Mind, the petals of the Throat centre embody the transformative potencies for the denizens of these realms. Effectively they project the emanative Words (mantras) that will convert the aberrant *saṃskāras* represented by the entities existing in the centres below the diaphragm wherein the Six Realms manifest.[47]

---

45 These pentads are concerned with cosmic purpose (north), factors of conversion of substance (south), spacious factors of Mind (east), and the substance of Mind (west).

46 Much is veiled here concerning the basis of the expression of the *nāḍī* system.

47 See Volume 4 for an explanation of these realms with respect to Avalokiteśvara.

The factors of the integrating intellect projected by a major petal of the Ājñā centre represent the potency to convert the domain wherein is found the activities of the gods of the *bhavacakra,* here taken as the domain of enlightened beings. To get there, all of the attributes concerning pride and ego-delusion *(āhamkara)* must be countered. Eventually super-human capabilities are developed. The sum of the mental-emotions developed by humans is countered by the mantric potencies from any major petal of the Throat centre. The conversion of the *prāṇas* of the 3 + 1 minor petals that can also be seen to support one major petal, deal with the *prāṇas* of the remaining realms. The more Watery attributes of the *asuras* (jealosy), animals (ignorance) and *pretas* (desires) relate to the three smaller petals. The more manasic *prāṇas* creating hell states (hatreds, intolerance, fanatical dogmatism, critical mind, spite, etc.) are dealt with by the larger petal. Their energies can be potently intensified via the Throat centre's Fiery proclivity, and more force will be needed to counter their effects. Herein lies the foundation for much evil *karma* generated via this centre and, by extension from the mouth.

From this perspective, the four main petals turn and each one comes under the influence of one of the petals of the Ājñā centre, so then the attributes of the four Elements can be directed and cleansed in this manner. We thus have (5 + 1) x 4 = 24 (or rather 4 + 20) potencies to be converted into enlightenment-attributes by this means for either the *iḍā* or *piṇgalā nāḍīs.* Thus when both *nāḍīs* are taken into account then 2 x 24 = 48 potencies must be converted by mantra. The significance of the esoteric science of Secret Mantra[48] is here indicated. (Mantras are force potencies organised, controlled and directed by mind/Mind.) When the complete number of petals to any quadrant of the Throat centre (1 + 3 + 7) is taken into account and integrated with one petal of the Ājñā centre then there are twelve potencies in each direction, making 4 x 12 = 48 altogether. Taking both *iḍā* and *piṇgalā nāḍīs* into account there are 2 x 48 = 96 attributes. The *saṃskāras* associated with all minor and major *chakras* can thereby be effectively processed by a *yogin* awakening higher perceptions. This number also represents the number of petals to the Throat tier of the Head centre.

---

48 See Dudjom Rinpoche, Jikdrel Yeshe Dorje, *The Nyingma School of Tibetan Buddhism* for the Nyingma perspective of the meaning of this term.

The Heart tier possesses 4 x 48 = 192 petals in order to refine four groupings of 48 *prāṇas* in terms of the four Elements before the proceeds are passed on to the Throat tier. When the combined number of petals to the Heart and Throat tiers of the Head centre is taken into account then we get 6 x 48 petals, which allow the refinement and conversion of the sum of the attributes of the Six Realms from all perspectives. It allows complete Mastery (transmutation) of the Watery Element.

The Solar Plexus tier of the Head lotus contains 8 x 96 petals altogether wherein the major processes of transformation of these *saṃskāras* occur in terms of the eight directions of space, or of the eight consciousnesses. (Note that the number 96 also equals 8 x 12.) Thus is the story of the gaining of enlightenment told *prāṇically*. Here we see the work of the eight Mahābodhisattvas and their Consorts, plus the four Guardians and Consorts to assist in this work. They govern and project the karmic ramifications of all that transpires. The number 8 + 4 produces the necessary number twelve needed to convey the qualities of the twelve signs of the zodiac,[49] the complement of twelve energies that express the *prāṇas* of the Heart of Life throughout space.

The relation between the Throat and the Ājñā centres is mainly found in the five Aetheric petals of the Ājñā centre, each of which possess eight petals. They offer a conduit for the development of the higher Mind from out of the domains of *saṃsāra*. When these five main Aetheric petals are multiplied by their eight subpetals then there are forty petals altogether. These forty petals manifest through any of the four Airy petals (responsible for processing the four Elements) and then a lobe of the Ājñā centre. It projects the sum of the *prāṇas* to the Throat centre. This then constitutes 40 + 1 + 1 = 42 petals, signifying the projection of the qualities of the Peaceful Deities for each of the four main Airy petals, which have an affinity to one or other of the four main petals of the Throat centre. Also, if we take the complete view and multiply the forty petals of the Aetheric tier by the four main Airy petals, then we get the number 160 = 10 x 16, signifying the ten stages of the evolutionary process that can manifest through the sixteen petals of the Throat centre to perfect the attributes of mind/Mind.

---

49 We also get the number 24 = 2 x (8 + 4) when the work of the Consorts are taken into account. This number completes the story in terms of the *iḍā* and *piṇgalā* expression of the turning of each wheel.

The forces of Mind also need to be numerically expressed in terms of the attributes of the five sense-consciousnesses, if they are to be borne and evolved by the human units that are the vehicles of consciousness in *saṃsāra*. They (the *tathāgatagarbha* attribute of humanity) have come into existence as converters of primordial *citta* into wisdom, as earlier explained. To do so, five secret Vidyādharas appear, to direct the *saṃskāras* of mind, as they are converted into elements of Mind in their appropriate centres in the domain of Mind. Here the *saṃskāras* can be spontaneously, desirelessly, and effortlessly processed in terms of the categories of their united wisdoms. The attributes of the Dhyāni Buddhas are consequently born. The Consorts of the Vidyādharas embody the karmic ramifications of all activities of mind within *saṃsāra*. The symbolic seventh day of the deceased's experience in Bardo marks entry into the abode of the *devas* (*ḍākinīs*), where all vicissitudes of *karma* are expressed as the manifestation of *saṃsāra*. Thus we have the statement: 'In the Outer Circle, round about these Knowledge-Holders, innumerable bands of *ḍākinīs—ḍākinīs* of the eight places of cremation, *ḍākinīs* of the four classes, *ḍākinīs* of the three abodes,[50] *ḍākinīs* of the thirty holy-places and of the twenty-four places of pilgrimage...will come to receive the faithful and punish the unfaithful'.[51]

One can take the number thirty for these 'holy-places' to refer to the 16 + 12 petals of the Throat and Heart centres, plus the two main lobes of the Ājñā centre that integrate and process their *prāṇas* before they are sent to the Head centre. The meanings of the number twenty-four have been described above and elsewhere in this book.

Counting the Vidyādharas and Consorts a total of 52 Peaceful Deities[52] appear in the domains of Mind to account for the above activity.

---

50 Concerning these 'three abodes' and 'eight places of cremation', Evans-Wentz's *The Tibetan Book of the Dead*, 128, states in a footnote that 'The eight places of cremation are the eight known to Hindu Mythology; the three abodes are the heart-centre, the throat-centre, and the brain-centre, over which, esoterically speaking, certain *ḍākinīs* (as the personification of the psychic forces resident in each centre) preside, just as other *ḍākinīs* preside over the holy-places and places of pilgrimage'. By the number eight we see that these places of cremation represent any grouping of eight petals in the various centres wherein *saṃskāras* are transformed yogically. They are charnel grounds indeed.

51 Ibid., 128. They represent the generalised accounting of all karmic forces governing all the minor *chakras*, the *saṃskāras* which the deceased must now experience as karmic due.

52 There is an interesting correlation here to the number of weeks to a year, the major

The four Guardians and their Consorts however manifest as the gates of exit or entry of *prāṇas* to an entire *maṇḍala*. They stand neither in or out of the structure. Their role is to absorb the *prāṇas* from the innermost groups of four petals delineated by an acorn of Gatekeepers of pristine cognition of either of the two lobes of the Ājñā centre. They are the foundation of support of all that is to transpire in a *maṇḍala* and are thus semi-wrathful. From this perspective they can be discounted from the list of the Peaceful Deities if need be. If we subtract the number 2 x 4 from 52 then we get the number 44, which as stated in part A relates to human evolution.

In presenting the liberated correlations to the main petals of the two major *chakras* above the diaphragm (not counting the Ājñā centre) we need to consult the information in part A in relation to the diagrams of the petals of the *chakras*. With respect to the twelve main petals of the Heart centre, the Ādi Buddha and Consort plus the five Dhyāni Buddhas embody the functions of the seven sacred petals (that process the *saṃskāras* of the seven Rays), whilst the Consorts of the Dhyāni Buddhas would play the role of processing the *prāṇas* (the refined characteristics derived from the five sense-consciousnesses) of the five non-sacred petals.

Discounting the Ādi Buddha and Consort we see that the remaining forty Peaceful Deities will find their expression governing the main petals of the Throat centre. There are thus 24 inner minor petals, plus 12 + 4 outer ones to this centre. Also, the internal arrangement of the petals of this *chakra* is seen in terms of four units of 7 + 3 petals, making the number 40 within the context of the four major petals, esoterically making the number 44 altogether. This number's relation to the Fiery Throat centre is one reason why humans are sometimes called divine *mānasaputras,* bearers of mind.[53] It is the centre they are learning to positively develop and control, so its *prāṇas* must be revealed and awakened, whereas the Heart centre is intrinsic to their development.

From another perspective, the four Guardians or their Consorts, depending upon whether one is viewing an *iḍā* or *piṅgalā* energisation, would naturally process the *prāṇas* manifesting via the four main petals

---

unit of time wherewith we reckon the cycles of activity during our sojourn upon the earth.

53 In the esoteric tradition established by H.P. Blavatsky. Another reason for this appellation being that the Sambhogakāya Flower exists upon the higher mental plane thus is constituted of the substance of Mind.

of the Throat centre, according to the orientation of the respective petals. The thirty-two remaining deities can be divided into two groups of sixteen entities each.

a. The *iḍā* grouping: the five Vidyādharas and their Consorts, plus the six Buddhas governing the Six Realms. They deal specifically with the *manasic* input (the wisdom attribute) into this centre from the centres below the diaphragm. They also process the *prāṇas* from the non-sacred petals of the Heart centre.
b. The *piṇgalā* grouping: the eight Mahābodhisattvas plus their Consorts. This group is responsible for processing the compassionate attributes of the *manasic* input from the centres below the diaphragm. They also process the *prāṇas* from the sacred petals of the Heart centre, plus the most refined Aetheric *prāṇas* from the non-sacred petals.

One could then make a case that either grouping comes into play for the sixteen main petals of the Throat centre, depending upon whether the prime nature of the *prāṇa* to be expressed is either *iḍā* or *piṇgalā*. The four Guardians are the overall determinants as to what *prāṇas* enter or leave this *chakra*. (The Guardians come specifically into activity when the individual manifests mantric forces in meditation, or when the stages of Initiation are undertaken.)

For the major *chakras* below the diaphragm we can include the Splenic centres (which together manifest as a major centre), plus the Diaphragm centre, which acts as the distributer of all major *prāṇas* above and below the diaphragm. Thus there are 4 + 6 + 10 = 20 petals for the three main *chakras*, 12 + 8 = 20 petals for the Splenic centres, plus 8 for the Diaphragm centre, making forty-eight altogether. The effect of the Peaceful Deities via these petals happens upon the stages of discipleship and Initiation when the individual is consciously working to control the related *saṃskāras* and to develop *bodhicitta*.

If the Diaphragm centre is omitted, because it is essentially a distributer of energies, then there are 40 major petals all told, which have a direct correlation to the 40 petals of the Throat centre. They relate to the 40 Peaceful Deities (minus the Ādi Buddha and Consort) and signify that all *saṃskāras* developed below the diaphragm have the propensity to develop into *manas* so that they can be incorporated into the mind, to make a human unit a 'man,' a thinker. The development of clear rational thought, rather than the irrational Watery emotions, is the objective and which is the function of the Throat centre to channel. It is designed to convey the pure Fires of the Mind. The eight petals of the Diaphragm centre have a similar function to the centres below the diaphragm as the Guardians and their Consorts have to the Throat centre.

Having accounted for the appearance of the Peaceful Deities with respect to the major *chakras,* the next chapter will explain the expression of mind/Mind in the centres below the diaphragm, where the mindful emanations of the Wrathful Deities can be found. Below the diaphragm we have the process of converting *prāṇas* where the associated wheels turn anticlockwise from right to left. The process of converting *saṃskāras* of desire, lust, attachment, etc., into those expressive of the *dharma,* changes the right to left movements of the swastikas clockwise towards the right. The *prāṇas* can then flow to the centres above the diaphragm, and the wrath of the various guardians of the *chakras* concerned can be overcome.

The cycles of 'seven days' of experience

Analysis of the cycles of seven 'days' that the deceased experiences in Bardo can now be briefly made. The focus shall be upon the more veiled significance of appearing phenomena the deceased would expect to encounter, rather than a psychological account. We see that the first five days are concerned with the manifestation of the attributes (lights) of the Jinas. To respond positively to these lights one has to develop the wisdoms that are the transmuted gain of the sense-consciousnesses. The sixth day sees the appearance of the remainder of the Peaceful Deities, with a focus being upon the Buddhas of the Six Realms, who provide the background to the rebirthing process wherein *karma* can be experienced and processed. The seventh day sees the appearance of the secret Vidyādharas and all of the *ḍākinīs* needed for the functioning of a human unit via the processing of *saṃskāras.*

On the first day Vairocana activates the entire *maṇḍala* of the Dhyāni Buddhas from the originating seed *(bīja).*[54] This relates to

54 The text provides the Consorts, symbols and associated Bodhisattvas, etc., to the various Jinas, but as they have already been detailed in Part A I shall omit them in this brief summary.

garnering the accumulated experiences of what has been developed in the Head centre. If this centre has been awakened then the person can enter into the domain of liberation veiled by the deep blue light of the *dharmadhātu,* if not then the dull white light of the god realm is said to be experienced because of fear. This god realm relates to the various *prāṇas* of the Head lotus that have not been converted into wisdom attributes. They are god-like because they represent the crown of the thought life, but as they have not yet been mastered and are imperfect, rebirth (of the qualities) is required so that the appropriate wisdom attributes can eventually be obtained. The associated energy conveyed is of the Element Aether.

On the second day the energy of Love-Wisdom manifests via Akṣobhya, acting as the supreme deity Vajrasattva, who energises the entire construct of the *maṇḍala.* At this stage, therefore, the *chakras* associated with the Peaceful Deities of the Heart and Throat centres are activated to bear the major impact of the incoming energy of the Wisdom of the Jinas. A dazzling white light is emitted, which if not heeded is said to propel the individual into a hell state through the onset of anger. Having started with the highest of the centres on the first day (the combined Head centres), the *Bardo Thödol* then focuses upon the existence of the lowest of the centres on the second day, the combined Sacral and Base of Spine centres. The hell states are generated through the evocation of the most forceful types of emanations. It is said to manifest before the deceased in the form of a smoke-coloured light to which he/she will be attracted if the *saṃskāras* are strong enough to impel the person thereto. It therefore necessitates the most loving energy in the most forceful, powerful, steadfast form of Vajrasattva (effectively the Ādi Buddha) to overcome these *saṃskāras.*

Note that the colours of the Elements (lights) of both Vairocana and Akṣobhya are transposed, with Vairocana taking the indigo blue of Akṣobhya, and Akṣobhya the white colouration of Vairocana. A reason for this is that either Jina can be found as the central *bīja* of the *maṇḍala*, depending upon the context and quality to be expressed.[55] The Elements of the other Jinas are as the colours assigned to each

---

55 Also, though Vairocana is white his radiance is blue, whereas Akṣhohya has a blue form with a white radiance.

Jina. The consciousness aspect can then be called forth from the cosmic Waters to play its appointed role in the *maṇḍala* to be.

Here the accounting of the Elements attributed to the Jinas as depicted in the *Bardo Thödol* shall be followed. This *differs* from how they have been assigned throughout this Treatise, where they are considered to be the substance of the dimensions of perception (the substratum of all levels of being/non-being). The *Bardo Thödol,* on the other hand assigns them to processes involving the appearance of things in relation to the way that consciousness manifests. This happens via the *skandhas,* the bundles of attributes constituting the human personality. In the *Bardo Thödol* the Elements therefore represent the nature of the manifestation of the *skandhas.*

As Vairocana is the synthesis of all the other Jinas, so his Element is Aether with the corresponding *skandha* being revelatory knowledge *(vijñāna).* This sets the stage for understanding the attributes of the remaining Jinas, as they are subsets of the qualities needed to develop such knowledge.

The Element attributed to Akṣobhya is Water, and the *skandha* is that of the form or body *(rūpa),* where the idea is the integration of the entire corporeal expression in terms of unity. One can presume that the Watery Element here relates to the conception of the energies that convert impressions gained from sense objects into consciousness-attributes. The entire bodily organism needs to be functioning as a unity to do so.

Having established the qualities of the polarities of existence the *Bardo Thödol* then fills in the rest of the body of manifestation. We thereby have the Logoic forces establishing the outline of the *maṇḍalic* construct on the first day. The establishment of the procreative forces that will cause all to manifest happens on the second day. The human lives that can bear the principle of consciousness and experiences it all within the Six Realms then appear on the third day, wherein the Equalising Wisdom of Ratnasambhava manifests. His energy is needed to establish the entire *nāḍī* system of the body, human, planetary or Logoic. All *chakras* must come into play if all of the five wisdoms are to be expressed via the sense-consciousnesses of an evolved humanity. The Ray energy governing the building of the *nāḍīs* and the general conveyance of the *prāṇas* within them is that of the golden fourth Ray of Beautifying Harmony overcoming Conflict. Esoterically, the sun of glory can now shine upon the *maṇḍala* in the form of the dazzling yellow light of *prāṇic* vitality, allowing all of the *chakras* to be vitalised with the living Breath of the light of Life.

The Element attributed to Ratnasambhava is Earth, to which is attributed the *skandha* of feeling and the emotions *(vedanā),* presumably because the emotions concretise ideas and relate them to everyday objects of perception via the self-identity of the personal-I. Ratnasambhava's purpose, therefore, is to overcome the forms of separateness and ill will often expressed through people's emotions, so that goodwill and loving dispositions are generated instead. Through emotional relationships the opposite sexes are brought together and via the associated sexual act human birth is possible. In relation to this, therefore, it is said that if one cannot receive the brilliant light from this Jina, then a dull bluish-yellow light manifests to which one flees because of egotism, the 'I' producing principle wherein consciousness abides.

On the fourth day the Discriminating Inner Wisdom of Amitābha and the expression of the Fiery Element is called into account. The fifth Ray of Intelligence and Scientific Reasoning manifests to govern the general activity of the way mind is expressed. The *skandha* is a faculty of discrimination *(samjñā).* As the red-orange Fires of Mind can now be effected, the centre activated is the Throat. Commanding mantras are evoked to allow the constructs of the attendant deities and forces that must inform the entire *maṇḍala* of mind to be generated. A dense form then appears, wherein all attributes of mind can be expressed.

In terms of the evolutionary process this represents the point of time when elementary *citta* is sought and galvanised into activity, to inevitably become the base substance for the development of the five sense-consciousnesses. The appearance of the phenomena associated with *saṃsāra* allows the establishment of all aspects of mind and the sum of human expression whereby people cling and attach to illusory forms they are desirous of possessing. Strong desire evolves because of the lure of that which is attractive, which causes attachment to phenomena. In the early stages of life such attachment produces the development of rudimentary mind via the sense-consciousnesses. For the most part, however, we have the way of intense desire for sensual pursuits and the accumulation of material objects. When one is deceased this desire attacks the individual, producing the proverbial thirst of the *pretas* for the things that can no longer be satiated. The intensity of the consequent developed desire-mind and its bewildered attachments then causes humans transiting in Bardo to be attracted to the dull-red light of the *preta loka* (the lower astral realms), which they consequently fear.

On the fifth day the All-Encompassing Wisdom of Amoghasiddhi is utilised to drive the entire process forward to its evolutionary conclusion. His green energy of enlightening, Mathematically Exact Activity empowers all of the ingredients associated with the forces of Nature. By this stage the mind has been developed and has begun the process of mastering phenomena. Everything known in the world of sense-perception manifests objectively so that they can be experienced, comprehended, and conquered. Inevitably, the entire path to enlightenment is produced. At first, however, the many competitive warring forces in human society are perceived and the mind plots, plans and schemes to obtain what it wills of the material domain for itself. Jealous of the riches and abundance others may possess, it is willing to make war to aggrandise its powers. Thus is the personal will developed, to carve for itself a personal empire at the expense of all competitive factors. Later, upon the path to light, self-will is converted to the Will-to-Love, which the development of the principle of compassion provides (invoking the mercy of Amoghasiddhi's Consort, Tārā). Thus the levels of yogic attainment awaken. Until then, the deceased person, with strong *saṃskāras* of jealousy and envy (towards the inhabitants of the 'god realm', the shining luminaries in thought, or the glamourous), is said to be attracted to the dull-green colour from the *asura loka*. There is found the miseries of non-stop quarrelling and warfare.

The Element attributed to Amoghasiddhi is Air, which here refers to the *nāḍī* system and the *prāṇas* of volitions, the *saṃskāras* that course through them. Their mastery is the basis to Amoghasiddhi's all-accomplishing power, the process of which is explained throughout this volume.

As a consequence of having the entire *maṇḍala* established, all of the Peaceful Deities can now empower its expression on the sixth day, and the field of Life is set for the role that human beings will play therein.

Thus the 'four colours of the primal states of the four elements',[56] the colours of the four primary wisdoms, of the six *lokas*, etc., will shine simultaneously. The sum of the effect of all these lights is seen in terms of the rosy colouration of the sixth Ray of Devotion, with respect to the manner of action that these deities apply themselves to the task at hand.

On this sixth day the deceased experiences the combined energies and benevolent qualities of these deities; of the complete body of expression of the forces transforming the propensities of *saṃsāra*. The deceased is asked not to be attracted to the illusory lights that would cause rebirth into the Six Realms. Rather, the inner light that leads to liberation must be recognised and striven for. The sum of the *maṇḍala* must be embodied in the awakened Mind, and Buddhahood thereby attained. If this is not possible then rebirth is ensured. The visions of the seventh and succeeding days now awaken.

On the seventh day the five secret Vidyādharas and their Consorts manifest. (Their role in establishing the kingdom of the *tathāgatagarbha* upon the higher mental plane, from which each new incarnation proceeds, has earlier been explained.) The entire *bhavacakra* (the wheel of birth and death), turning around the central hub of ignorance, everything associated with the rebirthing process, thus manifests. The response to the inevitable pain-filled domain of *karma*-formations leads eventually to the emanation of wisdom.

The Vidyādharas manifest the brilliance of the five colours that are associated with the wisdoms of the five Dhyāni Buddhas. If one fears these colours and listens not to the 'natural sound of the Truth' that 'will reverberate like a thousand thunders',[57] then the text states one will be attracted to the dull blue light of the animal world. This animal world is really that of the psychic constitution of the human body, and the development of animal-like *saṃskāras* that must eventually be battled with upon the path to liberation, thereby evoking the effects of the theriomorphic deities earlier explained. The entire path of liberation concerns building the right qualities into the petals of the Sambhogakāya Flower so that transformation of *samalā tathathā* (Suchness mingled with pollution) into *nirmalā tathatā* (Suchness apart from pollution)

56 Evans-Wentz, *The Tibetan Book of the Dead*, 119.

57 Ibid., 129.

occurs. The Śūnyatā Eye that is the door to liberation is thus opened. The Sound of Truth heard in the Heart centre must be listened to if such transformation is to occur and the Wisdom vectors (the Vidyādharas) awakened in consciousness. All of the animal-like forces of the body consequently will be defeated.

The seventh Ray of Ceremonial, Cyclic Activity generally governs the cycles of activity associated with our wandering through *saṃsāra*. It organises the power to overcome all obstacles to the path, and ritualises our endeavours to manifest the meditations, *dhāraṇīs* and *tapas* needed to invoke the necessary deities, visualisations and forces to transform *saṃskāras* into the brilliant lights of the Jinas. They can then be easily recognised and acquiesced to, preventing undesired rebirths. The 'deceased' here represents the *yogin* undergoing the ritual stages of dying to all bodily allurements associated with the Six Realms so that eventually a Jina is produced. Oṁ Svāhā!

The eighth and succeeding days produce the domain of the Wrathful Deities, wherein all of the *saṃskāras* are effected, experienced (suffered) and transformed on the road to the making of an enlightened being. They are the subjects of the next chapter.

2

The Bardo Thödol and the Natural State of Mind
Major Influences below the Diaphragm

Mind and the seven Rays

Having analysed the attributes of the Throat and Heart centres in relation to the 42 Peaceful Deities, our attention can be turned to the awakened centres below the diaphragm. The concern shall be how the *chakras* function when the activities of the Wrathful Deities are not needed because defiled *saṃskāras* no longer circulate. We shall start with the section entitled 'Observations Related to Examining the Nature of Mind'[1] in the fourth chapter of the *Bardo Thödol* from Gyurme's book. This information shall be supplemented by quotes in italics taken from W.Y. Evans-Wentz's *The Tibetan Book of the Great Liberation,* entitled 'The Yoga of Introspection'.[2] First there are seven statements that are an explanation of the seven Ray attributes of the Mind. They must be comprehended before proper consideration of the nature of the transmuted *saṃskāras* is possible.

1. Be certain that the nature of mind is empty and without foundation.
   One's own mind is insubstantial, like an empty sky.
   Look at your own mind to see whether it is like that or not.

1. The One Mind being verily of the Voidness and without any foundation, one's mind is, likewise, as vacuous as the sky. To

---

1 Gyurme, 44. The seven associated statements are from pages 44-45, and as usual I have added the numbers to facilitate explanation.

2 Evans-Wentz, *The Tibetan Book of the Great Liberation,* 214.

know whether this be so or not, look within thine own mind.[3]

2. Divorced from views which constructedly determine [the nature of] emptiness,
   Be certain that pristine cognition, naturally originating, is primordially radiant –

2/3. *Being of the Voidness, and thus not to be conceived as having beginning or ending, Self-Born Wisdom has in reality been shining forever, like the Sun's essentiality, itself unborn. To know whether this be so or not, look within thine own mind.*

3. Just like the nucleus of the sun, which is itself naturally originating
   Look at your own mind to see whether it is like that or not!

4. Be certain that this awareness, which is pristine cognition, is uninterrupted,
   Like the coursing central torrent of a river which flows unceasingly.
   Look at your own mind to see whether it is like that or not!

4. Divine Wisdom is undoubtedly indestructible, unbreakable, like the ever-flowing current of a river. To know whether this be so or not, look within thine own mind.

5. Be certain that conceptual thoughts and fleeting memories are not strictly identifiable,
   But insubstantial in their motion, like the breezes of the atmosphere.
   Look at your own mind to see whether it is like that or not!

5. Being merely a flux of instability like the air of the firmament, objective appearances are without power to fascinate and fetter. To know whether this be so or not, look within thine own mind.

6. Be certain that all that appears is naturally manifest [in the mind],
   Like the images in a mirror which [also] appear naturally.
   Look at your own mind to see whether it is like that or not!

6. All appearances are verily one's own concepts, self-conceived in the mind, like reflections seen in a mirror. To know whether this be so or not, look within thine own mind.

7. Be certain that all characteristics are liberated right where they are,
   Like the clouds of the atmosphere, naturally originating and

---

3 The quotes for the seven statements in italics are from Evans-Wentz, *The Tibetan Book of the Great Liberation*, 214-216.

naturally dissolving.
Look to your own mind to see whether it is like that or not!

7. *Arising of themselves and being naturally free like the clouds in the sky, all external appearances verily fade away into their own respective places. To know whether this be so or not, look within thine own mind.*

1. The qualities of *the first Ray of Will or Power* is exemplified in the first statement given in this 'Yoga of Introspection'. Being the most forceful, intense and refined of energy qualifications, it produces the spacious, empty aspect of mind. To 'look' into one's own mind, to perceive the Void of mind that is Mind, necessitates complete cleansing of all *saṃskāric* defilements and overcoming *saṃsāric* allurements. The Will must be used to yogically strip bare all aspects of mind so that what remains is emptied of the substance producing normal ratiocination. A rigorous one-pointed application of the yogic Will via many cycles of transforming *saṃskāras* thus produces the ability to allow one to 'look within to see' the nature of Mind as 'vacuous as the sky'. What has been eliminated is the weight of *manasic* substance that is limited by attachments to concepts of an 'I' and consequently slows down the speed of thought. What remains is spaciousness, luminosity, freedom to instantaneously perceive without limitations. There are no bounds to the nature of the thought. The Void, therefore, is not void of the ability to discern, but is Void because no anchorage anywhere in *saṃsāra* can be found. It is void of the attributes of *saṃsāra,* whose limitations have been eliminated. The mastery of *saṃsāra* necessitates the right use of the Will, and the attainment is the power of unfettered enlightenment.
2. The quality of *the second Ray of Love-Wisdom* is the 'Self-Born Wisdom', being that radiance (of Mind) which 'shines forever' and is 'divorced from views'. It is pure consciousness, the direct cognitive perception that knows the truth, hence needs not to form opinions or views. It is beyond the activity of the lower concretising mind. Love-Wisdom is the essentiality of the Heart of Life itself, the *bodhicitta* or power of compassionate action to liberate erroneous concepts from woe-producing karmic limitations. The wisdom of the Heart demonstrates the realisation of 'pristine cognition'.

This cognition then manifests its luminescence like the rays of an all-sustaining sun. Evans-Wentz's comment is that the Tibetan term provided, snying-po, means 'pith, heart, essence, or essentiality, with reference to the secret essence of the Sun as known to the occult sciences'.[4] The first and second Rays always work as a practical unity to produce the luminosity of such an internal sun. It is perceived in the mind's Eye of a beholder as a glorious radiant aura around the head of the awakened one. When applied amongst humanity such attainment manifests in terms of the activity of the third Ray—which represents the natural radiance of the Mind.

3. The *third Ray of Mathematically Exact Activity* is 'the Sun's essentiality'[5] that enlightens or illumines the all. This sun literally embodies the constitution of the Mind that one is asked to delve into in each of these *ślokas*. The second and third Ray statements can be combined, as Evans-Wentz's rendition does, because their qualities are found in the term Love-Wisdom. Here 'Love' is the expression of the 'nucleus of the sun', and the 'Wisdom' part necessitates the evolution and expression of Mind (governed by the third Ray) that manifests in the form of the expression of the Sun's rays. The Sun shines equally upon all beings, blessing them with beneficence in a precise, karmically appropriate formula of lighted perception.

   The phrase 'mathematically exact' refers to the ability of this wisdom to impeccably manifest logic to produce certain conclusions of outcome, like the application of a mathematical formula which is solved lightning fast. The expression of wisdom's logic is precise, cogent, prescient, and acutely penetrative.

4. The *fourth Ray of Beautifying Harmony Overcoming Conflict* manifests in the form of an uninterrupted flow of (pristine) energy qualifications. This is because it governs the flow of *prāṇa* in the *nāḍīs*. The movement of *prāṇa* harmonises the qualities of the entire system by bringing all attributes into line with the ordering energy of Life (*jīva*) from the Heart centre. Conflicting *saṃskāras*

4 Ibid., 215, footnote 2.

5 Ibid., 215.

are then converted into the bountiful, beauteous qualities of the Heart's Mind. The 'uninterrupted' series has been equated with the consciousness-stream of each human existence because it is the natural vehicle of all the Rays. Here the concept of the absolute (timeless) time is introduced as the torrent of a river, with its eddies and modifications of flow that manifest the qualities of finite cyclic time. This produces the *saṃskāric* modifications of mind that are formed as a consequence of the activity of the three lower (reflected) Rays. The river itself flows timelessly in the midst of the 'extremes' represented by the qualities of its banks on either side. The fourth Ray conveys the energies from the Heart of Life, as a Life giving flow that pacifies the emotive forces of Life, and consequently beautifies all around it. This Ray represents the middle between the 'banks' that are the triad of the Real and triad of the *saṃsāric* qualifications. It is the mediating mirror that reflects divinity into *saṃsāra*.[6]

5. *The fifth Ray of Intelligence, Scientific Reasoning* concerns the use of 'conceptual thoughts and fleeting memories', and all other logical attributes of the mind. It regulates the activities of the empirical mind. Each fleeting thought is 'a flux of instability' that is insubstantial in its motion. We are asked to look into this expression of the concretion of mind 'to see whether it is like that or not'. When analysing the mind, however, we eventually discover the Mind, wherein truth can be found. Our scientific, analytical skills are bought to the fore at this stage of the analysis of Mind.
6. *The sixth Ray of Devotion* concerns the right expression of all the fluid images generated by people's desire-minds and emotions centred around the concept of a 'self', or what they wish to obtain for such an 'I'. We thus have all the fleeting images, glamour, and turmoil of the world of human interrelationships; things that people devote themselves to, to fulfil their desires. We are asked to 'look within one's own mind' to properly ascertain the nature of this phantasmagorical play of *saṃsāra* all around us. To do so the emotional Waters must be stilled. The means is the practice of

6 For further insight into the significance of this flow of a river, consult the chapter entitled 'The River Simile' in Volume 2 of this *Treatise on Mind.*

calm abiding. Once attained it will allow one to observe a natural mirror-like expression in the mind, so that images from the realm of enlightenment can appear naturally without distortion.

7. Finally we come to *the seventh Ray of Ceremonial, Cyclic Endeavour, and of Demonstrable Power,* which governs all forms of activity upon the physical domain. Here all characteristics manifest, providing an opportunity to be liberated. All mental-emotional *saṃskāras* manifest like 'the clouds of the atmosphere' temporarily obscuring the natural clarity of the Mind. The *saṃskāras* bear their own karmic fruit, appearing and dissolving naturally again with each passing moment. It is important therefore to ritualistically observe one's own mind to assess the nature of this fleeting phenomenal appearance, and of the manifesting *karma*, so that it is cleansed of all tendencies that would necessitate further rebirth. Once the Mind is discovered and properly experienced then one will be able to 'see whether it is like that or not'.

The phenomena of Mind and the Jinas

The text continues with five further statements informing us (utilising the Yogācāra philosophy) that because no phenomena exists outside that which originates in the mind, the results of perceptions that originate from the five sense-perceptors are also expressions of what happens in the mind. As the primary basis to the establishment of these sense-expressions in Nature are the Dhyāni Buddhas, so this sets the basis to comprehend the nature of the five *prāṇas* that course through the *nāḍīs*. This must be clearly understood when observing such phenomena as the appearance of the Wrathful Deities and their Consorts, as well as of the expression and effects of any of the *saṃskāras* that one must experience through the course of one's life.

The seven Ray qualities in general, and the five attributes of mind, condition the sacred and non-sacred petals of the Heart centre. However, as they are clearly separated in the text we can presume that they refer to the main influences governing the evolution of the human psyche in general, indeed of all of Nature.

1. There are no phenomena extraneous to those that originate from the mind.

[So], how could there be anything on which to meditate apart from the mind?

2. There are no phenomena extraneous to those that originate from the mind.
   [So] there are no modes of conduct to be undertaken extraneous [to those that originate from the mind].
3. There are no phenomena extraneous to those that originate from the mind.
   [So], there are no commitments to be kept extraneous [to those that originate from the mind].
4. There are no phenomena extraneous to those that originate from the mind.
   [So], there are no results to be attained extraneous [to those that originate from the mind].
5. There are no phenomena extraneous to those that originate from the mind.
   [So], one should observe one's own mind, looking into its nature again and again.[7]

Evans-Wentz's rendition is similar, but equates the term translated as 'phenomena' above with 'the *Dharma*' (within),[8] which refers to everything obtained from our interrelation with external phenomena that teaches us what and what not to do, plus that gained inwardly through meditation by listening to the clear perceptions from the Heart. It is the effect of the Voice of the Heart speaking silently to our inner ears. The listing is straightforward, bringing us into the familiar territory of the qualities that are expressed by the five Jina families. The list, however, is not in its usual order, so we have to carefully analyse the properties given in each statement to find the placing of the Dhyāni Buddha concerned. We find that the three reflected attributes that deal directly with the three aspects of *saṃsāra,* of 'body, speech, and mind' that people normally mistake to be the external reality, are safely nestled within the protective qualities of the two Jinas whose attributes relate directly to the development of the meditation-Mind, Vairocana and Akṣobhya. Consequently, this produces liberation from *saṃsāric*

7 Gyurme, 45. As usual I have added the numbering.

8 Evans-Wentz, 217.

allurements. All aspects of *saṃsāra* are therefore safely contained within the precincts of this Mind.

When observing external phenomena, one effectively views the expression of the combined meditations of the Dhyāni Buddhas. Everything contacted experientially is a manifestation of their meditation-Minds, and are developed in the 'wombs' of their Consorts (as previously explained). Similarly, humans experience the results of contact with such external phenomena entirely in their minds. We can therefore say that 'There are no phenomena (or *dharma*) extraneous to those that originate from the mind'.

The first phrase therefore, 'how could there be anything on which to meditate apart from the mind?', refers to the manifested emanation of Vairocana. The Element expressed is Aether, and the sense-consciousness developed is that of *smell.* This represents the process of meditation by someone at a very advanced stage of consciousness, a *yogin* (or Bodhisattva) whereby the subtlest of discernments can be experienced. Comprehending that there is nothing but the Mind upon which to meditate sets the tenure of all the statements that are to follow in this entire section regarding the nature of *prāṇic* circulation below the diaphragm.

The second phrase, 'there are no modes of conduct to be undertaken extraneous [to those that originate from the mind]', refers to the emanation of Ratnasambhava, and thus with the expression of the Watery Element that so many humans wallow in. The sense-perceptor expressed is that of *touch*, and involves the sum of human social interrelationships, 'modes of conduct', that are generally expressed in an emotional, desirous, or sensual manner.

The third phrase, 'there are no commitments to be kept extraneous [to those that originate from the mind]', refers to the manifested emanation of Amitābha. Commitments are formulated in the mind that concern mental, social, ritualistic, and religious observations. They are generally a necessary adjunct to life, such as the (ritualistic) commitment of having to go to work to earn a living. The Element generated is that of Fire and the sense-consciousness utilised is *sight.* Evans-Wentz presents the statement: 'there is no other place of truth for the observation of a vow'[9] (*samaya*), confirming that the principal concern in studying all

9 Ibid.

of these precepts is our religious meditative observations (*tapas*), where we manifest a sacred pledge to never cease striving until liberation is obtained. This becomes the sum of the commitments that will pave the way to comprehend the complete extent of the nature of Mind.

The fourth phrase, 'there are no results to be attained extraneous [to those that originate from the mind]', refers to the manifested emanation of Amoghasiddhi and the consequences of mastering the various *saṃsāric* attributes and tasks one is involved with. All (physical) accomplishments are really mental formations, seeded by mind, expressed by mind, and reaped by mind. Nothing can be considered extraneous to mind, as the sum of our world view concerns the expression of *cittavṛtti*, the substance of mind. The Element expressed is Earth, and the sense-consciousness developed is *hearing*. Evans-Wentz's version is: 'there is no Dharma elsewhere whereby Liberation may be attained', informing us that the 'results to be attained' are everything related to gaining freedom from *saṃsāric* allurements. This involves the transmutative processes associated with the Wrathful Deities to accomplish the needed results.

Finally we have: 'one should observe one's own mind, looking into its nature again and again'. This refers to the manifested emanation of Akṣobhya, and the Mirror-like Wisdom, that allows one to repeatedly observe in its own mirror all attributes of mind/Mind, abstracted, concrete, or its luminous sun-like expression (the Sambhogakāya Flower). The Element expressed is the Air (which conveys the emanation of the five *prāṇas* in their totality), and the sense-consciousness is *taste*. Having discovered all forms of ephemera contained within the confines of the meditation substance of the mind/Mind, one can proceed with the rest of the examination of this chapter of the *Bardo Thödol*. The energies of the seven Rays, combined with those of the Jinas (or more appropriately, with that from their Consorts) then represent the twelve main factors of the energy of Life (*jīva* or *bodhicitta*) directed from the centres above the diaphragm to effect the *prāṇic* transformations in the centres below it.

The Mind and the Diaphragm centre

This section deals with the way that the eight-petalled *Diaphragm centre* directs *prāṇas* to and from the centres above and below the diaphragm in relation to the emanations of mind. Our focus thus concerns the nature of the phenomena experienced and processed by the centres below the diaphragm. The resultant *prāṇas* must be converted through yogic discipline and proper control of the mind so that they can be experienced by the centres above the diaphragm. This involves the work of the Wrathful Deities in the latter stages of the process, when the individual is clearly aspiring to gain liberation from *saṃsāra*. The *chakra* that passes *prāṇas* to either side of the diaphragm is the Diaphragm centre, which concerns this part of the 'Observations Related to Examining the Nature of Mind'. This incorporates the completion of the transformative processes effected with the help of the eight Mātaraḥ (the natural mastery and conversion of mental constructs associated with the eight classes of consciousness), as analysed in Part A.

1. If, upon looking outwards towards the external expanse of the sky,
2. There are no projections emanated by the mind,
3. And if, on looking inwards at one's own mind,
4. There is no projectionist who projects [thoughts] by thinking them,
5. Then, one's own mind, completely free from conceptual projections, will become luminously clear.
6. [This] intrinsic awareness, [union of] inner radiance and emptiness, is the Buddha-body of Reality,
7. [Appearing] like [the illuminating effect of] a sunrise on a clear and cloudless sky,
8. It is clearly knowable, despite its lack of specific shape or form. There is a great distinction between those who understand and those who misunderstand this point.[10]

1. The *northernmost* petal of the Diaphragm centre conveys the most refined *prāṇas* from the lower portion of the body to the Heart centre. In doing so it looks 'outwards towards the external expanse of the sky'. The 'expanse of the sky' then represents the sum total of the consciousness principle, where its most expansive, clarified vistas are embodied by the Heart centre's compassionate embrace. The energies from the Heart centre of this 'external expanse' can

10 Gyurme, 45-46. As usual I have numbered the statements.

also be projected downwards to help cleanse the lower centres from impediments and to awaken them.

2. The next phrase concerns the polar opposite of this petal, the *southernmost* orientation, which directs rejected *prāṇas* from the Heart centre to Splenic centre II (via Splenic centre I) for processing *saṃskāras*. Coming from the Heart centre therefore, there are 'no projections emanated by the mind', rather they are from the Heart of Life. In this case the directing mind/Mind utilises the energies from the Heart centre to effect the necessary transformations of *saṃskāras*. The compassionate effects of *bodhicitta* then manifest. The entire *prāṇic* flow (as viewed from below the diaphragm) from the southern to the northern petal (and vice versa) is treated as one expression in the text, hence Evans-Wentz's rendering: 'When looking outwards to the vacuity of space, there is no place to be found where the mind is shining'.[11] As Splenic centre II is the place for the transformation of general muddied *saṃskāras*, so therein is found the defilements and obscurations of mind needing converting, thus though the mind may exist there, it does not shine.
3. We now have the process of 'looking inwards at one's own mind', which relates to the *eastern* direction of this lotus. Here the *prāṇas* from the Heart centre admixed with those from the Diaphragm centre are directed towards the Liver centre to be integrated into the general *piṇgalā* circulation. The circulation below the diaphragm can then be controlled by the meditator, necessitating thinking with the Heart as far as the lower centres will allow, and cleansing the defilements of the general *piṇgalā* circulation. Residing in the natural spaciousness of the Heart the meditator need no longer ask the question; 'Who is the projector of the thought stream?', as there is no 'self' to query with.
4. This realisation comes once one's mind has been sufficiently purified, necessitating directing, rectifying *prāṇas* to the *western* direction embodied by the Stomach centre. Here the impediments of the general *iḍā nāḍī* stream of a determinant *manasic* nature are cleansed. The developed mind is then completely freed from

11 Evans-Wentz, 218.

conceptual projections, to become 'luminously clear'. This *iḍā* stream conveys the general intellectual, *manasic*, desire-mind conceptualisations, concretions and attachments to concepts. It principally feeds illusory identifications with an 'I' and with *saṃsāra*. The major battles concerning the transformation of mind into transcendental awareness happen in relation to this *nāḍī* stream. Once *manasic saṃskāras* are thoroughly refined by mind then what remains is Mind. Freeing one's mind from 'conceptual projections' is a long process involving all the battles associated with the entire panoply of wrathful protectors. In general, the Wrathful Deities are emanations of the *iḍā nāḍī* qualities, whilst the Peaceful Deities are expressions of *piṇgalā nāḍī* attributes.

5. The question concerning the projector of the thought is answered from the *southeast* direction, because by now *piṇgalā prāṇas* returning from the Liver centre have been sufficiently generated, integrated with the *manasic* stream, and refined with the *prāṇas* flowing from the Heart centre. Consciousness then recognises that 'There is no projectionist who projects [thoughts] by thinking them'. The *piṇgalā* stream deals specifically with the flow of consciousness (realisations of the group awareness and spaciousness of the Heart), rather than intellectual discourse centred around an 'I' (which is relegated to the *iḍā nāḍī* stream). The mind that would project is not active and therefore cannot be found. Evans-Wentz's rendering unites these two statements into one: 'When looking inwards into one's own mind in search of the shining, there is to be found no thing that shines'.[12] 'The shining' here refers to the concept of an 'I' that clearly stands distinct from any other such entity. Consciousness-streams progressing from the past to the future can, however, be found within the embrace of the 'mindfulness' that is no-mind.

6. Observing the polar opposite of this southeast direction, we come to the *northwest,* where the gain of all meditative revelations are expressed in the form of the emanative Will-to-Good that is enlightenment. Here the integrated *iḍā* and *piṇgalā nāḍī* streams within the central *suṣumṇā* channel produces the 'intrinsic

12 Ibid.

awareness, [union of] inner radiance and emptiness' that is 'the Buddha-body of Reality' *(dharmakāya).* 'Intrinsic awareness' is the expression of the *piṇgalā prāṇas* once they have been cleansed of defilements, whilst 'inner radiance' is similarly the effect of purifying the *iḍā* stream. Emptiness (*śūnyatā*) is the seal of their union, revealed as part of the nexus between *śūnyatā* and *saṃsāra.* In this northwest direction of the Diaphragm centre we have the outward expression of *prāṇas* to the Right Lung centre, preparatory to integration with the *prāṇas* from the Heart centre proper, wherein the full radiance of emptiness can be found.

Evans-Wentz fuses the attributes of both this petal and that of the seventh statement into one in his account: 'Being of the Clear Light of the Voidness, one's own mind is of the *Dharma-Kaya;* and, being void of quality, it is comparable to a cloudless sky'.[13] 'The Buddha-body of Reality' is the *dharmakāya*, which necessitates the fusion of all transmuted *prāṇas* into a unity, preparatory to projection into cosmos, via this direction of the compass.

7. The *northeast* direction concerns the incoming *prāṇas* from the Left Lung centre, channelling *prāṇic* directives from the Throat centre, to be integrated into the general *prāṇic* flow below the diaphragm. Their purpose is to empower the minor *chakras* with higher directives so that *siddhis* can be awakened. The entire *iḍā* stream must be transformed into illuminating light. The luminous radiance of the Mind must control every source of ideation that these centres represent if the person is to be truly liberated. The incoming *prāṇas* are the combined energies of the Peaceful Deities, and appear 'like [the illuminating effect of] a sunrise on a clear and cloudless sky'. This passage describes the luminous nature of Mind itself that irradiates all aspects of the manifest body (the *maṇḍala)* with light.
8. The final phrase concerning the Diaphragm centre's circulation is associated with the incoming energies from the Stomach centre (the *southwest* direction), once they have been appropriately cleansed

13 Ibid.

through the assistance of all the *prāṇas* from the 42 Peaceful Deities flowing via the polar opposite of this direction. The sum total of the *iḍā* stream is 'not a multiplicity, and is omniscient'[14] once the Head lotus is awakened by it. This means that though thoughts appear as a multiplicity they are really one omniscient stream of ideation manifesting prescient wisdom. They are 'clearly knowable' despite their 'lack of specific shape or form'[15] by the mind, whilst an enlightened Mind uses them to help awaken many beings. They represent the foundation for the enlightenment of all the attributes of the Stomach centre, once the qualities of the Peaceful and Wrathful Deities have coalesced and integrated.

The paragraphs numbered 3, 4, 5, and 8 imply a direct connection to the Solar Plexus centre and the method of converting its powerful Watery energies by means of *prāṇas* from the Heart centre, the Heart's Mind, via the minor centres. They represent the battleground of the conversion of *saṃskāras*. These paragraphs also represent the *iḍā* and *piṇgalā* connection between these two major centres.

From the above one can discern why the activity of the eight petals of the Diaphragm centre is summarised by the statement 'There is a great distinction between those who understand and those who misunderstand this point'. This concerns the difference between the enlightened, who have undergone the transmutation process of all the *saṃskāras* associated with the elevation of all *prāṇas* from below the diaphragm to above it, and those who are still battling at any stage of the process. This passage also hints that the eight statements of this section relate to the Diaphragm centre, as it is the centre that clearly differentiates between that which is above the diaphragm (hence comparatively enlightened attributes) to that which is below, wherein the obscuring *saṃskāras* are generated.

---

14 Ibid.

15 This statement is true for the average thinker, who can't see them, but to an awakened one their shape and form, as well as colours are quite clearly discernable. Such attributes allow their content to be easily interpreted. Thoughts are things, however the thoughts upon the domains of Mind are abstract and radiant, and thus effectively formless *(ārupa)*.

Mind and the *tathāgatagarbha*

Until now this chapter has dealt with the main enlightening factors that influence the *chakras* below the diaphragm. These factors were the seven Ray influences, the permutations of Mind from the Dhyāni Buddhas, plus the mechanism of transference of these energies to below the diaphragm. The next nine verses continue along this vein, with a brief overview of the qualities coming from the Sambhogakāya Flower via the mind.[16] They are important factors that cannot be overlooked by the *yogin*, as they govern the overall flow of *saṃskāras* and the *karma* needing attention.

The statements present the background to the processes transforming the empirical mind into the abstract Mind. The attributes of the *tathāgatagarbha* that exists upon that realm can then be visualised and directly experienced. Evans-Wentz's version presents eight statements under the title 'The Wondrousness of these Teachings',[17] indicating that at this level of analysis (of the Clear Light of Mind) the most wondrous or amazing revelations are possible. The hint also lies in the need to master the eight directions in space, if appropriate navigation of the way of Mind is to manifest, working up from the *chakras* below the diaphragm. Many amazing revelations come through understanding the nature of the domain of the radiant Sambhogakāya Flower, incorporating also the constitution of the Mind. Gyurme's version states:

1. This naturally originating inner radiance, uncreated from the very beginning,
   Is the parentless child of awareness—how amazing!
2. It is the naturally originating pristine cognition, uncreated by anyone—how amazing!
3. [This radiant awareness] has never been born and will never die—how amazing!
4. Though manifestly radiant, it lacks an [extraneous] perceiver—how amazing!
5. Though it has roamed throughout cyclic existence, it does not degenerate—how amazing!

16 See Volume 3, chapter 7 for detail concerning the nature of this Flower, also Volume 4, Figure 27.

17 Ibid.

6. Though it has seen buddhahood itself, it does not improve—how amazing!
7. Though it is present in everyone, it remains unrecognised—how amazing!
8. Still, one hopes for some attainment other than this—how amazing!
9. Though it is present within oneself, one continues to seek it elsewhere—how amazing![18]

1. The first and most refined of the petals of the Sambhogakāya Flower is the Will-Sacrifice—Will-Sacrifice petal. It stores the most abstracted qualities of the *tathāgatagarbha,* which can be described as the 'naturally originating inner radiance, uncreated from the very beginning'. It is 'naturally originating' since it is the 'child' of the *śūnyatā-saṃsāra* nexus, the expression of the purpose from the Śūnyatā Eye at the heart of this lotus and the impact of its energies upon the domain of Mind. A nine-fold whorl of petals is consequently established to contain the developed attributes of mind as they are converted to Mind. It is radiant because this is the energy field of any 'form' that manifests upon the highest, subtlest level of the domain of the abstract Mind. It therefore is the radiance assigned to the Clear Light of Mind. Intrinsically, the quality of this energy manifests as the hub of the wheel of the eight-armed cross of direction.

   Evans-Wentz uses the phrase 'self-originated Clear Light, eternally unborn'[19] and states in his footnote that only 'the Thatness, transcendent over form, birth, being, existence, is non-*sangsāric'*,[20] where *saṃsāra* refers to the transitory domain wherein things are born. The Thatness refers to the Heart's essence (the ever-present Mind). It is that which was in existence prior to the origination of time, i.e., prior to the origination of any thought, because thoughts originate in time and are the cause of the concepts of time. Though it has no origination, all forms of luminous thought (clear,

18 Gyurme, 46.

19 Evans-Wentz, 218.

20 Ibid., footnote 4.

instantaneous rational thought) spring from it, and although it is 'parentless' it is the 'child of awareness' once those thoughts cognise it. This is indeed an amazing or wondrous concept. 'Awareness', the Love-Wisdom that is the hallmark of all enlightened beings, can also be conceived of as *bodhicitta*, which is the natural substance of this Flower. It is therefore experienced as the meditating one travels inwards towards the Heart centre. This experience comes once the transmutative battles concerning the base *saṃskāras* have been accomplished in the centres below the diaphragm.

2. The second of the petals of the Sambhogakāya Flower is the Will-Sacrifice—Love-Wisdom petal. This is naturally associated with the *eastern* direction, which exemplifies the pure way of the Heart. The Heart is Life itself, whose expression is sacrificial in intent,[21] and the Heart's Mind is here denoted as 'naturally originating pristine cognition, uncreated by anyone'. Such a wondrous Mind is the fount of Wisdom that is not centred around an 'I' concept, as implied by the term 'anyone'. (That which creates in relation to itself, and which therefore causes the expression of *karma*.) Having no 'I' at the centre of its volition, its entire expression is therefore karmaless. The concept of manifesting spontaneous thought, 'Natural Wisdom', as Evans-Wentz puts it, without producing any resultant material *karma*, is indeed amazing, but such is the way with the clear-Mindedness of the wise. It spontaneously manifests in 'the field of expression' whenever a seed (*bīja*) appears to act in relation to it, producing that *bīja's* natural expansion and expression. The purpose of the expansion of the *bīja,* however, is to drive all *saṃskāras* to liberation, producing freedom from *karma's* limiting binds. This introduces the third statement.

3. We now come to the concept of a radiant awareness that 'has never been born and will never die',[22] which brings into perspective the quality of Mind viewed as the radiance of transcendent perception. Such awareness is conveyed by the Will-Sacrifice—Knowledge petal of the Sambhogakāya Flower. The direction relegated is

---

21 The way that compassionate wisdom manifests.

22 Evans-Wentz's version is 'Not having known birth, it knows not death. Wondrous is this'. (Ibid., 219.)

north, of upward aspiration to the *dharmakāya*. It involves the transformation of knowledgeable *saṃskāras* obtained through *saṃsāric* involvement into the experience of *śūnyatā,* which represents the void of all consciousness-attributes. The activity of the mind (knowledgeable pursuits) hence is sacrificed to experience the Void. Such development is a product of first establishing a 'container of thoughts', or mind, in the southern direction. (The incarnation of a human unit that struggles to gain enlightenment by awakening Mind.)

The liberated attributes of Mind manifesting as the real, absolute Truth eternally exist and can be *invoked* to help awaken the mind. These attributes can be contrasted to the relative truth derived from the volitions of the peregrinations of mind that are the gain of the long involvement with *saṃsāra* by the Flower. The liberating attributes of Mind also need to be *evoked* through the crucible of experience and by meditative attitudes. The relative and absolute then merge into unity. Together through a process of invocation and evocation the enlightened Mind becomes thoroughly substantiated as the integral equipment ('manifestly radiant') of the individual. Myriad are the experiences that have been processed and refined into the attributes of Mind. Wisdom characteristics have developed that shine as the Mind's luminescence. Much must transpire via the evolutionary process to produce the transmutation of empirical gain into the Clear Light. The application of invocation and evocation constitutes a science producing the liberation of evolutionary being. Through its processes a Jina inevitably comes into manifestation.

Thoughts can be directed in any way desired by the thinker. As thoughts are expressed they are born, and that which propels the 'thoughts' or incarnations of each personal-I from the domain of the Sambhogakāya Flower is the principle of Love-Wisdom. They are impelled by the Sambhogakāya Flower's need to sacrifice itself so that further knowledge (the basis of expanding wisdom) can be gained. Inevitably this containment of consciousness (the Sambhogakāya Flower) sacrifices its aeonic residence upon the abstracted domain of Mind, to enter *śūnyatā*, once *saṃsāra* offers no further gain for a reincarnating personal-I.

The quality of the force directed into *saṃsāra* by the *Will* of the Sambhogakāya Flower is *bodhicitta* (Love-Wisdom) which is the fundamental energy of this Flower. (The focus of *bodhicitta* is via the western direction of the fourth, Love-Wisdom—Will-Sacrifice petal.) As *bodhicitta* is not born, it simply is, so there is no time of birth and thus 'will never die'. Its radiance that is seeded to govern the central jewels of the *chakras* via which the personality works may be ever-existent, but the forms *(chakras)* through which it works have an evolutionary life span. *Bodhicitta* arranges itself automatically into the needed permutations of revelatory awareness that have no definite boundaries, but incrementally expand. Though such expansion implies a beginning there is no locus for the concept of origination.[23] There is, however, a succession of births and deaths of the instruments for such expansion, as each personal-I undertakes its cycles of experience. Indeed, this is a wondrous state of being/non-being in which to reside.

4. Next considered is the Love-Wisdom—Will-Sacrifice petal, which is 'manifestly radiant' of and by itself. This radiance is an emanation of the Will to compassionately sacrifice for the benefit of the all and finds its expression in the *western* direction. Here the Sambhogakāya Flower manifests its form of the Bodhisattva vow as it sacrifices itself in the entire field of human endeavour to help transform the conditions of human society via the personal-I that is its instrument.

   Though this radiant essence manifests as the magnetic field of the *chakras,* the average human unit thoroughly obscures it with strong desire and emotion based *saṃskāras (kleśas).* We therefore have the entire pain and pleasure filled domain inhabited by a personal-I. Inevitably, the internal force of *bodhicitta* overcomes

---

23 There is a cycle for the birthing of the Sambhogakāya Flowers *(tathāgatagarbha)* out of an animal kingdom (called Individualisation). However, the substance of Love-Wisdom that it is composed of is the subject of discussion here. This energy field was integrated with the elementary *citta* of nascent animal mind so that the subtle Soul-form could come into existence. Though that form will eventually 'die' at the fourth Initiation, the essence (Mind) persists, manifesting an intensified radiance. The evolution of the *citta* (mind substance) expands the expression of wisdom when integrated with Love. In any case, from the perspective of the personal-I (which is the view taken here) the *tathāgatagarbha* is eternally existing.

the *kleśas* and liberation is ardently sought by the personality.

We are told that despite the appearance of such perceivers, the incorporating Mind is 'manifestly radiant' ('Total Reality' according to Evans-Wentz[24]), that there is no extraneous perceiver of it. This is because whatever revelations happen with respect to the mind/Mind within it, therefore are not extraneous to it, consequently no 'extraneous perceiver' can be found. This mind/Mind analyses by being absorbed in any particular thing, and being in all things, there is no 'I' to be thus absorbed. This is a truly amazing observation.

In the domain of the Sambhogakaya Flower, group consciousness, the way of thinking with the Heart (the Heart's Mind), is the natural field of expression. Collectively the Sambhogakaya Flowers can be considered extraneous perceivers of the course of the entire human experience of the coming and goings of civilisations. The intricacies of this topic of analysis however concerns us not here.

5. Next we have the central Love-Wisdom—Love-Wisdom petal, presenting the pure characteristic of the *tathāgatagarbha* upon its own level, which 'does not degenerate',[25] despite having continuously cycled through manifestation in the form of *samalā tathatā*. (Which as earlier explained is Suchness covered over or concealed with impurities.) The rebirthing principle of the *tathāgatagarbha* has seeded many 'I's' in *saṃsāra* over uncounted millennia for the duration of each successive incarnation of the consciousness stream. The purpose requires developing the desired qualities and converting elementary *citta*, yet all the time the fundamental quality of the Flower, the 'Buddha-womb',[26] remains undefiled by the *saṃskāras* of *saṃsāric* involvement.

   The northeast direction of 'unity' is here implicated, where the Sambhogakaya Flower integrates a united meditation with the sum of the membership of its domain in order to direct the evolutionary

24 Evans-Wentz, 219.

25 Evans-Wentz's version is that 'Although wandering in the *Sangsāra* it remains undefiled by evil. Wondrous is this'. Ibid.

26 The meaning of the term *tathāgatagarbha*, for which I generally use the descriptive term the Sambhogakāya Flower.

course of the human personalities that are their incarnate expressions roaming in *saṃsāra*. The objective is to convert the knowledgeable pursuits gained through normal activity into Love-Wisdom by means of bathing the personality life with the principle of Love. The gain is absorbed into the general constitution of the Flower, which then becomes the seed for the next incarnation. The process of absorbing the gain of the experiences from *saṃsāra* without being in any way corrupted by these experiences is indeed a wondrous thing, visualised as an amazing phenomena in the mind/Mind of one gaining liberation.

6. The *northwest* direction of outward emanatory expansion (of consciousness) allows the *tathāgatagarbha* to interrelate with all others of its kingdom, plus reach out to all liberated beings. The related petal of the Sambhogakāya Flower is that of Love-Wisdom—Knowledge. The phrase provided is 'Though it has seen buddhahood itself, it does not improve'. The implication here is that it aught to improve upon seeing the Buddha nature. In fact it does 'improve' in terms of developing increased luminosity, however it remains untainted by the most material aspects of the *saṃsāric* impurities developed by the personal-I. What 'does not improve', however, is the intrinsic quality at the heart of the Flower, veiled by the Śūnyatā Eye. The intrinsic attribute (that perceives the Buddha-nature, *tathatā)* of this Flower cannot be improved upon, but the *samalā tathatā* (the defiled aspect) must be gradually removed, to reveal its undefiled *nirmalā* form. This necessitates transforming the refined *saṃskāras* that are projected to the Sambhogakāya Flower by the incarnate personality.

Evans-Wentz's version is that 'Although seeing the Buddha, it remains unallied to good'.[27] The Sambhogakāya Flower's wisdom comprehends that both good and evil are part of *saṃsāra*, all produce knowledgeable attributes, hence have their cycles of usefulness. What people consider to be 'good and evil' are both forms of *karma* that keep one tied to *saṃsāra,* to the cycle of birth and death. In considering the type of *karma* to be cleansed by any personal-I the *tathāgatagarbha* is only interested in that which will

27 Ibid.

eventually produce Buddhahood. This necessitates cleansing all forms of *karma* that tie one to earth, after the requisite knowledge and wisdom has been obtained that is the cause for the incarnation process. All forms of *karma,* good and bad, must be experienced by the personal-I to transmute them into the qualities of Love and Wisdom. All *saṃskāras* are to be cleansed of defiling attributes and elevated from the lower centres to those above the diaphragm. Many incarnations are needed before the personal-I recognises this fact and strives to convert the *saṃskāras* that bind one to all types of phenomena. Evil is that which prolongs *saṃsāric* activity for far longer than need be, and which therefore must be countered. Love-Wisdom is the gain.

We see in the above how two translations of the same text can produce differing lines of enquiry. The question of interpretation of sacred texts, as dealt with in the first chapter of Volume 1, could be considered with respect to this.

7. In the *southern* direction the Knowledge—Will-Sacrifice petal is activated to sustain the duration of the life (and the lives) of an incarnate human unit, so that eventually higher revelatory perceptions of what is veiled by Mind can be obtained. This direction concerns the descent into incarnation, where things are born and undergo an evolutionary expression known as 'Life'. The Sambhogakāya Flower has sacrificed its blissful self-absorption in its domain in order to project into incarnation and process the experiences of a personal-I. The process produces the birth of an 'extraneous perceiver' that then analyses things. The entire phenomenal world is at the command of such perceivers, but no matter how they try with their intellects they do not discover the divinity present within them.

   Despite having caused the appearance of the incarnate human unit, who manifests a busy schedule of self-discovery, it is indeed an amazing phenomena that though the *tathāgatagarbha* 'is present in everyone, it remains unrecognised'. People normally know nothing about this sublime form, considering its fundamentality to everyone's lives. Many religionists have postulated the existence of a 'soul', however few have directly experienced its transcendence, or recognise the true signs of its directive purpose within their minds. The nature of the *tathāgatagarbha* remains unrecognised because most people have not developed the necessary sacrificial Will to penetrate the veils that allow them to know the radiant luminosity that represents Mind. They develop versions of selfish personal will instead, and this directs them in the opposite direction to domains that intensify *saṃsāric* bondage. Transforming battles must be fought in the Solar Plexus arena that will convert forms of self will to the Will-to-Love. Through meditation and via yogic direct perception they then discover there is no extraneous perceiver, yet the truth pertaining to the *tathāgatagarbha* exists. Only as they aspire upwards to *dharmakāyic* heights comes the refinement of mind that allows perception of this Buddha-germ within.

Evans-Wentz's version is: 'Although possessed by all beings, it is not recognized. Wondrous is this'.[28] The interpretation here in light of the above is obvious, for though the signs of the existence of the *tathāgatagarbha* may appear, very few actually recognise their true import.

8. We now come to the Knowledge—Love-Wisdom petal, relegated to the *southeast,* the field of the expression of inner plane energies into outer manifest activity. This petal absorbs loving, considerate, compassionate, devotional and well meaning *saṃskāras* from the personal-I, and assists their further development. The accompanying phrase is 'Still, one hopes for some attainment other than this'. (Evan-Wentz's version: 'Those not knowing the fruit of this yoga seek other fruit. Wondrous is this'.) Despite these salutary characteristics, significantly further striving for the attainment of liberating wisdom needs to be achieved in the domain of mind/Mind if the Sambhogakāya Flower is to be directly experienced. Also, an overhaul is needed in the way religion and philosophy is taught by the various teachers devotees follow. Various forms of attainment are taught, but rarely is the way of revelation of the nature of the Buddha-germ adequately provided. Despite the vast amount of doctrines that purport to be truth, that which is the radiant source of the rebirths of the individual amazingly remains generally unrecognised.

28 Ibid.

All philosophical speculations (the 'attainment other than this' that is hoped for) need to be eliminated, if the natural state of Mind is to shine forth from the rubble of speculative opinions.

9. Finally we have the *southwest* direction of 'understanding', and the Knowledge—Knowledge petal garnering the *saṃskāras* of knowledgeable things that are sought out for their own accord. This is the base level of all experiences to be gained, from which wisdom may eventually be derived. It is thus the foundation for the unfoldment of all the petals of this flower when the attributes to be developed are increasingly experienced. The associated phrase is 'Though it is present within oneself, one continues to seek it'. In the elementary stages of the search for truth or the meaning of life most people seek it everywhere but within themselves, which is the only place where truth can really be found. The path of knowledge for its own sake and so that the things pertaining to *saṃsāra* can be experienced and amassed for pleasurable pursuits is sought instead.

The repetitious activity of those that are bewildered thus by *saṃsāra* is amazing. Only when love is evoked (seeking out the eastern way) can the wisdom be developed that will cause seekers to do the appropriate meditations that will allow Mind to be observed for what it is, and thereby the Buddha-germ found within. There, as Evans-Wentz's version states, the 'Clear Light of Reality shines within one's own mind'.[29] This Clear Light is the essence of the substance of Mind, and though it is present within one, it needs to be cleansed from defilements and perturbations of mind (by relaxing the mind and transforming base *saṃskāras*). Because aspirants are ensconced with various forms of mental activity that shield them from higher perceptual thought, so the attributes of Mind elude them. They seek by utilising emotional and often opinionated thoughts which hinder such a search.

From this *southwest* direction the human unit must aspire to understand the nature of the 'son of Mind' (the Sambhogakāya Flower), and how it functions. The Sambhogakāya Flower similarly learns what occurs within the kingdom of which it is a part, and later its view must be directed upwards towards *śūnyatā*. Its kingdom is

29 Ibid., 220.

responsible for the existence of human units constituting the sum of our civilisation, consequently the collective meditation is vast.

The petals of the Sambhogakāya Flower effectively manifest in terms of a fixed cross of steadfast purpose to project the fundamental attributes of the Flower. The central point of this cross is occupied by the Sūnyatā Eye that provides the ability to perceive multidimensionally and to direct the purpose of this Flower in any of the four directions. The northern direction is occupied by the three bud petals, whose focus is the domains of liberation. The eastern direction is governed by the Sacrifice petals, whose focus is the attainment of Initiation, The southern direction is occupied by the Knowledge petals, where the focus is gaining *manasic* attributes in *saṃsāra*. The western direction is empowered by the Love-Wisdom petals, where the focus is the generation of wisdom by each personality it sends into incarnation, and the eventual expression of compassionate activity.

Mind and Splenic centre I

The next section of the text is titled 'Intrinsic Awareness as View, Meditation, Conduct, and Result' by Gyurme.[30] We are first presented with three groups of four, relating to the functioning of the twelve petals of Splenic centre I (see Figure 3). The first list provides the qualities of the *prāṇas* channelled by the four cardinal petals of this *chakra*. They distribute what might be depicted as the *suṣumṇā* functioning of one or other of the four Elements, as conveyed by the respective petal. Evans-Wentz comments that this concerns 'the fourfold Mahāyāna. The four preceding aphorisms reveal the four parts of this Great Path of the "*Yoga* of Knowing the Mind", which are (1) the actual teaching, (2) the actual meditation, (3) the actual practice, or practical application, and (4) the actual fruit, or result attained'.[31]

The text states:

1. EMA! This immediate awareness, insubstantial and radiant,
   Is itself the highest of all views.

---

30 Gyurme, 46.

31 Evans-Wentz, 220, footnote 1.

2. This non-referential, all-encompassing [awareness] which is free in every respect
   Is itself the highest of all meditations,
3. This uncontrived [activity based on awareness], simply expressed in worldly terms,
   Is itself the highest of all types of conduct.
4. This unsought [attainment of awareness], spontaneously present from the beginning,
   Is itself the highest of all results.

[Now], the four great media, which are errorless are presented:
[First], the great medium of errorless view
Is this radiant immediate awareness—
Since it is radiant and without error, it is called a 'medium'.
[Second], the great medium of errorless meditation
Is this radiant immediate awareness—
Since it is radiant and without error, it is called a 'medium'.
[Third], the great medium of errorless conduct
Is this radiant immediate awareness—
Since it is radiant and without error, it is called a 'medium'.
[Fourth], the great medium of errorless result
Is this radiant immediate awareness—
Since it is radiant and without error, it is called a 'medium'.

[Now] the four great nails, which are unchanging, are presented:
[First], the great nail of the unchanging view
Is this radiant immediate awareness—
Since it is firm throughout the three times, it is called a 'nail'.
[Second], the great nail of the unchanging meditation
Is this radiant immediate awareness—
Since it is firm throughout the three times, it is called a 'nail'.
[Third], the great nail of the unchanging conduct
Is this radiant immediate awareness—
Since it is firm throughout the three times, it is called a 'nail'.
[Fourth], the great nail of the unchanging result
Is this radiant immediate awareness—
Since it is firm throughout the three times, it is called a 'nail'.[32]

32 Gyurme, 46-47. I have added the numbers 1 to 4.

The four types of awareness refer to the fundamental meditations of which both the mediums and the nails are attributes. They can be considered the cardinal, *suṣumṇā* quality, that sets the direction of the energy flow of the meditation-Mind.

The 'four great media which are errorless' relate to the *piṇgalā nāḍī* attributes of their respective directions. Thurman uses the phrase 'the teaching of the universal vehicle's four inerrancies',[33] implying therefore that these media are the applied wisdom of the Mahāyāna doctrines. Within *saṃsāra* the *saṃskāras* conveyed by this *nāḍī* require mental effort on the part of the personal-I to produce the right expression of the Heart's wisdom. Enquiries are made whether the imparted empirical information is correct or not, and if correct, are there any part truths or omissions to consider upon the path that leads to the Heart of Life wherein one is liberated from illusion's *(māyā's)* thrall. An enlightened perspective is thereby developed. Once developed, the nature of the enlightened Mind perceives all information in an error-free manner, quickly omitting any falsifications. The media represent the four fixed cross directions of the wheel because they express the way of the Heart as applied to *saṃsāra's* turmoil.

The 'four great nails which are unchanging' refer to the *iḍā nāḍī* attributes that no longer change with respect to *saṃsāra's* expression. The implication is that formerly there was much mental activity in the conversion of aberrant *saṃskāras,* but now such activity has been completed, 'nailed down', fixed in enlightened consciousness. The *saṃskāras* have been thoroughly transmuted, hence there is no further change. The course of *saṃsāric* wandering over many millennia has produced such an eventuation after the developed *saṃskāras* have outlived their usefulness. The nail represents a developed *antaḥkaraṇa* (consciousness link) that integrates the higher attribute of Mind with the *saṃskāras* that need to be converted into its clarified form in the Clear Mind. This *nāḍī* creates the mechanism by which one travels to gain the wisdom needed to mount the steed of enlightenment. As the Bodhisattva path is reached and the great transmutations occur on the way to complete expression of the Heart's Mind, then the enlightened one manifests effortless activity. The mutable cross is implicated in the

33 Robert A.F. Thurman, *The Tibetan Book of the Dead*, 236.

nature of the transmutative process of the base *saṃskāras* into their liberated correspondences.

There is no need to reiterate what has already been stated regarding the functioning and qualities of the petals of Splenic centre I in the former volumes of this Treatise, with respect to the activities of the five Wrathful Buddha-Herukas and Consorts. Figure 5 in part A of this volume (on the twelve-petalled lotus of Splenic centre I) should be consulted for reference.

Splenic centre I is the place of the integration of the energies from the Heart centre (the east-west direction) with those from the Throat centre (the north-south direction). The purpose is to purify and transmute all remaining undesirable *saṃskāras* so that the lower centres can bear the attributes of Mind. Being 'nailed down' in these centres, these attributes thereby govern those *chakras.* The view, therefore, is the end result of the transformation of *saṃskāras,* effected with the help of the Wrathful Deities.

This analysis shall treat the petals of Splenic centre I in terms of triads of petals, focussed upon the cardinal directions. The *suṣumṇā* expression of the triad then dominates, incorporating the other attributes of awareness. Therefore it is the highest of all views, meditations, conduct and results. A *suṣumṇā* petal is integrated with the corresponding 'great media' of the *piṇgalā* stream and the associated 'great nail' of the *iḍā nāḍī.* These triplets of energies (or aspects of Mind) directed to the four quadrants of space can then be relegated to an overall Element, and therefore to the attributes of one or other of the Jina families. Thus the eastern triad conveys the Airy Element, as embodied by the functions of Akṣobhya and Consort. The southern triad represents the Watery Element conveyed by Ratnasambhava and Consort. The western triad conveys the Fiery qualities of Amitābha and Consort. Finally, the northern triad conveys the Earthy qualities of Amoghasiddhi and Consort.

The triads in question are oriented around the cardinal directions. For the Airy triad the Arian petal directs its attribute of awareness as the *suṣumṇā* stream. The Taurian petal directs its energies as the *piṇgalā* stream, and the Pisces petal projects the *iḍā* stream (or 'nail').[34] They

34 The petals of any direction are arranged according to the pattern of the central petal for that direction (in this case Aries) and the two contiguous petals. (Here Taurus and Pisces.)

can also be viewed in terms of the three *guṇas*. This wheel moves from the eastern direction associated with Akśobhya's Mirror-like Wisdom, here depicted as 'immediate awareness', to the northern position of Amoghasiddhi's All-accomplishing Wisdom. At first we would expect this wisdom to refer to the 'all-accomplishing [awareness]' of the second statement of Gyurme's translation, however this is not so. This can be deduced when comparing this section to that of Evans-Wentz's translation, which he titles 'The Four-fold Great Path'. We have for the first four statements:

> All hail to this Wisdom here set forth, concerning the invisible, immaculate Mind!
> The teaching is the most excellent of teachings.
> This meditation, devoid of mental concentration, all embracing, free from every imperfection, is the most excellent of meditations.
> This practice concerning the Uncreated State, when rightly comprehended, is the most excellent of practices.
> This fruit of the *yoga* of the Eternally Unsought, naturally produced is the most excellent of fruits.
> Herewith we have accurately revealed the Fourfold Great Path.[35]

The correlating phrases of Evans-Wentz's statement of the meditation being 'devoid of mental concentration, all embracing, free from every imperfection' and statement 2 from Gyurme, of it being 'the all-accomplishing [awareness]' that is 'the highest of all meditations' directly relate to the Discriminating Inner Wisdom of Amitābha. His *mudra* is 'the gesture of meditation' hence he embodies the meditative function of a *yogin,* who at the stage implied need no longer concentrate the mind, but is naturally absorbed in meditative poise.

In his footnote to this passage Evans-Wentz states that 'the Fourfold Great Path' is also termed 'the fourfold Mahāyāna. The four preceding aphorisms reveal the four parts of this Great Path of the *"Yoga* of knowing the Mind", which are (1) the actual teaching, (2) the actual meditation, (3) the actual practice, or practical application, and (4) the actual fruit or result attained'.[36] Evans-Wentz combines the two groups

35 Evans-Wentz, 220.

36 Ibid., footnote 1.

of four media and nails of Gyurme's translation into four statements, which need not be quoted here.

Having established the basis to assigning the attributes of the Jinas to this list we can proceed to the interpretation of its meanings. The related paragraphs shall be numbered according to the four quadrants governed by the Jinas. This means that the easternmost (Arian) petal shall be enumerated first, followed by the contiguous southeast *piṇgalā* (Taurean) petal of this triad, then the northeast *iḍā* (Piscean) petal, etc. By *iḍā* is meant the qualities related to the development and mastery of *manas* (mind), whereas *piṇgalā* relates to the development of compassion that converts *manas* into wisdom. *Suṣumṇā* is that which integrates both into a non-dual unity.

The interrelation between the four cardinal directions and the corresponding nails and media should be noted. The first statement for instance, the 'immediate awareness, unsubstantial and radiant', is related to Akṣobhya's Mirror-like Wisdom, which is said to be 'the highest of all views'. The 'all-encompassing [awareness]', the 'highest of all meditations', we saw has a reference to the Discriminating Wisdom of Amitābha (the western direction). The associated media is given as 'errorless meditation' and the associated nail as 'unchanging meditation'. The third awareness given, of 'uncontrived [activity based on awareness], simply expressed in worldly terms' refers to the activity of Ratnasambhava's Equalising Wisdom. It is stated to be 'the highest of all types of conduct'. The corresponding media is of 'errorless conduct', and the nail is 'unchanging conduct'. Finally, the 'unsought [attainment of awareness], spontaneously present', or 'the *yoga* of the Eternally Unsought, naturally produced' as Evans-Wentz styles it, refers to Amoghasiddhi's All-Accomplishing Wisdom that manifests in this spontaneous fashion. It is said to be 'the highest of all results'. The corresponding media and nail are of 'errorless result' and 'unchanging result'.

The *mudras* (gestures) attributed to the Jinas can now be correlated to some of their attributes found in the text. Amoghasiddhi's 'gesture of fearlessness'[37] is that which produces the highest of all results or

37 The quotations related to the gestures of the Jinas are taken from the diagram of the five Dhyāni Buddhas provided by Govinda in his book *Foundations of Tibetan Mysticism*, 121.

fruits. The highest of all conducts (or practices) directly refers to Ratnasambhava's *mudrā*, which is the 'gesture of giving'. The highest of meditations, refers to Amitābha's 'gesture of meditation'. The concept of errorless or unchanging view (or teachings) is correct for Akṣobhya's 'gesture of earth touching', and Mirror-like Wisdom. This gesture (*bhūmisparśa mudrā*) has reference to the Buddha when he utilised it to invoke the Mother Earth to witness the 'errorlessness' of his enlightenment. It should be noted here that Akṣobhya also takes the guise of the supreme Buddha, Vajrasattva in this text. Mastering the dialectics of all views is symbolised by the gesture of earth touching, signifying complete control of all aspects of the material domain and the world of opinions derived from those that interrelate with it. The term 'views' refers to the philosophical speculations of the various Buddhist schools, informing us that thinking with the Heart represents the highest possible mode of such meditative discernments (to establish correct syllogisms and pristine logic).

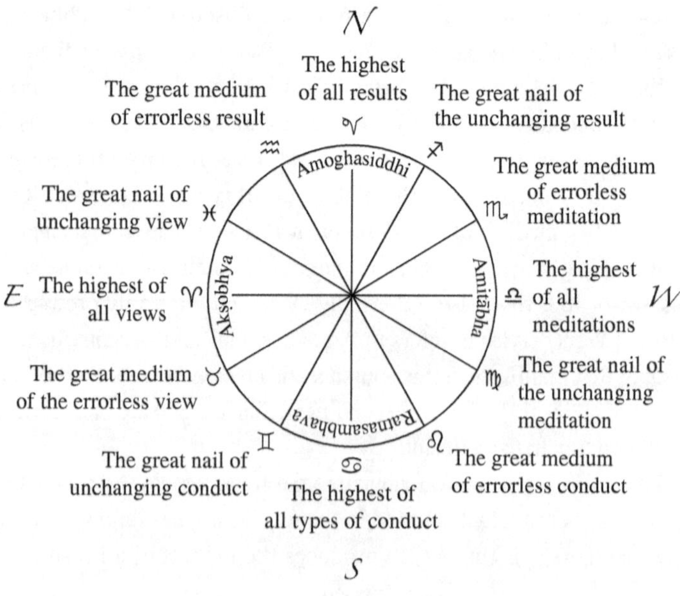

Figure 3: Splenic centre I and Meditation

Following the definitive or intended meaning of a sacred scripture[38] generates the inclination to meditate. The process of developing *yoga*-meditation (Amitābha) necessitates the manifestation of right conduct in all aspects of life. The results of striving to be compassionate are spontaneous giving (Ratnasambhava) and following the Bodhisattva path. Meditation also produces a fearlessness in all aspects of life (Amoghasiddhi). Inevitably, the fruit of all this activity is his All-accomplishing Wisdom.

The eastern triad of petals of Splenic centre I manifests the way of the Will-of-Love, which produces immediate radiant awareness that enables the Heart centre's awakening. This triad consists of the Arian, Taurean and Piscean petals. It is governed by Akṣobhya and the attributes of the *vajra* family. Evans-Wentz's translation is: 'All hail to this Wisdom here set forth, concerning the invisible, immaculate mind! The teaching is the most excellent of teachings'.[39] Immaculate indeed is the Heart's Mind.

1. Aries presents an abstracted Airy-Fiery emanation that constitutes the initial beginning of all that is to follow by way of the Mind. This petal, signifying 'the middle path'[40], can therefore be coupled to the first statement because the way of thinking with the Heart manifests as 'the highest of all views'. It is immediately aware, 'insubstantial and radiant'. The *suṣumṇā* aspect of Akṣobhya's wisdom allows the compassionate aspect of the *dharmakāya* to be reflected into manifestation, to produce the initial awakening of the abstraction of Mind. The entire wheel of Splenic centre I can then be appropriately empowered by means of this *suṣumṇā* energy of immediate awareness and its subsidiary qualities of unchanging and errorless views.
2. The Taurian *southeast* petal completes the triad. Earlier titled 'without one extreme', it manifests here as a *piṅgalā* expression denoted as 'the great medium of the errorless view'. Taurus, the sign into which the Buddha was born, represents the principle of wisdom, of the opening of the All-seeing Eye that sees all events through the three

38 See chapter 1, Volume 1 for the meaning of these terms.

39 Evans-Wentz, 220.

40 See Part A, Figure 5 for the earlier assignments to the petals of this *chakra* and their relationship to the Herukas and their Consorts.

times. The three times are thereby one immediate radiant awareness of the eternal Now. If there are no extremes in thought because the absolute Truth has been cognised, then the view one possesses does not change, it is errorless and flows in accordance with the *piṇgalā* (wisdom-evoking) qualities of the stream of *dharma*. All doctrinal opinions have been rectified and integrated as a unified philosophy, now abiding in the truth of the *dharma* that is immediately available for inspection in the Mind's Eye.

3. The Piscean petal, the contiguous northeast part of the Arian triad, earlier titled 'without discursive thought', expresses the *iḍā* quality denoted as 'the great nail of the unchanging view'. This quality represents the sum of the *manasic* input derived from the *dharma* as integrated by the Mind. Literally we have the sum of the ontological deductions of the Buddhist *dharma* that produce enlightenment. This is because this Piscean petal represents the end of the great cycle concerning the refinement and transformation of these teachings. Their bondage to *saṃsāra's* Watery environment has been severed. As all different views have been errorlessly integrated into the Mind, consequently there is no need for discursive thought. There is but one unbounded vista of enlightenment's expanse that has its basis in *śūnyatā*.

The northern triad of Capricorn *(suṣumṇā),* Aquarius *(piṇgalā)* and Sagittarius *(iḍā)* can now be analysed. Amoghasiddhi's All-accomplishing Wisdom governs the expression of this triad.

4. The *northernmost* Capricornian petal signifies the height of attainment upon the mountaintop of revelation that manifests 'without ceasing'. This *suṣumṇā* part of the triad representing aspiration upwards is presented as the 'unsought [attainment of awareness], spontaneously present from the beginning' and is 'the highest of all results'. The sum of the *ālayavijñāna* environment therefore comes into the ken of the meditating one. When 'non-referential' then the *saṃsāra-śūnyatā* nexus is the place of residence of the enlightened Mind. Consciousness can then be integrated with the *dharmakāya*. Evans-Wentz's version is: 'This fruit of the *yoga* of the Eternally Unsought, naturally produced is the most excellent of fruits'.[41]

41 Ibid.

5. The *northeast* Aquarian petal represents the *piṅgalā* aspect of this northern triad. This petal of Splenic centre I was earlier designated 'without constructive thought' and manifests as 'the great medium of errorless result' because it stems from *dharmakāyic* absorption, or else is grounded in the *tathāgatagarbha*. Such a result pours into the meditator's Mind in the Airy form of the (cosmic) Waters of Life (*bodhicitta*) as compassionate expression to assist the development of the Bodhisattva path for all, enlightening them with errorless views.
6. The *northwest* Sagittarian *iḍā* petal of this northern triad, earlier designated 'without arising' refers to 'the great nail of the unchanging result'. It is unchanging because it is the result of one's one-pointed arrow-like aspiration to experience the *dharmakāya*, or else to integrate with the domain of the *tathāgatagarbha*. To do so it utilises the gain of the mind's conversion to Mind. The arrows fired by the Archer (Sagittarius) act as nails empowering any of the aspects of the *dharma*. They signify ceaseless, effortless striving[42] to produce the highest possible revelations.

The western triad, signifying manifesting outwards to the field of service representing humanity, has Libra the balances demonstrating the *suṣumṇā* force, Scorpio the scorpion as the *piṅgalā* attribute and Virgo the virgin as the *iḍā* petal of Splenic centre I. Amitābha governs the overall expression of this triad.

7. The Libran *westernmost* petal, 'without nihilism', here concerns the 'non-referential, all-encompassing [awareness] which is free in every respect'. Such awareness is all-encompassing because it includes all thought structures and meditation streams that can be found wherever people exist. This direction involves observing the minutiae of all experiences undertaken in *saṃsāra*. Every experience must be cleansed from contrived *manasic* activity preparatory to being expressed as an attribute of the Discriminating Inner Wisdom embodied by Amitābha. The Throat centre's potency can thereby be empowered. This direction therefore represents the meditative equipoise between all attributes of Mind as directed to the field of service, thus 'the highest of all meditations.' Evans-Wentz's version

42 Effortless striving works like instinct at a certain stage of the path whereby the momentum of many former cycles of achievement flow on to produce progressive further attainment.

is: 'This meditation, devoid of mental concentration, all embracing, free from every imperfection, is the most excellent of meditations'.[43] Libra the balances governs the interrelation between all streams of consciousness. It determines the timing between their various cycles of activity, therefore it signifies the meditative interlude, gathering in all forces and thoughts before a new cycle of action can commence. It governs thereby the entire process of the art of meditation, producing its all-embracing freedom.

8. The Scorpionic *piṇgalā* petal of the western triad, 'without eternalisation', is expressed by 'the great medium of errorless meditation' because no matter what distractions may occur in the field of testings upon the path of discipleship (governed by Scorpio), or in yogic discipline, the meditator persists in the fundamental pursuit of liberation. Thus ensures the transmutation of *manasic saṃskāras* into the compassionate basis of the Bodhisattva path. All sentient beings can then gain the educational and compassionate benefits developed by the meditator.
9. The Virgoan *iḍā* petal of this western triad, presented earlier as 'without apprehension', is 'the great nail of unchanging meditation'. Here one's meditative unfoldment (relating to the proper appreciation of any or all attributes of Nature's kingdoms) can be made to persist for the necessary duration without any distractions whatsoever. Being *iḍā* means that all attributes of mind ('views') have been fully developed and integrated into Mind so that meditation upon any subject can be errorless. Virgo is the mother of the entire material domain, and no matter what the meditation-Mind is focussed upon, the 'nails' hammered in *saṃsāra,* it is but a minor part of a vast meditation-stream that changes not.

The final southern triad is focussed downward to the little ones in *saṃsāra*. Cancer represents the *suṣumṇā*, Leo the *piṇgalā,* and Gemini the *iḍā* expression. Ratnasambhava's Equalising Wisdom governs the form of activity for the awakened ones in this direction.

10. The *southern* Cancerian petal of Splenic centre I earlier denoted 'without apprehensible' concerns the 'uncontrived [activity based on awareness], simply expressed in worldly terms'. It becomes 'the

43 Evans-Wentz, 220.

highest of all types of conduct' because from here, in the depths of *saṃsāra,* the yogin must learn to climb the mount of attainment. Consciousness turns away from Watery material concerns to reach up to *śūnyatā* or the *dharmakāyic* heights (for the most advanced), or to the *tathāgatagarbha* (for the majority of meditators). Its blissful revelations are then spontaneously integrated into the meditation-field. This represents the *suṣumṇā* way for this direction, leading straight up from the southern arm of the cardinal cross to its northernmost Capricornian position. This entire path concerns the methodology whereby *saṃskāras* can be converted, as described in part A of this volume. Evans-Wentz's version refers to the mechanism that will eventually produce the fruit (*phala*) of such meditative striving: 'This practice concerning the Uncreated State, when rightly comprehended, is the most excellent of practices'.[44]

11. The *southwest piṅgalā* Leonine petal, designated 'without apprehender', manifests as 'the great medium of errorless conduct'. Such conduct is errorless because it is dedicated to the service of others with view of their gaining liberation from all concepts of self-hood. (Leo being the sign of the self-conscious individual.) Once accomplished, it is the medium for them to develop the Bodhisattva path, which equilibrates people's opinions of concepts of an 'I' into concepts of the egolessness of oneness. The sum of the gain of one's experiences is therefore directed towards the great Bodhisattvic service of enlightening all. (Demonstrated in the polar opposite of this sign, Aquarius.)
12. The *southeast iḍā* petal of this triad is Gemini the twins, earlier designated 'without two extremes'. It is represented by 'the great nail of unchanging conduct'. The concern is the conduct enacted by the wise whilst they interact with material substance. The form of activity that unceasingly works to produce liberation from the various domains of *saṃsāra* is 'unchanging'. What is 'nailed' is the path between the extremes of life. The extremes posited can refer to the extremes of the two truths. (The mortal brother representing conventional truth, whilst the immortal one embodying the absolute Truth.) We also have that which produces right conduct by travelling

44 Ibid.

the Dharmakāya Way, where the nexus between *saṃsāra* and *nirvāṇa* is found. Gemini embodies the ritual activity associated with gaining access to the sacred adytum of the Temple of Life. Here all dualities (inevitably abstracted in terms of the two truths) can be resolved into a unity. The symbolism can then be seen in terms of the twins (the *piṇgalā* male, signifying the absolute Truth of *śūnyatā,* and the *iḍā* female, relating to the conventional truth) holding hands as they enter the temple. The two truths become merged into one integral fusion *(suṣumṇā),* or third truth that integrates one relative to the other. (Meaning there is a separation in consciousness between *saṃsāra* and *śūnyatā,* which become fused in *suṣumṇā.*) They become both at once when *dharmakāya* manifests. That beyond is the All and the All is the One. The *saṃsāra-śūnyatā* nexus is then the place of residence. Here the masculine view refers to the ultimate gain of the *piṇgalā* path (*śūnyatā*). The feminine represents the material domain through which this path manifests (and which is inherently empty). The *dharmakāya* integrates the two in terms of the universality of the all-encompassing Mind.

All forms of yogic disciplines and meditation processes must be ritualistic if enlightenment is to be obtained. The forms of cyclic activity (conduct) must therefore be nailed by the Will of the *yogin* if all obscuring *saṃskāras* are to be eventually converted into enlightenment attributes.

The three times in one

Next to be considered are 'the esoteric instructions which reveals the three times to be one'.[45]

> Abandon your notions of the past, without attributing a temporal sequence!
> Cut off your mental associations regarding the future, without anticipation!
> Rest in spacious modality, without clinging to [the thoughts of] the present.
> Do not meditate at all, since there is nothing upon which to meditate.
> Instead, revelation will come through undistracted mindfulness.[46]

45 Gyurme, 47-48.

46 Ibid.

Evans-Wentz's version is:

The essence of the doctrine concerning the Three Times in at-one-ment can now be expounded.

The yoga concerning past and future not being practised, memory of the past remains latent. (Footnote: 'Literally "is relinquished"'.)

The future, not being welcomed, is completely severed by the mind from the present.

The present, not being fixable, remains in the state of the Voidness.[47]

This seemingly straightforward passage of the *Bardo Thödol* is a little more ambitious than first meets the eye. It manifests a shorthand esoteric account of the three times, the four *female Gatekeepers of pristine cognition,* and the five *skandhas,* all from the perspective of the enlightened Mind. The numbers 3 + 4 + 5 = 12, signifying functions that relate to the way that the Heart centre's activities can govern the activity of the *prāṇas* generated from the Base of Spine centre. The powers of the Heart must come to totally govern these twelve different attributes that inevitably determine the nature of the manifestation of phenomena.

This manifestation is governed by the three times, which relate to the way consciousness experiences a sequence of changing phenomena in the three worlds of human livingness: the dense physical, the emotional and mental bodies. The five *skandhas* govern the way consciousness appropriates the attributes of these three worlds. The Gatekeepers of pristine cognition govern the nature of the manifestation of the four main Elements, which condition consciousness as it evolves. They are the basis of the substance utilised by the *saṃskāras* that arise as a consequence of the reaction of consciousness to *saṃsāra's* mutability over time. All of this activity is grounded by the four petals of the Base of Spine centre. Each of the petals convey the *prāṇas* generated from one or other of the kingdoms of Nature, which are incorporated in the bodily consciousness. They qualify the attributes of the *saṃskāras* generated.

General teachings on the nature of the manifestation of time were provided in Volume 2 in the chapter entitled 'The Examination of Time in the *Mūlamadhyamakakārika*'. Also, Volume 1, chapter 2 explained the way the term *skandhas* (bundles of aggregates embodying the attributes of consciousness) is utilised throughout this series, where the esoteric

47 Evans-Wentz, 222.

account is provided, relegating them more purely to consideration of form *(rūpa)* and of the mental substance that incorporates the body of expression of the material world. Hence *saṃskāras* have been differentiated from the *skandhas,* whilst the term *kāma-manas* is used instead of *vedanā* (feeling-emotions) and *samjñā* (faculty of discrimination).[48]

It was earlier stated that the *four female Gatekeepers of pristine cognition* close the 'doors of the four types of birth' and represent the 'face of the four immeasurable aspirations'. They embody the functioning of the four petals of the Base of Spine centre. They also guard the functioning and modality of time (intricately interwoven with the generation of *karma)* with respect to its appearance, expression and being/non-being, as everything comes to be rightly sequenced in the *maṇḍala* of the enlightened Mind.

The *past* refers to the petal related to the mineral kingdom, therefore to dense physical involvement with *saṃsāra* wherein all forms of action concerning the three times occur. Here humans are caught up with the illusionality of the concepts of time. 'A temporal sequence' refers to the commonplace way of viewing time, of happenings through time, necessitating a past that leads inevitably to the future. One is asked here to abandon one's attachments to the past (i.e., former *saṃskāra*-creating practices). As no pathways thereto are created, so no temporal sequence can be followed. The enlightened view relates to comprehension of the law of cycles. The *skandha* associated is *rūpa,* of the objects of perception experienced by the sense-consciousnesses. This work is regulated by the northern Gatekeeper and as all *prāṇas* head north from this base centre, so the attribute developed is the 'immeasurable aspiration of equanimity'.[49] In a completely serene Mind no volitions that could possibly create the conditions of attachment to *saṃsāric* allurements are possible.

---

48 There are five *skandhas*: 1. form, or body, the sense organs, sense objects and interrelationships (*rūpa*), 2. perception or sensation, feelings and emotions (*vedanā*), 3. aggregates of action, or the motives to thus act (*saṃskāras*), 4. the faculty of discrimination (*samjñā*), 5. revelatory knowledge (*vijñāna*). In the account below I shall utilise the conventional terminology, in which case the limitations will be perceived by the discerning reader.

49 Gyurme, 394, similarly to all other references to the Gatekeepers.

The *future* then refers to the petal qualifying the animal kingdom, and therefore to all of the theriomorphic animal-like propensities that relate to the development of mind, with its ability to envision all future possibilities of what the desire-mind wishes. We are therefore asked to cut away our 'mental associations regarding the future, without anticipation'. The propensity to create such *manasic saṃskāras* must be severed and transformed into enlightenment attributes if the Now is to be properly experienced. This concerns the guardianship of the western Gatekeeper. The gain then is 'boundless sympathetic joy'[50] of being freed from the tyranny of one's former animal nature, allowing one to help others to free themselves. The associated *skandha* is *saṃskāra.*

The *present* refers to that petal related to the plant kingdom, and therefore to the mechanism of conveying the various types of *prāṇa* flowing in the *nāḍīs* by means of the *chakras.* This describes the Watery quality of the general *prāṇas* that course through the *nāḍīs* by normal human activity (clinging to thoughts of the present). 'Spacious modality' manifests as the natural state of Mind that will be accomplished as a consequence of the process of transmutation of *saṃskāras* and developing the states of natural abiding associated with these *chakras.* If no *saṃskāras* are generated, and no consciousness-attribute is being attached to, then there is no 'present' that can be considered 'fixable', so consciousness experiences Voidness. The southern Gatekeeper and the *skandha* of feeling perceptions *(vedanā)* is here implicated.

The ability to reside in the *eternal Now,* wherein one does not need to 'meditate at all' because 'revelation will come through undistracted mindfulness' is a propensity of the enlightened members of the human kingdom. This notion of eliminating all concepts of time, and therefore of *saṃsāric* attachment and affiliation, is what all aspirants aspire to. It is the 'essence of the doctrine concerning the Three Times in at-one-ment'. We need to remember here that the focus of this entire chapter relates to the end attainment of meditation and of the transmutation of *saṃskāras,* thus the attainment of 'calm abiding' in the naturalness of Mind that perpetually experiences the eternal Now. We are asked to not meditate at all because 'there is nothing upon which to meditate' since

50 Detlef Ingo Lauf, *Secret Doctrines of the Tibetan Books of the Dead,* (Shambhala, Boston, 1989), 150. See also Gyurme, 394.

all is Void. The meditation-Mind is then self-absorbed in that Void. Evans-Wentz's description of the 'present' 'not being fixable, remains in the state of the Voidness' also has reference to this eternal Now.[51]

Time is void of discernable attributes to the enlightened Mind, other than having relevance to the domain of ephemera. Within this domain cycles of time come into perspective to a conscious mind. Indeed, all forms of sentience are conditioned by it one way or other. The function of the eastern Gatekeeper, governing the 'immeasurable aspiration to compassion', come to the fore when time is voided in consciousness because the Airy *prāṇas* from the Heart centre is the governing experience. The timelessness of the eternal Now is consequently experienced. At this stage the faculty of discrimination (*samjñā*) manifests in terms of the wisdom of the Heart's Mind, seen in terms of the intuitive faculties that transcend the ratiocinations of the mind. 'Discrimination' then becomes the non-conceptual direct yogic perception *(pratyakṣa)* that sees in an instant the truth regarding anything.

The final statement of Gyurme's account ('Instead, revelation will come through undistracted mindfulness') relates to the 'pristine cognition' guarded by the female Gatekeepers governing the petals of the Base of Spine centre. This centre is the foundation of everything that transpires to awaken the 1,000 petalled lotus, its polar opposite at the other end of the spinal column. An unbroken *prāṇic* interconnectedness from the jewel in the heart of the base centre right through to the five tiers of expression of the Head lotus produces the ability to manifest 'undistracted mindfulness', necessitating the awakened *chakras* that come as a consequence of *kuṇḍalinī* flow. Inevitably we have the Aetheric dispensation that is the true fruit of the flow in the *suṣumṇā nāḍī*. The seeds of enlightenment *(vijñāna)* have then fully flowered.

51 Evans-Wentz, 222.

3

Mind and the Īśvarī

Mind and the twenty-eight theriomorphic female deities

In Volume 5A, chapter 5, we saw that the twenty-eight Īśvarī help refine and transform *saṃskāras* from below the diaphragm into enlightenment-attributes. In this present chapter the nature of their transmuted *prāṇas* shall be analysed. Their main division into five groups is repeated below, to facilitate correlating the sections relating to the natural state of Mind in the present chapter to what was previously presented. In chapter five it was stated that each of the five groups deals with one or other of the *prāṇas* of the five Elements. We come now to the domain of the Solar Plexus centre, which is arranged in two groups of five petals, so it can properly assimilate and process the consciousness bearing Watery *prāṇas* of the *iḍā* and *piṅgalā nāḍīs*. We have:

1. The four female Gatekeepers enacting *emanational rites* govern the petals of the in and outgoing *iḍā* and *piṅgalā nāḍīs* to and from the Solar Plexus centre (*maṇipūra chakra)*. This arrangement utilises four of the ten petals of the Solar Plexus centre. Their control is of the most refined Fiery-Airy-Watery *prāṇas* the Solar Plexus is capable of expressing. This leaves six petals free. The associated Jina is Vairocana, therefore the sense-consciousness associated is smell.
2. The six 'Queens of Yoga' enacting the *rites of pacification* (the east) governing the remaining six petals of the Solar Plexus centre. These petals control the main body of the Watery-Fiery-Earthy emotional

prāṇas of the Solar Plexus. The associated Jina is Akṣobhya, with the sense-consciousness being taste.

3. The six 'Queens of Yoga' enacting the *rites of subjugation* (the west) embody the functions of the left Gonad centre. This centre is a six-petalled lotus. These petals control the Earthy-Fiery form-building *prāṇas.* The associated Jina is Amitābha, with the sense-consciousness being sight.
4. The six 'Queens of Yoga' enacting the *rites of enrichment* (the south) embody the functions of the six-petalled right Gonad centre. This centre controls the Earthy-Watery desire grounding *prāṇas.* The associated Jina is Ratnasambhava, with the associated sense-consciousness being touch.
5. The six 'Queens of Yoga' enacting the *rites of wrath* (the north) embody the functions of the Sacral centre. The six petals of the Sacral centre control the Earthy-Watery-Fiery desirous sensation-seeking *prāṇas* causing attachment, as well as general bodily vitalisation. The associated Jina is Amoghasiddhi, with the associated sense-consciousness being hearing.

Gyurme states:

Revelation will come through undistracted mindfulness—
Since there is nothing by which you can be distracted.

1. Nakedly observe [all that arises] in this modality, which is without meditation and without distraction!
2. When this [experience] arises,

   Intrinsically aware, naturally cognisant, naturally radiant and clear,

   It is called 'the mind of enlightenment'.
3. Since [within this mind of enlightenment] there is nothing upon which to meditate,

   This [modality] transcends all objects of knowledge.
4. Since [within this mind of enlightenment] there are no distractions,

   It is the radiance of the essence itself.

5a. This Buddha-body of Reality, [union of] radiance and emptiness,

5b. In which [the duality of] appearance and emptiness is naturally liberated,

5c. Becomes manifest [in this way], unattained by the [structured] path to buddhahood,

5d. And thus Vajrasattva is [actually] perceived at this moment.[1]

Point number one of the list from chapter 5 can now be analysed, relating to the various *Gatekeepers enacting emanational rites*. They govern the petals of the *iḍā* and *piṇgalā nāḍīs* to and from the Solar Plexus centre. This group controls the Fiery-Airy-Watery *prāṇas* of the Īśvarī. The four statements 5a to 5d of Gyurme's list, however, refer to the result of the work of the four *Gatekeepers of pristine cognition* who guard the gates of the Base of Spine centre. This represents a continuation of the information provided regarding the three times in one. What is implied in the combination of all these phrases concerns the effect of the liberation of *kuṇḍalinī*. We thus have the flow of the Fires (representing the transmuted qualities of the four main Elements), as governed by the four petals of the Base of Spine centre up the *iḍā* and *piṇgalā nāḍīs,* awakening the petals of all the *chakras* through which the Fire flows.

Each of the *iḍā* and *piṇgalā nāḍīs* are inherently dual, there being an *iḍā* aspect to the *piṇgalā nāḍī,* and a *piṇgalā* aspect to the *iḍā nāḍī.* This is also represented by the north-south, east-west orientation of the Base of Spine centre. This orientation is seen, for instance, in terms of the four types of birth governed by the Gatekeepers of pristine cognition that were explained in part A, chapter 5. Here we see that birth by womb and egg are similar processes, effected by an animal body (including therefore the human). Also, the birthing by 'heat and moisture' of the plant kingdom and the 'miraculous birth' via *chakras* are also similar. In the first case we have an *iḍā* stream, where the womb birth represents the *piṇgalā* aspect and the egg birth the *iḍā.* In the second case we have a *piṇgalā* stream wherein 'miraculous birth' is the *piṇgalā* aspect, and the germinating seed the *iḍā.*

The actual place of generation of these *nāḍīs* is the Sacral centre, as earlier depicted. This follows through to the four petals of the Solar

1 Gyurme, 48. Vajrasattva, the bearer of immutable power, in this text is equated with Akṣobhya. He also takes the role of the Ādi Buddha. As usual, I have provided the numbering to the quote.

Plexus centre that receive and transmit the energy flow of the natural radiance of the liberated Fires of Mind. As all of the petals of the Sacral centre at this stage have been purified of the aspects of desire, they become the meeting place of the energies of radiance and emptiness, so parts 5a-5d of this tract are concerned with the effects of the continuation of the work of the Gatekeepers of pristine cognition. Considering that the Sacral centre is wherein the union between a Buddha and his Consort is eventuated, so parts 1-4 of Gyurme's statement relate to the effects of that union experienced in the field of consciousness governed by the Solar Plexus centre. This includes the sum of the perceptions garnered below the diaphragm. Such experience is generally regulated by the Gatekeepers enacting emanational rites.

The four statements of the Gatekeepers of pristine cognition related to the three times and the 2 x 4 statements of the section that we are now analysing, are integrated by the passage 'Revelation will come through undistracted mindfulness', which we saw previously relates to the *skandha* producing the seeds of enlightenment *(vijñāna)*. Undistracted mindfulness therefore is the key to the awakening of *kuṇḍalinī*. The succeeding passage: 'Since there is nothing by which you can be distracted' concerns the factor allowing this experience to arise.

Again twelve statements are presented, if the four associated with the three times, plus the eight of this section are combined.[2] This signifies the evocation of the qualities of the twelve petals of the Heart centre (which could be correlated with these twelve statements). Providing that there is nothing by which one can be distracted, *bodhicitta* can then be projected, allowing *kuṇḍalinī* to safely arise.

When the number of times groups of twelve have been observed to appear in the text so far, we will see that this is the fifth time:

1. The first is provided in the list of the twelve subsidiary petals to the Throat centre. They relate to the Vairocana aspect of the

2 The three times were explained at the end of the last chapter, starting with the phrase 'Now follows the esoteric instructions which reveals the three times to be one'. That section and the present one are directly tied together by the phrases: 'Do not meditate at all, since there is nothing upon which to meditate. Instead, revelation will come through undistracted mindfulness.' (Gyurme, 47-48.) 'Undistracted mindfulness' then becomes the centre of the twelve-spoked wheel, delineating its major characteristic.

demonstration of the properties of Mind. The directive power stemming from the *dharmadhātu* is then expressed to all of the other centres wherein Mind is to be conveyed.

2. Next we have the statements relating to the twelve petals of the Heart centre. Here the Mirror-like Wisdom of Akṣobhya reflects the attributes of *bodhicitta* via all of the centres concerned.
3. The section dealing with the seven Rays and the five attributes of Mind express the qualities of the Discriminating Inner Wisdom of Amitābha. Here the major characteristics of the Heart's Mind are conveyed in terms of the attributes of the seven sacred and five non-sacred petals of the Heart centre. The aspects of the esoteric meaning of the compound word *bodhicitta* are thereby delineated in these two characteristics, where the seven Rays relate to the *bodhi* part of this compound word, and *citta* to the awakened *manasic* part. All of these attributes represent the major qualifiers to what is known as Mind.
4. The twelve petals of Splenic centre I are appropriated with these energies. Their purpose is to direct their potencies to the centres below the diaphragm. Ratnasambhava's Equalising Wisdom now comes to the fore, integrating aspects of Mind from above the diaphragm to what exists below.
5. The twelve statements concerning the interrelation between the Base of Spine, Sacral and Solar Plexus centres, whereby *kuṇḍalinī* can be awakened. Here the All-Accomplishing Wisdom of Amoghasiddhi is expressed so that the living Fire of the powers of Mind are awakened throughout the body of manifestation, and the associated *siddhis* are empowered.

The attributes of the Jinas then empower the liberated one, and these five levels of twelve energies project their potency through the Solar Plexus centre (the abdominal brain), which then manifests in the effective twelve-petalled arrangement explained in part A (see Figure 12). The energies of the Heart centre *(bodhicitta)* can then flood the sum of the minor *chakras* (the Inner Round). All power over *saṃsāra* is then possible for the awakened One. When this group of twelve is controlled by the twelve innermost petals of the Ājña centre we then have seven groups of twelve, which are governed by the attributes of the seven Rays. Here Ray one of Will or Power governs the Throat centre which rules the directive impulses of mind/Mind and the evocation of Secret Mantra (statement 1). Next we have Ray two of Love-Wisdom governing the expression of the Heart centre (statement 2). Statement 3 concerns the major forces governing the entire *maṇḍala* of the *nāḍī* system with respect to Mind, hence the Head centre is implied with the overriding Ray quality being the third of enlightened, Mathmatically Exact Activity. Ray four of Beautifying Harmony overcoming Strife reflects all seven Ray energies generated by mind/Mind. It therefore empowers the coordinating activities of the Ājñā centre, the All-seeing Eye. Its petals are uniquely organised to direct the movement of the faculty of Mind in any direction vision is required. The twelve petals of Splenic centre I (statement 4) acts to empower the centres below the diaphragm (where the sixth Ray of Devotion or aspiration comes into play) with the energy of the Heart's Mind. Statement 5 concerns the interrelation between the Base of Spine and Sacral centres viewed as an eight petalled lotus (as explained in part A) and their integration with the four petals of the Solar Plexus centre that are concerned with the flow of *iḍā* and *piṇgalā nāḍīs*. This interrelation is governed by the seventh Ray of Ceremonial or Cyclic Activity. Once the Watery attributes of the Solar Plexus centre are controlled, then the fifth Ray of Scientific Reasoning governs the activity of the resultant twelve-petalled arrangement.

The statements from Gyurme's book can now be analysed. First the Gatekeepeers enacting emanational rites.

1. The first phrase asking us to 'Nakedly observe [all that arises] in this modality' refers to the *iḍā* stream generated by the Sacral centre and directed to the Solar Plexus centre. The Sacral centre governs the principle of desire conditioning all human relationships and therefore the sexual function. We are thus asked to observe in its intrinsic purity all attributes of this function, which will inevitably lead to the highest form of union. This concerns the *southwest* arm of the mutable cross that is formed (said to be the northern gate in the text), once the snake-headed Vajrā Lambodarā has properly controlled the little serpents of desire that were generated through *saṃsāric* activity. The implication is that the rites of wrath have manifested and the six 'Queens of Yoga' have thoroughly trampled

upon and subjugated all base sensual impulses. 'All that arises' relates to the generation of all forms of *saṃskāras* which must be observed and cut at the root by transmutation into their higher correspondences. At this stage one is so thoroughly ensconced in the meditation-Mind that the formal processes of meditation are no longer needed. They are automatic, therefore the statement 'without meditation' is given. In his exposé Evans-Wentz calls this process: 'The Yoga of the Nirvāṇic Path'.[3]

2. 'The mind of enlightenment'[4] concerns the projection of the arisen Sacral experiences towards the Throat centre via the *northeast* petal of the Solar Plexus centre (the western gate in the text), after the lion-headed Vajrā Mahākumbhakarṇī has completed her function. The Throat centre governs the direction of the *prāṇas* of the Fires of Mind, that are 'Intrinsically aware, naturally cognisant, naturally radiant and clear', which when combined with those from the Heart centre produce this 'mind of enlightenment' (*bodhicitta*), the wisdom part of the Ray of Love-Wisdom.
3. When the enlightened Mind manifests so that 'there is nothing upon which to meditate' then the reference is to the ability to meditate within the Heart centre to experience *śūnyatā*. The experience of this non-dual bliss 'transcends all objects of knowledge'. The Gatekeeper that is represented here thus controls the eastern gate (also the *northwest* petal of the *maṇḍala* of the Solar Plexus centre) that controls the *piṇgalā nāḍī* flow to and from the Heart centre. This Mind is generated after the work of the cuckoo-headed Vajrā Mahākālī has been accomplished.
4. 'The radiance of the essence' refers to the *piṇgalā nāḍī* flow to and from the Sacral centre. This represents the energies that vivify the Solar Plexus centre generally. (The radiant essence effectively being the energy of *bodhicitta* that flows through this *nāḍī* once impurities have been cleansed.) Unruly passions, desires, or emotions no longer arise at this stage of evolution of the *yogin*, so no distractions can

3 Evans-Wentz, *The Tibetan Book of the Great Liberation*, 222.

4 This is effectively a translation of the term *bodhicitta*. Evans-Wentz (Ibid., 222) here states: 'Without meditating, without going astray, look into the True State, wherein self-cognition, self-knowledge, self-illumination shine resplendently. These, so shining, are called "The *Bodhisattvic* Mind"'.

affect his Mind. The *southeast* petal of this *chakra* is now activated after the work of the goat-headed Vajrā Mahāchāgalā guarding the southern gate in the text, has been successfully achieved. The types of emanations normally associated with sacral activity do not distract because now the essence of the compassionate Mind that manifests via it produces right human relations with the view of liberation from form. This centre then acts as a pure energy distributor for all *prāṇas* bearing enlightenment-attributes in the body. It is a vital, dynamically active distributor of radiant energy.

Next we have the work of the four *Gatekeepers of pristine cognition.* They are treated in the sections labelled 5a-5d, concerning 'undistracted mindfulness'.

5a. The 'Buddha-body of Reality', the *dharmakāya,* is said to be the union of 'radiance and emptiness'. *Radiance* is the natural expression of the energies of the Mind, once the mind has been cleansed from the *saṃskāras* of mental-emotional attachments. Radiance emanates from the processes that liberates the *iḍā nāḍī* stream from the impediments of mind. Once all emotional and desire volitions of the defiled mind associated with the *piṇgalā nāḍī* flow have also been utterly cleansed by the mechanisms earlier explained then the united, highly refined *prāṇas* can be absorbed by the Heart centre and further processed. The *iḍā nāḍī* stream is processed by the five non-sacred petals of the Heart, and the *piṇgalā nāḍī* by the seven sacred petals. The full processing of the *iḍā nāḍī prāṇas,* however, happens in the Throat centre, which is designed for this purpose. From there they are either directed to the Head Lotus, for the expression of Wisdom, or to the Heart centre and then the Solar Plexus centre, where they assist in the generation of *siddhis.* When the *iḍā and piṇgalā prāṇas* are accommodated in a non-dual form in the Heart centre, emptiness can then be accessed, with radiance and emptiness as one conjoined expression being the result. Radiance being the outcome of conventional truth and emptiness of the ultimate truth, in relation to following the Dharmakāya Way, as was explained in Volume 1, chapter 2 of this treatise. It causes the appearance of Vajrasattva 'at this moment'. The process necessitates the progressive integration of the attributes concerning the four statements (5a-5d), linking the Base of Spine centre, the Heart centre, and the Heart in the Head centre. This interrelation then brings into conscious activity the energies of the Sambhogakāya Flower or the Monad (the *dharmakāyic* form integral to a human unit allowing the appearance of a Buddha).

The integration of wisdom (the appearance of radiance) and compassion (in the form of the expression of emptiness) manifests at the *saṃsāra-śūnyatā* nexus. The Dharmadhātu Wisdom of Vairocana is a product of this nexus in the form of 'boundless compassion'. The foundational work is provided by the horse-headed Aṅkuśā (signifying the eastern petal of the Base of Spine centre), whereby all of the base *saṃskāras* associated with the development of compassionate attributes of the human kingdom are mastered.

5b. Wisdom and radiance is 'naturally liberated' to condition the entire *nāḍī* system after the work of the sow-headed Pāśā (the southern direction of the Base of Spine centre) has been accomplished. It then manifests in the form of 'boundless kindness' and the Equalising Wisdom of Ratnasambhava. The *dharmadhātu* is not attained by any structural (mindful) path to Buddhahood. It spontaneously manifests rather than being brought about arbitrarily by the activity of mind. First the lion-headed Sphoṭā (the western petal of the Base of Spine centre) must overcome all animal-like propensities and the natural egoism of the human persona. This awakens 'boundless sympathetic joy' and the Discriminating Inner Wisdom of Amitābha. When the way of the Heart and Throat centres are united then the revelation of Vajrasattva, representing the adamantine power of the All-accomplishing Wisdom of Amoghasiddhi, comes about naturally in the form of 'infinite equanimity'. The foundation for this revelation necessitates the work of the snake-headed Ghāṇṭā (the northern petal of the Base of Spine centre) to have been successfully undertaken.

One should note that part 5a compliments the first statement, where the 'naked' observation of all that arises (via Sacral centre activity) will inevitably result in the expression of the Buddha-body of Reality, the union of the feminine (wisdom) and masculine (compassionate) energies in the body. This is symbolised by the yab-yum (coital) integration of a Buddha and his Consort via the

Sacral centre. It can also be viewed in terms of the integration of the work of the Gatekeepers of pristine cognition and those that enact the emanational rites. Once this yab-yum expression has been achieved in the meditator's Mind, then the result of the union is 'naturally liberated', as explained in sentence 5b. These attributes must then be coupled to the second statement, which informs us that what is thus liberated (via integration with the energy from the Throat centre) is 'the mind of enlightenment'.

5c. Next comes the generation of an 'unstructured' path to enlightenment. (To contrast it with the structured path associated with the way of the development of the wisdom derived from the Throat centre's output.) This sentence is therefore to be coupled with the third statement, where there is 'nothing upon which to meditate'. This is the way of the evocation of the power of the Heart centre *per se* (the fruition of the emanation of the *piṇgalā nāḍī),* wherein the Void is experienced. The 'radiance of the essence' (*bodhicitta*) that comes as an expression of the union of Heart and Throat—the Heart's Mind, is then produced. To do so, the five levels associated with the number twelve explained above come into play. The entire body of manifestation of the enlightened one is then a *nirmāṇakāya* governed by the Mind, and the Heart is what directs its expression.

5d. The above represents the gain of the *saṃsāra-śūnyatā* nexus, which is the Dharmakāya Way that allows experience of Vajrasattva (who veils the constituency of cosmos).

The eight statements also relate to the eight arms of the cross of direction in space, upon which they can be placed, where statements one and 5a represent polar opposites, as also statements two and 5b, etc.

With respect to the above, Evans-Wentz states: 'In the Realm of Wisdom, transcendent over all meditation, naturally illuminative, where there is no going astray, the vacuous concepts, the self-liberation, and the primordial Voidness are of the *Dharma-Kāya'.* In their true state all concepts are essentially vacuous, devoid of form and of *saṃsāric* content. 'Without realization of this, the Goal of the *Nirvāṇic* Path is unattainable. Simultaneously with its realization the *Vajra-Sattva* state is realized. These teachings are exhaustive of all knowledge, exceedingly deep, and immeasurable'.[5] His comment here being: 'Text: *mthah-drug* (pron. *Tha-drug*), literally 'six directions', namely, the four cardinal points, the zenith and nadir; here taken in a figurative sense as implying completeness, or exhaustion, of all knowledge'.[6]

It should also be noted that the Wisdoms of the Jinas may also be ascribed to the statements numbered 1-5, where the first statement relates to the Dharmadhātu Wisdom of Vairocana. Statement two refers to the Mirror-like Wisdom of Akṣobhya, statement three to the Discriminating Inner Wisdom of Amitābha, and the fourth statement to Ratnasambhava's Equalising Wisdom. The four levels of statement five refer to the ability of Amoghasiddhi's All-accomplishing Wisdom to master the qualities of the four etheric sub-planes wherein exist the *chakras*.

Mind and the Solar Plexus centre

The remaining six petals of the Solar Plexus centre can now be analysed. They can be correlated to the end attainment of the work of the first of the four groups of six theriomorphic deities, the six 'Queens of Yoga' concerned with the pacification rites explained earlier. These six petals from the Solar Plexus centre control the Watery-Fiery ego-building *prāṇas* of the list of the twenty-eight Īśvarī. The passage from Gyurme's text that corresponds to this section is:

> Now follows the instruction which brings one to the point where the six extreme [perspectives] are exhausted:[7]
>
> 1a. Though there is a vast plethora of discordant views,
>
> 1b. Within this intrinsic awareness or [single nature of] mind,
>
> 1c. Which is the naturally originating pristine cognition,
>
> 1d. There is no duality between the object viewed and the observer.

---

5 Ibid., 223.

6 Ibid., footnote 3.

7 Gyurme's footnote here is: 'The two extremes of which the view is free are open and closed or high and low perspectives; the two extremes of which meditation is devoid are hope and doubt; the two extremes of which conduct is free are renunciation and acceptance; and the two extremes of which the result is free are beginning and end. These eight extremes may be reduced to six by omitting the category of the result'. Ibid., 410, note 16.

2a. Without focussing on the view, search for the observer!

2b. Though one searches for this observer, none will be found.

2c. So, at that instant, one will be brought to the exhaustion point of the view.

2d. At that very moment, one will encounter the innermost boundary of the view.

3a. Since there is no object at all to be observed,

3b. And since one has not fallen into a primordial vacuous emptiness,

3c. The lucid awareness, which is now present,
Is itself the view of the Great Perfection.

3d. [Here], there is no duality between realisation and lack of realisation.

4a. Though there is a vast plethora of discordant meditations,

4b. Within this intrinsic awareness,

4c. Which penetrates ordinary consciousness to the core,

4d. There is no duality between the object of meditation and the meditator.

5a. Without meditating on the object of meditation, search for the meditator!

5b. Though one searches for this meditator, none will be found.

5c. So, at that instant, one will be brought to the exhaustion point of meditation.

5d. At that very moment, one will encounter the innermost boundary of meditation.

6a. Since there is no object at all on which to meditate,

6b. And since one has not fallen under the sway of delusion, drowsiness, or agitation,

6c. The lucid uncontrived awareness, which is now present,
Is itself the uncontrived meditative equipoise or concentration.

6d. [Here], there is no duality between abiding and non-abiding.[8]

The first four statements, which I have labelled 1a-1d, relate to the flow of *iḍā prāṇas* from the Solar Plexus centre to the Stomach centre.

8 Gyurme, 48-49. I have added the numbering.

The *iḍā* stream conveys the *prāṇas* of mind, whilst the Stomach centre acts as a charnel ground for the admixing of its *prāṇas,* the *saṃskāras* of which are often considerably concretised, assertive, egotistical or inflamed. It thereby processes the 'vast plethora of discordant views', which though sometimes prosaic are generally insistent or the most discordant and reactionary of the mental-emotional conceptualisations or attitudes of mind developed by the personality. Consequently, the forcefulness of these energies is difficult to master. The trident wielded by the leopard-headed Raudrī is then needed to pacify and convert them into enlightenment-attributes.

[1a-1d] When the intrinsic awareness of the unitary nature of Mind has consequently been obtained, then the forces, images and processes that constitute mind have been controlled. The observer is then unified with that which is observed.[9] The perturbations of mind therefore no longer arise. There is simply a clear calm observation that produces a complete identification with whatever was contacted by Mind.

Evans-Wentz's version is 'Although they are to be contemplated in a variety of ways, to this Mind of self-cognition and self-originated Wisdom, there are no two such things as contemplation and contemplator'.[10]

The points 1a to 1d follow the way of the qualities of the fixed cross. Thus the phrase: 'Though there is a vast plethora of discordant views' is placed at the southern direction of downwards into *saṃsāra's* domains. Here a plethora of clashing concepts and ideas are found. They must be equilibrated, harmonised into a unity of truth, by means of Ratnasambhava's Equalising Wisdom. The phrase: 'Within this intrinsic awareness [or single nature of] mind' can then be placed at the western direction of outwards to the field of service representing humanity, wherein the single nature of Mind must be found and expounded. This work comes under the auspices of Amitābha's Discriminating Wisdom. The knowledge base of the Solar Plexus centre can then be increased in a non-volatile, non-glamoured way by the *prāṇas* returning to it. The next phrase: 'Which is the naturally originating pristine cognition' relates to the northern direction of upwards to the heights of *dharma.* Here

9 One could, if desired, make a case that each of the statements a-d for each of the six groups relate to the sub-Elements: Earthy, Watery, Fiery, and Airy, of the *prāṇic* flow associated with each major grouping.

10 Evans-Wentz, 223-224.

we have Amoghasiddhi's All-encompassing Wisdom enthroned, which demonstrates the power of the 'pristine cognition' after the single nature of Mind has been discovered. (Utilising thus the awakened qualities of the Gatekeepers directed upwards towards the Throat centre.) Finally, 'no duality between the object viewed and the observer' relates to the eastern direction of inwards to the Heart of Life. All dualities become stripped bare of their contrasting contradictions, and are seen to be but attributes of the ultimate truth. They become integrated into the Void that manifests in the form of Akṣobhya's Mirror-like Wisdom.

[2a-2d] The 'observer' relates to the concept of an 'I', which thinks about things in relation to itself at the centre of a self-focused universe of experiences. The central powerhouse for the generation of such concepts is the Solar Plexus centre. Once, however, this centre has been fully mastered and cleansed of its obscuring clinginess and aberrations, then nothing remains with which to structure an 'I' around or in relation to. The Solar Plexus creates boundaries, limits of expression, focussed upon self-centred concepts. When these boundaries are eliminated through the emasculation of an 'I', then this is referred to as 'the exhaustion point of the view'. This concept also posits the existence of limited durations of any experiential object, image or thought ('the view') by means of which an observer can come to know something, and to correlate it accordingly with perceptive wisdom. The view here refers to all concepts of mind, which are processed by the Stomach centre, via the weasel-headed Vaiṣṇāvī and the wheel that turns this *chakra*. The *prāṇas* are then incorporated in the Solar Plexus centre for complete integration into the Inner Round system of *chakras*. Later all of these views (incorporating also that of all Buddhist and non-Buddhist schools of thought earlier explained) must be refined, then abstracted into Mind, where concepts of an 'I' have been exhausted by means of the Heart's expression.

Points 2a-2d can be treated in the same manner as 1a-1d, by placing them upon the arms of the fixed cross, starting with the southern position. The results are similar for all of the points of the remaining phrases (as well as their relation to the Jinas), therefore comment will be minimal. The reader can make the necessary detailed correlation if desired. In the southern direction we find the 'search for the observer'. When in the western direction the mind carefully examines what actually constitutes an observer, and finds that 'none will be found'. The aspiration of consciousness towards the northern direction will exhaust all 'points of view'. Finally, as the way of the Heart comes into expression, then the 'innermost boundary of the view' will be found.

Evans-Wentz's version is: 'When exhaustively contemplated, these teachings merge in at-one-ment with the scholarly seeker who has sought them, although the seeker himself when sought cannot be found'.[11] This means that the seeker *per se,* the Mind in its natural state, has no individualised personal existence, therefore the seeker is not perceptible.

[3a-3d] The *piṅgalā* aspect of this meditation that is concerned with the pacification of the Solar Plexus centre can now be focussed upon. This necessitates emotional energies to be directed to the Liver centre where the *saṃskāras* are processed in such a way that they become quietened. This control happens via the work of the brown bear-headed Kaumārī and her short pike, representing the personal will that needs to be generated to control these potent emotional impulses. Once controlled, the *prāṇic* flow can be directed to the Heart centre, wherein true 'emptiness' can be found that is not nihilistic. Once the Solar Plexus centre is thereby mastered, necessitating cleansing of the entire Inner Round *prāṇas,* then the manifestation of *siddhis* are possible. They are the product of non-obstructed and transformed *saṃskāras,* as governed by each minor *chakra.* When all the *chakras* of the *nāḍī* system are thus transformed and incorporated into a completed *maṇḍala* of Mind, then this constitutes 'the Great Perfection'. Evans-Wentz's version has: 'This beginningless, vacuous, unconfused Clear Wisdom of self-cognition is the very same as that set forth in the Doctrine of the Great Perfection'[12] (rDzogs-Chen).

The focus here are the objects of perception that are integrated into consciousness by means of the pentads of the Solar Plexus centre. When we are told that 'no object at all is to be observed', then this refers to perception in the southern direction. From here via the perspective of relative truth such objects exist everywhere. However, with respect to absolute Truth (found in the Heart centre – the eastern direction), no object can be observed at all. Points 3b-3d then posit the method of validation of such an observation. The western direction informs us of a mentalistic trap to which a *yogin* can succumb; 'a primordial vacuous emptiness',

---

11 Ibid., 224.

12 Ibid.

which refers to the forceful denial or mental suppression of images to produce a state of mindlessness, rather than transforming ideas into lucid wisdom-attributes. (The Solar Plexus is the source of the intense personal will.) What results is an appearance of a void, but is not *śūnyatā*. The northern direction defines the aspect of Mind that must manifest if the Void is to be recognised: 'the lucid awareness' that is 'itself the view of the Great Perfection'. This manifests because a valid method[13] has been sought and utilised. The eastern direction then defines what this Void is: 'there is no duality between realisation and lack of realisation'. This also defines the stance at the *śūnyatā-saṃsāra* nexus that enables one to stand poised to serve the all. Being lucid and spacious the Mind is simply empty, unless made to act to perceive (something).

[4a-4d] This section refers to the *saṃskāras* ('discordant meditations') that arise in the Liver centre and which are directed to the Solar Plexus centre. The Liver centre specifically absorbs all *prāṇas* concerning normal human relationships, which the *yogin* has also lived through. Hence the *saṃskāras* conveyed by the *piṇgalā* stream naturally evoke the meditation-Mind and its related images associated with such relationships at this advanced stage of development. The entire panoply of Life is visualised during the active meditative life. Myriad are the forms of discordant as well as harmonious interactions with humanity that have evolved the consciousness of the *yogin*. Every incident that arises from human contact must be meditated upon to produce an 'intrinsic awareness' that ascertains all streams of karmic purpose and direction, so that liberation from karmic entanglements ensues. The normal mundane consciousness, symbolised by the noose of entrails held by the black bear-headed Indrāṇī, containing the gain of everything *saṃsārically* interrelated with is then quickly interpreted and counteracted.

Evans-Wentz states here 'Although there are no two such things as knowing and not knowing, there are profound and innumerable sorts of meditation; and surpassingly excellent it is in the end to know one's mind'.[14] We can interpret this in terms of the doctrine of the Void, wherein 'there are no two such things as knowing and not knowing', however, within the emptiness of the Clear Mind can exist many 'profound and innumerable sorts of meditation'.

---

13 The various yoga paths, culminating in rDzogs-Chen, or the Dharmakāya Way.

14 Evans-Wentz, 224.

Therefore, upon the path of meditation in the southern direction 'a vast plethora of discordant meditations' (emotions) can at first be encountered. Then as one grows accustomed to the vicissitudes of mind it allows discovery of the 'intrinsic awareness' of the way of Mind in the western direction. Thorough comprehension of 'ordinary consciousness' can then occur in the northern direction, and the Void realised in the eastern direction when the *prāṇas* flow to the Heart centre. Here there is no 'duality between the object of meditation and the meditator'.

[5a-5d] This section is similar to the second grouping where one is asked to try to find an observer, however now the search is focussed upon the mental domain *(ālayavijñāna),* where it is queried if a meditator engaged in mediation can be found therein. If the meditation is intrinsic, natural, spontaneous, then a meditator cannot be found, because the Mind is freed from all conceptual bounds, including that involving a central 'I'. Here we have the phrase 'the innermost boundary of the result' rather than 'the innermost boundary of the view' presented earlier. The views of the various Buddhist schools are now irrelevant because the truth is plainly seen for what it is. The result is concerned with a thorough cleansing of all *saṃskāras* of attachments to material forms, including all attributes of mind. Hence the *nāḍī* that leads from Splenic centre II to the Solar Plexus is now subjectively the focus. As stated earlier, this Splenic centre is the natural sewer system in the body and works to transform unruly *saṃskāras* ('the object of meditation'), and therefore eliminate ungainly types of *karma* ('the result'). Here the yak-headed Manurākṣasī needs the power of a *vajra* to control the input from these defiling *saṃskāras.* Once all materialistic *prāṇas* are cleansed then the *vajra* can be applied to the domain of the mind, allowing a natural spontaneity of the meditation process to occur. There is no clinging substance to slow down or impede its activity.

This worthy meditation is the natural effect of all interrelationships in our human societies, as the *saṃskāras* of many forms of contact and social engagement must be eliminated. All such *saṃskāras* are analysed and transformed by the mind. When the mind rests in its natural state there is no 'I' that is the focus of this meditation, simply the effects of the meditation-Mind spontaneously cleansing all impediments to meditation. Where then can a meditator be found? To find such an entity one would have to go outside of the mind that is enquiring, and as this is not possible by utilising the mind, the question 'where is an entity that can be called a meditator meditating?' can thus be validly asked.

Searching for an object of meditation (which inevitably is found to be non-existent), the meditator in the southern direction is then asked 'who or what' is meditating. Having thoroughly analysed the nature of mind by the time the western direction has been reached such a meditator will not be found in terms of a 'personal-I'. The 'exhaustion point of meditation' is then discovered by following the path that leads to the Throat centre, and then full integration into the 1,000 petalled lotus in the northern direction. In order to lose perception of a meditator one must travel the eastern way via the Heart centre, and in that domain experience becomes 'the innermost boundary of meditation'. All exists within the expansive inclusiveness that the Heart reveals.

Evans-Wentz's version is 'There being no two such things as object of meditation and meditator, if by those who practise or do not practise meditation the meditator of meditation be sought and not found, thereupon the goal of the meditation is reached and also the end of the meditation itself'.[15] The cleansed *prāṇas* from Splenic centre II flow to the Solar Plexus centre (the source of the 'I' concept and the principle of self will). They inevitably find their way to the Heart centre when self will is converted to the Will-of-Love *(bodhicitta*—the Heart's essence). The Heart knows only of Oneness and integrates all into the one non-dual modality, where no meditator can be found in its embracive Void.

[6a-6d] This final section deals with the sum of the body of manifestation that represents the meditator's equipment of response, which is the entire *nāḍī* system, inclusive of the Inner Round of minor *chakras*. This circulation is concerned with deriving the experiences needed from all objects in the material world. These *chakras* properly process the effects of normal sense-contact with things and with the basic emotions. Therefore the phrase 'there is no object at all on which to meditate' falls into line with standard Yogācāra philosophy, wherein all things in the phenomenal world are illusions, existing in the mind only and have no reality of their own.

Next the major obstacles to meditation are introduced; 'the sway of delusion, drowsiness, or agitation', which are predominantly caused

15 Ibid.

by the impediments contained within and channelled by the minor *chakras*. Once these impediments have been eliminated with help from the corresponding protective theriomorphic deity, the snake-headed Brahmaṇī, then the 'lucid uncontrived awareness' that fuses all objects and images into one unbounded meditative experience is possible. The lotus that Brahmaṇī holds symbolises the sum of the Inner Round *chakras* that are mastered at this stage.

'No object at all on which to meditate' refers to the southern direction wherein such objects are found conventionally but not in terms of the absolute Truth. Falling under 'the sway of delusion, drowsiness, or agitation' refers to the western direction where these enemies of the meditation process must be overcome. As a consequence, the 'lucid uncontrived awareness' that is the 'uncontrived meditative equipoise or concentration', is attained in the northern direction of upward aspiration to *dharmakāyic* realms. The sequence is finally completed in the domain of the Heart centre, where 'no duality between abiding and non-abiding' is discovered.

Evans-Wentz's version reads: 'There being no two such things as meditation and object of meditation, there is no need to fall under the sway of deeply obscuring Ignorance; for, as the result of meditation upon the unmodified quiescence of mind, the non-created Wisdom instantaneously shines forth clearly'.[16]

Because the Solar Plexus centre is the driving powerhouse of all *saṃskāras* generated below the diaphragm, it is interesting to note that each of the four parts to each section can also be related to the expression of a corresponding Gatekeeper of pristine cognition. Thus the doors to the four types of birth can be closed to awaken the four immeasurable cognitions.

Mind and the Sacral centre

The next section concerns the result of the work of the theriomorphic deities that govern the flow of *prāṇas* to and from the six petals of the *Sacral centre* (governed by the six 'Queens of Yoga' manifesting the 'rites of wrath'). These petals control the Watery desire enhancing *prāṇas* of the twenty-eight Īśvarī. Gyurme states:

16 Ibid., 224-225.

1a. Though there is a vast plethora of discordant modes of conduct,

1b. Within this intrinsic awareness,

1c. Which is the unique seminal point of pristine cognition,

1d. There is no duality between the action and the actor.

2a. Without focussing on the action, search for the actor!

2b. Though one searches for this actor, none will be found.

2c. So, at that instant, one will be brought to the exhaustion point of conduct.

2d. At that very moment, one will encounter the innermost boundary of conduct.

3a. Since, from the beginning, there has been no conduct to undertake,

3b. And since one has not fallen under the sway of bewildering propensities,

3c. The lucid uncontrived awareness, which is now present,
Is itself pure conduct, without having to be contrived, modified, accepted or rejected.

3d. [Here], there is no duality between purity and impurity.

4a. Though there is a vast plethora of discordant results,
Within this intrinsic awareness,

4b. Which is the true nature of mind, (4c)[17] the spontaneous presence of the three buddha-bodies,

4d. There is no duality between the object of attainment and the attainer.

5a. Without focussing on the attainment of the result, search for the attainer!

5b. Though one searches for this attainer, none will be found.

5c. So, at that instant, one will be brought to the exhaustion point of the result.

5d. At that very moment, one will encounter the innermost boundary of the result.

6a. Since, whatever the [projected] result, there is nothing to be attained.

---

17 This number has been inserted here to keep intact the quaternary pattern of the text.

6b. And since one has not fallen under the sway of rejection and acceptance, or hope and doubt,

6c. The naturally radiant awareness, which is now spontaneously present,

6d. Is the full manifest realisation of the three buddha-bodies, within oneself.

6e. [Here], there is the result, atemporal buddhahood itself.[18]

[1a-1d] Here the focus is upon the *prāṇas* that flow from Splenic centre II to the northernmost petal of the Sacral centre (governed by the qualities of the snake-headed Varuṇanī). This Splenic centre's purpose is to process all of the *prāṇas* associated with the Inner Round series of *chakras*. Those that can be incorporated into the circulation of the major *chakras* find their door of opportunity via this particular petal of the Sacral centre. By representing the type of *saṃskāras* associated with the principle of desire and attachment to all forms of *saṃsāric* allurements they convey 'a vast plethora of discordant modes of conduct'. This manifests in the southern position of the fixed cross, because as before, all of these statements can be placed upon the four arms of this cross, starting from the south. Statement 1a therefore refers to the plethora of sense-consciousnesses, the sensual and desirous impressions associated with contact with the material world that is processed by the Sacral centre. Statement 1b directs us to the western orientation, wherein all things must be analysed by the Mind's 'intrinsic awareness'. They are thus instantaneously analysed by the meditator's awareness that intrinsically works to overcome all aspects of desire. By the time the person has learnt to meditate by aspiring upwards, the mind's discretion has developed into a unique seminal point for the 'pristine cognition' of Mind (1c). In mastering all attachments to objects of desire by travelling inwards by the way of the Heart (1d) then there will be no 'duality between the action and the actor', as desire (for something other in relation to the concept of 'self') is what causes such a duality. The 'action and the actor' become one effortless fusion of unitary purpose.

Continuing under the heading of 'The Yoga of the Nirvāṇic Path' Evans-Wentz's version is: 'Although there is an innumerable variety of

18 Gyurme, 49-50.

profound practices, to one's mind in its true state they are non-existent; for there are no two such things as existence and non-existence.'[19] Existence and non-existence are merely conventional designations, where the phenomena appearing in the mental continuum of *saṃsāra's* domain is designated 'existing', and when it disappears from that domain it is then designated 'non-existing'. In reality, we simply have one vast duration of being/non-being that persists, despite changes in transient phenomenal appearances.

[2a-2d] The process of searching for an actor (2a) refers to the petal of the Sacral centre that projects the generated *iḍā nāḍī* stream to the Solar Plexus centre. (Governed by the proclivities of the crow-headed Cāmuṇḍī.) Here the *manasic* principle is developed that conceives of things in terms of a central 'I', a central actor. This *manasic* propensity directed to the Solar Plexus, the centre of the emotions, makes it the central actor of all personality dispositions and activities. Every concept of 'self' revolves around Solar Plexus manifestation. It dramatises all attributes of 'I' and 'me' through its dominant place of normal human relationships and its control of the Watery emotions. The Solar Plexus centre effectively stands as the Head centre from the perspective of Sacral centre awareness, because the Sacral centre is situated below the Solar Plexus centre that absorbs its main *prāṇas*. As the *prāṇas* of all of the minor *chakras* are processed and synthesised by this major *chakra*, so it is the most powerful actor in the human persona. It is consequently the 'abdominal brain', the basis of all forms of ego-clinging. Thus in exploring this *chakra,* all forms of conduct, as governed by the desire-mind, all things that create an illusion of an 'I', will become comprehended, and thus exhausted. In cogently exploring the Solar Plexus by means of the development of the mind, one first finds that no actor can be found (2b), and as one enquires northward, one is inevitably brought to 'the exhaustion point of conduct' (2c) by investigating the manifold forms of emotions and attachments to ephemera that the Watery environment of this *chakra* provides.

When the Solar Plexus is completely mastered, by bringing it under the control of the *prāṇas* (*bodhicitta*) from the Heart centre, then 'the innermost boundary of conduct' (2d) will have manifested. *Bodhicitta*

19 Evans-Wentz, 225.

has replaced desire-mind, producing unfettered enlightenment.

Evans-Wentz's version is: 'There being no two such things as practice and the practitioner, if by those who practise or do not practise the practitioner of practice be sought and not found, thereupon the goal of the practice is reached and also the end of the practice itself.[20] We should note that the practice and the practitioner are one, inasmuch as all manifests as a *saṃsāric* play. *Saṃskāras* are generated in the process of the 'non-practice' of normal everyday activity, when the mind becomes identified with any *saṃsāric* attribute. These *saṃskāras* are transformed when the Mind is developed and it focuses upon them for this purpose. As this happens automatically with respect to the expression of Mind, so then the appellation of 'non-practice' can be also applied here. In between these two forms of 'non-practice' lies the *sādhana* of the practitioner, who works at the practice of developing the stages of the meditation technique, until it has become automatic, spontaneous, hence a 'non-practice'.

[3a-3d] 'The sway of bewildering propensities' refers to the southeast petal of the Sacral centre (governed by the activities of the wolf-headed Vāyudevī) which processes the *prāṇas* coming from the right Gonad centre. Here the principle of desire and how it affects all aspects of sexuality is generated. We therefore have concepts of union with the opposite sex, as well as many of the base appetites of which the human personality is capable. The phrase 'from the beginning, there has been no conduct to undertake' (3a) refers first of all to the conduct of the average desirous person (in the southern orientation of the fixed cross). They are undisciplined and controlled by unabated desire so no conduct of any value can be found there. Eventually, when the Mind holds sway over the Sacral centre's entire activity, then the process of sexual control becomes automatic and spontaneous, therefore there is no (disciplining) 'conduct to undertake'. In the western orientation, wherein the Mind comes to rule all activity, we then see in the proficient meditator that it has not 'fallen under the sway of bewildering propensities' (the sum total of sexual urges and desires that the normal person is faced with) because all of these allurements have been properly rationalised and apotropaically dealt with.

20 Ibid.

Once all such desire is mastered (by the time the northern orientation has been reached) then 'lucid uncontrived awareness' (3c) is the gain. As one then resides in the Mind, so that in itself is 'pure conduct, without having to be contrived, modified, accepted or rejected'. In developing the way of the Heart (the eastern direction), wherein the Void is revealed (3d) then 'no duality between purity and impurity' can persist. (The consequent fusion of male and female *prāṇas* at the *śūnyatā-saṃsāra* nexus assures the non-dual status of one's resultant awareness.)

Evans-Wentz's version is: 'Inasmuch as from eternity there is nothing whatsoever to be practised, there is no need to fall under the sway of errant propensities, The non-created, self-radiant Wisdom here set forth, being actionless, immaculate, transcendent over acceptance or rejection, is itself the perfect practice'.[21] This practise then is an expression of *śamatha*, calm abiding or tranquility meditation. This produces actionless, 'self-radiant Wisdom' (via *vipassana*) because the mind is no longer agitated by desire-impulses.

[4a-4d] We now proceed to 'the vast plethora of discordant results' representing the southwest petal, governed by the sow-headed Varāhī, and which also receives *prāṇas* from the left Gonad centre, related to general physical urges, appetites, and attraction amongst the sexes. The concern is with what brings them together to manifest their forms of sexuality, in conjunction with the development of elemental *manas*. This then produces a confusing plethora of assumptions concerning life in *saṃsāra*. Discordant indeed are the manifold results of normal human relationships based upon the sexual urge.

This petal is the foundation for all the knowable aspects of life, and which inevitably produce the appearance of the Buddha-Mind via the forms that can be perceived by mind/Mind. The three Buddha-bodies can then be experienced.

When the mind is utilised to analyse the nature and purpose of the entire sexual function upon the yogic path, then eventually its intrinsic awareness is developed (the western orientation of the fixed cross) which sees this entire plethora in perspective. This allows the higher yoga Tantras to be followed (the northern direction) whereby the non-dual *śūnyatā-saṃsāra* nexus can be discovered (via the eastern direction).

21 Ibid.

'The spontaneous presence of the three buddha-bodies' here also has an indirect reference to the birthing of the child that is the normal result of male-female interrelationships. When this process of 'birthing' is rightfully controlled, yogically, then the entire process of life will have been mastered. This allows the simultaneous appearance of the bodies of a Buddha (*trikāya*) by the *yogin,* which represents the 'child' of following the Tantras to conclusion.

Evans-Wentz presents: 'Although there are no two such things as pure and impure, there is an innumerable variety of fruits of *yoga*, all of which, to one's mind in its True State, are the conscious content of the non-created *Tri-Kāya'.*[22]

[5a-5d] Searching for the attainer without 'focussing on the attainment of the result' refers to the northeast direction of this petal ('unity'), governed by the ibex-headed Agnāyī. Here one projects the generated *piṇgalā prāṇas* of the Sacral centre upwards to the Solar Plexus centre. The upward motion manifests because what is normally viewed as 'the attainer' is really the effect of the Solar Plexus centre that has attained whatever the 'actor' (the ego, the 'I' concept) has set out to achieve. 'The attainment of the result' would normally refer to the attainment of whatever the ego desires, but here it refers to the continued projection of the consciousness-stream of the *piṇgalā nāḍī* flowing to the Heart centre. The resultant expression of the Heart's Wisdom is 'the innermost boundary of the result'. (The eastern orientation of the fixed cross.)

However, before this complete absorption into the Void of the Heart happens, the search necessitates the use of the mind in the western field of outward service to humanity, wherein no attainer will be found, other than the illusional concept of an 'I', which is insubstantial in and of itself. (The activity of the Solar Plexus centre has thus been superseded by the awareness of the higher centres.) Such realisation is then the 'exhaustion point of the result' (5c), and represents the northernmost point of this quest. When coupled with further refinement of meditative absorption via the eastern direction, of the Heart's awareness to 'encounter the innermost boundary of the result' (5d), then no ego exists to attain anything in relation to itself. 'The attainer' can, however, still be considered a transitory vehicle of the Heart's wisdom when seen to interrelate with

22 Ibid., 226.

normal (emotionally polarised) humanity, according to the dictates of the Bodhisattva vow. The Solar Plexus centre is then completely inundated with *piṅgalā prāṇas* from the Heart centre. When this effect flows on to dominate the entire Sacral centre activity, then also an 'innermost boundary of the result' is produced. Consequently, the *yogin* is liberated from the constraints of *saṃsāra,* the entire plethora of action-reaction activities associated with the *chakras* below the diaphragm.

Evans-Wentz presents: 'There being no two such things as action and performer of action, if one seeks the performer of action and no performer of action be found anywhere, thereupon the goal of all fruit-obtaining is reached and also the final consummation itself. There being no other method whatsoever of obtaining the fruit, there is no need to fall under the sway of the dualities of accepting and rejecting, trusting and distrusting these teachings'.[23]

[6a-6e] The overlapped petal of the Sacral centre with the Base of Spine centre petal can now be considered. It is governed by the elephant-headed Bhujanā. The 'full manifest realisation of the three Buddha-bodies, within oneself' is the natural expression of the accomplished *yogin* who has successfully united the Fires of the *iḍā* and *piṅgalā nāḍīs* with *suṣumṇā.* This process is accomplished via this petal. (The lowest correspondence within the body of the place wherein the *saṃsāra-śūnyatā* nexus can be found.) It is therefore the place where *kuṇḍalinī* is evoked. Yogically, these three fused Fires via the natural expression in the enlightened one's life are 'the three Buddha-bodies within oneself'. The result is 'atemporal buddhahood' (6e), which refers to the complete awakening of the Base of Spine centre, in conjunction with the liberation of the energies of the Head lotus, which makes one a Buddha.

Sections 6a-6c deal with the meditative process relating to following the middle between extremes (*mādhyamā pratipad*) that develops the 'naturally radiant awareness' of Mind necessary for liberation of the inner Fire. The entire phraseology of these statements is from the point of view of the accomplished *yogin* that has awakened *kuṇḍalinī,* and who therefore consciously resides in terms of the 'three buddha-bodies'. The visualisation of the statements, therefore, is from the northern position of the fixed cross. In 6a then, the '[projected] result' refers to the work

---

23 Ibid.

pursued in *saṃsāra* (the south) via meditation, which in terms of the ultimate truth is that nothing is 'to be attained'. Neither has one 'fallen under the sway of rejection and acceptance, or hope and doubt' (6b), which is the way of the expression of mind (the western orientation). The 'naturally radiant awareness, which is now spontaneously present' (6c) then relates to the eastern orientation that is the way of the Heart centre's expression. The stance of this entire verse is from residence in the *trikāya* of a Buddha (the north). All is the expression of such a Mind.

Evans-Wentz's version is: 'Realization of the self-radiant and self-born Wisdom, as the manifestation of the *Tri-Kāya* in the self-cognizing mind, is the very fruit of attaining the Perfect *Nirvāṇa*'.[24]

The seven Rays and the centres below the diaphragm

The next section is entitled 'Synonyms for Awareness' by Gyurme.[25] They refer to the seven Ray qualities that govern the experiences and awareness derived from the domains ruled by mind/Mind. Consequently, the influence of the Rays upon the sub-planes of the mental plane are implicated. The last five statements (stemming from the eighth statement) deal with the conditionings of the sub-planes of the empirical mind as related to experiences derived from the physical domain. Gyurme states:

1. This awareness, free from the eight extremes, such as eternalism and nihilism [and so forth],

   Is called the 'Middle Way', which does not fall into any extremes.
2. It is called 'awareness' because mindfulness is uninterrupted.
3. It is given the name 'Nucleus of the Tathāgata'

   Because emptiness is [naturally] endowed with this nucleus of awareness,
4. If one understands this truth, one reaches perfection in all respects,
5. For which reason, this [awareness] is also called the 'Perfection of Discriminative Awareness'.
6. Furthermore, it is called the 'Great Seal' because it transcends the intellect and is atemporally free from extremes,

24 Ibid.

25 Gyurme, 50. Evans-Wentz's version is 'The Explanation of the Names given to this Wisdom'. (Ibid, 226.)

7. And, further, it is called the 'Ground-of-all',

   Because [this awareness] is the ground of all joys and sorrows associated with this cyclic existence and nirvāṇa –

8. The distinction between these being contingent on whether or not this [awareness] is realised.

8a. [Further], this radiant and lucid awareness is itself referred to as 'ordinary consciousness',

8b. On account of those periods when it abides in its natural state in an ordinary non-exceptional way.

8c. Thus, however many well-conceived and pleasant-sounding names are applied to this [awareness],

8d. In reality, those who maintain that these names do not refer to this present conscious awareness,

   But to something else, above and beyond it,

8e. Resemble someone who has already found an elephant, but is looking for its tracks [elsewhere].[26]

1. The 'Middle Way' that does not fall into extremes would normally be considered an expression of the fourth Ray of Harmony in the midst of Conflict. However, in terms of the Buddhist context (which is governed by the fourth Ray) it is taken as an expression of the first Ray of Will or Power, as it lays bare all obstacles to enlightenment. It is the razor-edged path to Truth, the sword-bearer of enlightenment, the quickest, most efficient way to liberation. It represents the way of development of high spiritual power when utilised via Tantric methodology. Nothing can stand in its way as it passes through the centre of things (i.e., 'between the extremes') on the upward way to liberation. Yogically the focus on the 'Middle Way' is upon the centre of each of the *chakras* (the *suṣumṇā nāḍī*) through which *kuṇḍalinī* must flow when awakened. It is the path therefore that liberates. Evans-Wentz states that: 'This Wisdom delivers one from the eternally transitory Eight Aims.[27] Inasmuch as it does not fall

26 Gyurme, 50-51.

27 Evans-Wentz's footnote 3 (226-227): '*Mtaḥ-brgyad* (pron. *Tha-gay*), "Eight Limits", or "Eight Frontiers (or ends)", with reference to the Eight Worldly Aims,

under the sway of any extreme, it is called "The Middle Path"'.[28]

With respect to the centres below the diaphragm, the first Ray potency must be toned down (by means of the fourth Ray medium), otherwise its force would be too destructive, causing the petals of the *chakras* to spin far too rapidly. Too many aberrations of *saṃskāric* propensity would be caused if it were not for the harmonising quality of the 'Middle Way'.

2. The second Ray of Love-Wisdom is the fusion of the vast expanse of the blue ocean that is an uninterrupted awareness of Love with the added gain of an evolutionary epoch (Wisdom). Yogically this is produced by the flow of the *piṇgalā nāḍī* that awakens the unbounded duration of being/non-being experienced in the Heart centre. The mind is not active in an empirical fashion, as the comings and goings of mindful observations have been stilled. The gain of former activity has been abstracted and absorbed into a never-ending duration of awareness. The Heart's Mind (Love-Wisdom) thus supplants mind. The separative, ego-forming, emotional and clinging attributes of desire-mind that would naturally form in the centres below the diaphragm are negated by the unifying, expansive, non-localised energy of the Heart's awareness.

   Evans-Wentz's version: 'It is called "Wisdom" because of its unbroken continuity of memory'.[29] In terms of the livingness of all past experiences that have contributed to the gaining of wisdom, memory can be instantaneously evoked by the uninterrupted awareness of the Heart centre. It manifests as a continuum of the Mind-stream that is the Heart's Mind, wherein everything that was experienced previously can be recalled exactly as it actually happened. Nothing whatsoever is lost from the past except the corruptible form. All the seed *bījas* of what was remain, and when evoked, a *bīja* will reveal its complete *maṇḍala* in context with any epoch of the subject of enquiry.

---

which, taken in four parts, are: gain and loss, good name and bad name, praise and defamation, happiness and misery'.

28 Ibid., 226-227.

29 Ibid., 227.

3. The third Ray of enlightening, Mathematically Exact Activity is the 'nucleus of awareness' because it governs the flow of all the *prāṇas* of mind (of the *iḍā nāḍī* system) and their transformation into those of Mind. The complete development of this enlightened, abstracted Mind allows one to understand the truth that produces 'perfection in all respects'. Such perfection manifests with mathematical exactitude. The comprehension of this truth necessitates the transformation of all *saṃskāras* associated with desire-mind. The downpour of the energies of Mind to the *chakras* below the diaphragm facilitates this process, as has been explained. The five main *chakras* (where the Head and Ājñā centres are seen as a unity, as well as the Base of Spine and Sacral centres) become the recipients for the five Jina Wisdoms. Each *chakra* then manifests in the form of a 'nucleus of the Tathāgata'.

In these first three statements we have the three major *nāḍīs* exemplified. From a yogic perspective they are the triple jewels of: the Buddha (the *suṣumṇā nāḍī*), the *dharma* (the *piṇgalā nāḍī*) and the *saṇgha* (units of *manasic* integration, the *iḍā nāḍī*). The 'Nucleus of the Tathāgata' is also another way of describing the *tathāgatagarbha*-Sambhogakāya Flower, which exists upon the abstracted levels of the mental plane, the domain of Mind. The emptiness that is '[naturally] endowed with this nucleus of awareness' from this perspective refers to the *saṃsāra-śūnyatā* nexus. It must therefore eventually control every minor *chakra* through converting base *saṃskāras*.

Evans-Wentz's version: 'Being the essence of the vacuity of mind, it is called "The Essence of the Buddhas"'.[30]

4. The fourth Ray of Beautifying Harmony overcoming Conflict refers to the 'Perfection in all respects' because such perfection comes only via the resolution of all fields of conflict in *saṃsāra*. Discriminating awareness (the fifth Ray) lays the foundation for the attainment of such perfection, as it eschews that which is not viable for the path of enlightenment. Upon perfection of the path discrimination becomes automatic, as consciousness rests in the middle between extremes, facilitating transmission from one extreme *(nirvāṇa)* to the other *(saṃsāra)*, like an unsullied mirror. The Airy fourth Ray

30 Ibid.

governs the evolution of the *nāḍīs* in general, regulating the flow of *prāṇas* from below the diaphragm to above, and vice versa. When the *chakras* below the diaphragm are fully controlled by the *prāṇas* from above then this perfection is accomplished. The path of perfection therefore refers to the mode of conversion of *prāṇas* from defiled to undefiled states by means of evocation of the energies from the Heart centre.

Evans-Wentz's version (integrating both the fourth and fifth Rays): 'If the significance of these teachings were known by all beings, surpassingly excellent would it be. Therefore, these teachings are called "The Means of Attaining the Other Shore of Wisdom [or The Transcendental Wisdom]"'.[31]

5. We now proceed to the fifth Ray of Scientific Reasoning governing all attributes of mind and its manifold forms of activity. It finds the right harmonising, enlightened view within the often conflicting ideas in the domains of thought. As the potency of more knowledgeable impressions (*saṃskāras*) are increasingly developed in this process, then the various petals of the *chakras* awaken. Awakening the variegations and ordering of these petals reveals the awareness and *siddhis* they contain. One discriminates as per the type of *saṃskāras* (*manasiç* ideations) to be developed and cleansed of defilements. As discriminative attributes become perfected so the *chakras* appropriately awaken and automatically manifest enlightenment-attributes of their own accord.

The remainder of this extract from Gyurme concerns aspects of the fifth Ray because the mind/Mind rules the sum of the conditionings of *saṃsāra*. The abstract portion (Mind) of its dual expression possesses three sub-planes, signified by points 5 – 7. The concreted, empirical aspects are lettered a – e. The sixth and seventh Ray attributes fall under the jurisdiction of the domain of Mind. The effects of the sixth Ray of Devotion is usually wed to the expression of mind in the form of the desire-mind *(kāma-manas),* and the seventh Ray grounds its expression in *saṃsāra* in terms of cyclic endeavour and the power or force of material activity. The sixth Ray is seen as an energising bridge of devotion and idealism

31 Ibid.

that drives the *prāṇas* to produce the fulfilment of the objectives of mind/Mind. The seventh Ray provides the form or clothing of the impression or idea, thereby producing the tangible result.

6. The perfected expression of the manifestation of Mind produces the 'Great Seal' that 'transcends the intellect and is atemporally free from extremes'. The Mind seals or fixes in space all enlightenment-attributes derived from *saṃsāric* involvement. It integrates *saṃsāra* with *śūnyatā* in one great *saṃsāra-śūnyatā* nexus. The Mind cannot function in a discordant way, as it is freed from the emotions (that produce extreme views of all types). Total emotional control is thus implicated, where all petals of the *chakras* are fully awakened and empowered with the triune Fire of the major *nāḍīs*. The Mind yogically moves all *prāṇas* to awaken the powers of the *chakras* through the process of right discrimination, utilising the sixth Ray inspiration or driving power *(tapas)* that sustains the meditation practice. *Prāṇa* is thereby appropriately controlled and directed, making Mind and *prāṇa* synonymous terms. Once the *chakras* are functioning to full capacity, awakened, they can then be sealed with the complete capability of their potential.

   When all *chakras* (above and below the diaphragm) are empowered in the full glory of their potency, then we have the 'Great Seal', or 'the great perfection'. Such glory necessitates a complete unadulterated flow of liberated qualities between the centres above and below the diaphragm. They are sealed with the *mahāmudrā* of that which is above the diaphragm (the 'masculine') fused with that which is below the diaphragm (the 'feminine'). Evans-Wentz's version: 'To Them who have passed away into *Nirvāṇa,* this Mind is both beginningless and endless; therefore it is called "The Great Symbol"'.[32] (The symbol of Mind in its true or natural state.)

7. The sixth and the seventh Rays work as a practical unity, where the sixth Ray of Devotion controls all that can be considered Watery in one's system. (The emotions, desire principle, and all forms of attachment.) The focus is upon the activity of the centres below the diaphragm, which deal with the *prāṇas* of people's normal day to day consciousness. The seventh Ray of Ceremonial or Cyclic

32 Ibid.

Activity and demonstrable Power incorporates such attachment into the expression of the physical domain. This constitutes an interpretation of the 'Ground-of-all', because the awareness gained from the fact one has a physical body that interrelates with the forms constituting *saṃsāra* grounds 'all joys and sorrows associated with this cyclic existence and nirvāṇa'. Evans-Wentz's version: 'Inasmuch as this Mind, by being known and by not being known, becomes the foundation of all the joys of *Nirvāṇa* and of all the sorrows of the *Sangsāra*, it is called "The All-Foundation"'.[33] From this Sacral and Solar Plexus centre background comes the entire path to liberation once *saṃskāras* have been mastered.

All experiences are contained and resolved in the mind, and inevitably Mind is awakened, which determines the distinction between one and the other, because all is accomplished in the mind/Mind, which in the form of the *ālayavijñāna,* can also be considered the 'Ground-of-all'. The awareness that is centred upon the *ālayavijñāna* then becomes the first level of enlightenment. To realise this level, however, necessitates the awakening of all of the petals of the *chakras*, as all convey the *saṃskāras* of consciousness.

Devotion to the *dharma* and yogic precepts, aspiration to high ideals and enlightenment, and the application of the creative imagination (the highest aspects of the sixth Ray) are needed to visualise the *maṇḍalas,* deities, and Tantric processes if enlightenment is to be achieved. These processes then determine whether or not 'this [awareness] is realised'. They anchor all activities via cyclic or ritualistic means, utilising therefore the effect of the seventh Ray of Ceremonial Cyclic Activity—Demonstrable Power, which governs all forms of activity concerning physical plane interrelationships. The panoply of *saṃsāric* phenomena thus comes under its sway. 8a to 8e deal with the expression of such activity in a corporeal body in terms of the five Elements, starting with the Aetheric Element (hence the mastery of the smell sense-consciousness).

8a. The intelligence derived from such interrelationships can produce a 'lucid awareness' if the processes that awaken the abstract Mind

33 Ibid.

here relegated to the Aetheric Element are effected. When such a consciousness is directed to experience *saṃsāra* in the normal way then it can be referred to as 'ordinary consciousness'.

8b. Such awareness concerns all phenomenal involvement that cause the mind to abide 'in its natural state in an ordinary non-exceptional way'. The mental sub-plane implicated here is the fourth, governed by the fourth Ray. It represents the zone of transition between the abstract and the empirical mind and embodies the subtlest, more Airy, generally philosophical and aspirational, universalised concepts that are still orientated to the material domain. It is therefore easily impregnated by lucid impressions from the higher strata of Mind, which facilitates the engendering of compassionate idealism and the expression of *bodhicitta*. The specific sense-consciousness is taste, concerning subtle discernments.

8c. We now proceed to the domain of pure *manas,* of the mind ensconced in its most Fiery aspect, the fifth sub-plane of mind counting from above down, and the third from below up. Here the intelligent, logical, deductive methodology of the fifth Ray reigns supreme. Consequently, significant commentary could be provided because it incorporates the experiences pertaining to conscious life in *saṃsāra,* thus to the way the mind names things via intellectual discursiveness and the logical deductive assumptions of the scientific community. All humans utilise the 'many well-conceived and pleasant-sounding names' in order to traverse the exigencies of everyday life. Myriad are the languages that have arisen to convey the names bearing information about 'things', allowing humans to converse intelligibly with each other. Illogical concepts to high philosophic speculations can also arise through this faculty of the empirical mind. The entire scientific and technological civilisation we presently live in arises from the expression of this strata of the substance of mind. The sight sense-consciousness is here implicated.

8d. The sixth mental sub-plane that processes *kāma-manasic* impressions, comes to the fore in the disputes, controversies, arguments, assertive rhetoric and muddied thinking of those ensconced in 'this present conscious awareness'. They must learn to aspire 'to something else, above and beyond' the desire or emotional mind. The sixth Ray of

Devotion or Aspiration and the Watery Element plays its role here. The touch sense-consciousness is implicated.

8e. The entire history of such development is invariably complicated, because the intellect is often tricked into believing illusions are real. The text alludes to this by the allegory of the one 'who has already found an elephant, but is looking for its tracks [elsewhere]'. The elephant refers to the natural state of mind that is inherent, yet the individual abides not in it because of the many illusory pathways the intellect follows. People are too focussed upon the 'tracks', the imprints of the elephant of mind made upon the earth, the gross material domain, instead of perceiving the vastness of the subjective domain, where the true value of those tracks can be found.

The symbolism of the elephant also implicates Bhujanā, the elephant-headed Īśvarī, who we saw earlier governed the petal of the Sacral centre that interrelates with the four petals of the Base of Spine centre. This represents the foundation of all experiences in *saṃsāra,* of our ability to symbolically 'walk on the earth'. Consequently, the hearing sense-consciousness is implied.

All of these attributes refer to the nature of conscious development focussed upon the types of awareness associated with the *chakras* below the diaphragm. When lucid awareness is to be sought then consciousness must shift its focus away from the generation of *saṃskāras,* to that which works to transform them into enlightenment-attributes.

The statements 8a-8e are veiled references to the wisdoms of the Jinas, and therefore to their ability to transform the five poisons (ignorance, hatred, pride, passion, and envy) associated with ordinary consciousness. The key phrases relating to each of the Jinas are: firstly; 'lucid awareness' (8a), which refers to the ability of Vairocana's Dharmadhātu Wisdom to transform the ignorance of ordinary consciousness. Next we have the phrase 'natural state' (8b), which refers to the serene equipoise of Akṣobhya's Mirror-like Wisdom, which is said to transform the various permutations of hatred. The term 'awareness' (8c) refers to Amitābha's Discriminating Wisdom that transforms the poison of pride, which can be considered to derive from the ability to articulate 'pleasant sounding names'. Looking 'to something else, above and beyond' (8d) refers to Ratnasambhava's Equalising Wisdom, which works to integrate all incongruous attitudes into a harmony. The poison countered here is passion. Finally, the concept of having 'found an elephant' (8e) has reference to Amoghasiddhi's All-accomplishing Wisdom, which is said to overcome the various permutations of envy.

These poisons are generic terms for a large range of *saṃskāras* that possess similar basic qualities or energies as the poison in question. Ignorance is basic and refers to lack of comprehension of any aspect associated with the *dharma* or of the nature of things as they actually are. Hatred refers to any *saṃskāric* quality that opposes compassionate considerations, or the development of Love and Wisdom. Pride refers to all attributes developed by the ego to bolster its opinion of 'self'. Passion refers to all forms of emotionality that empower people to act irrationally. Envy refers to all the forms of jealousy or thwarted desire over other people's material possessions, looks, accomplishments, etc. It then can produce attributes of the critical mind, malicious scheming, and theft.

Evans-Wentz's version: 'The impatient, ordinary person when dwelling in his fleshy body calls this very clear Wisdom "common intelligence". Regardless of whatever elegant and varied names be given to this Wisdom as the result of thorough study, what Wisdom other than it, as here revealed, can one really desire? To desire more than this Wisdom is to be like one who seeks an elephant by following its footprints when the elephant itself has been found'.[34] Here the elephant, the largest of all animals, is referred to because the wisdom demonstrated in the Buddhist *dharma* (the elephant) is exceedingly clear to all discerning people. It is, however, obvious that most people are so bewildered that they effectively continue looking at the tracks in the dirt of their mental-emotional attitudes for revelations, rather than acknowledging what should be so plainly obvious.

Mind and the left Gonad centre

The next grouping of six theriomorphic deities, that relate to the expression of the left Gonad centre, can now be analysed. Here we

34 Ibid., 228.

have the six 'Queens of yoga' who enact the 'rites of subjugation', so that procreative forces do not run rampant. Their purpose is to control the Watery-Earthy form-building *prāṇas* of the twenty-eight Īśvarī. Gyurme states:

1. Though one were to scan the [entire] external universe,

   [Searching for the nature of mind], one would not find it.

   Buddhahood cannot be attained other than through the mind.

   Not recognising this, one indeed does search for the mind externally.

2. Yet, how can one find [one's own mind] when one looks for it elsewhere?

   This is like a fool, for example, who, when finding himself amidst a crowd of people,

   Becomes mesmerised by the spectacle [of the crowd] and forgets himself,

   Then, no longer recognising who he is, starts searching elsewhere for himself,

   Continuously mistaking others for himself.

3. [Similarly], since one does not discern the abiding nature,

   Which is the fundamental reality of [all] things,

   One is cast into cyclic existence, not knowing that appearances are to be identified with the mind,

   And, not discerning one's own mind to be buddha, nirvāṇa becomes obscured.

4. The [apparent] dichotomy between cyclic existence and nirvāṇa is due to [the dichotomy between] ignorance and awareness,

   But there is [in reality] no temporal divide between these two, [even] by a single moment.

5. Seeing the mind as extraneous to oneself is indeed bewildering,

   Yet bewilderment and non-bewilderment are of a single essence.

   Since there exists no [intrinsic] dichotomy in the mental continuum of sentient beings,

   The uncontrived nature of mind is liberated just by being left in its natural state.

   Yet if you remain unaware that bewilderment [originates] in the mind,

   You will never understand the meaning of actual reality.

6. So you should observe that which naturally arises and naturally originates within your own [mind].

   [First], observe [the source] from which these appearances initially originated,

   [Second, observe the place] in which they abide in the interim,

   And [third, observe the place] to which they will finally go.

   Then, one will find that, just as, for example, a pond-dwelling crow does not stray from its pond,

   Even though it flies away from the pond,

   Similarly, although appearances arise from the mind,

   They arise from the mind and subside into the mind of their own accord.[35]

1. This section concerns the petal that leads to a minor *chakra* at the left testicle or ovary that directly controls its secretions, and which projects *iḍā* type Earthy *prāṇas* into the rejected pool from Spleen II circulation into the next level of minor *chakras*. They control the entire form-building propensity of these organs, signified by the carrion that the vulture seeks to consume. The first section, therefore, where we are asked to 'scan the [entire] external universe' to search for the nature of mind (the 'carrion' of its basic, and also subsidiary thoughts), refers to the functioning of this petal after the red vulture-headed Bhakṣasī has finished her work. This concerns disposing the offal of desirous images via thorough consumption, then crushing the remainder (its 'bones') with the primitive club she holds. Once the illusional phenomenal objects of this external universe have been scanned, one cannot find the source of mind in any of the fleeting images. Enlightenment (Buddhahood) cannot be obtained through *saṃskāra*-generating identifications (impelled by desire for union with or to be attached) to any phenomenal attribute. Enlightenment is not gained through mistaking phenomena as real, but rather by a thorough analysis of the naturalness of Mind. Even the most insignificant thoughts and ideas must be thoroughly dissected and consumed by mind to analyse whatever intrinsic worthiness there may be. Having done so, enlightenment can only be found if what has been consumed has been transformed and transmuted into elements of Mind.

35 Gyurme, 51-52. As ususal, I have added the numbers.

Under the title he gives for this section ('The Yoga of the Thatness') Evans-Wentz presents: 'Quite impossible is it, even though one seeks throughout the Three Regions, to find the Buddha[36] elsewhere than in the mind. Although he that is ignorant of this may seek externally or outside the mind to know himself, how is it possible to find oneself when seeking others rather than oneself?'[37]

2. Next we have that petal regulated by the red horse-headed Ratī, who carries the impulses of the *piṇgalā* attributes of the Earth Element that develop the desire aspect of *manas* associated with the small *chakra* that governs the control and function of the sexual organ. The development of the desire-mind is here likened to 'a fool' that finds 'himself amidst a crowd of people', and becomes 'mesmerised by the spectacle [of the crowd] and forgets himself' and searches 'elsewhere for himself'. This small centre herds these basic human emotional and sexual exchanges associated with the general pool of minor centre circulation. The average individual becomes so totally inebriated with the morass of desire based interactions thus generated that this miasma becomes the basis for their concept of reality. The concept of 'self' is then an expression of the combined opinions of people similarly engaged integrated with the individual's own awareness of him/herself.

   One therefore should not seek 'reality' in forms of (sexual) relationships. Enticing though it may be, nothing permanent exists there. Better to look within oneself and there discover the pathways to Mind. Ratī then assists in the generation of *saṃskāras* that teach the truth concerning the nature of social interactions, so that all forms of attachment to societies' mores and sexual indulgences can be eliminated.

   Evans-Wentz presents: 'He that thus seeks to know himself is like a fool giving a performance in the midst of a crowd and forgetting who he is and then seeking everywhere to find himself. This simile also applies to one's erring in other ways'.[38]

36 Evans-Wentz (footnote 2, 228) states that the term for the Buddha, '*Sangs-rygas* (pron. *Sang-gay*) also signifies "being liberated from the beginning and by nature full of knowledge"'.

37 Ibid.

38 Evans-Wentz, 228-229.

3. Next we have the Watery *iḍā nāḍī prāṇas* to and from the small organ governing the pleasure of the sex act. This is the main cause of the production of the children (or child of desire) that perpetuates cyclic existence; thus the awareness of appearances that are thought of as separate from the nature of mind. The pale-red Garuda-headed Rudhiramadhī holds a cudgel to pound the little serpents of desire-impulse that cause such impressions, so that she can consume and completely transform them into a knowingness of the fundamental unity of appearances. Inevitably then, on the highest stages of the path, the Buddha-Mind can eventually be discerned for what it is. We see here that such a Mind has its genesis in the transmutation of even the tiniest perceptions derived from the material world, and also from the most intense pleasurable experiences, once those perceptions have been properly processed by mind. However, for the most part, most people are completely ensnared by lust for pleasurable experiences to the extent that it prevents knowingness of the nature of Mind, and obscures the possibility of knowledge of the Void. Through repetitious sexual activity people perpetuate 'cyclic existence' (and cause children to be born in *saṃsāra).* Cycles of happiness and misery ensue, and to find their causes they must understand that all such experiences are extensions of their own minds and they must seek to comprehend the nature of mind in order to master all attributes of phenomenal life.

   Evans-Wentz's version: 'Unless one knows or sees the natural state of substances [or things] and recognizes the Light in the mind, release from the *Sangsāra* is unattainable. Unless one sees the Buddha in one's mind, *Nirvāṇa* is obscured.'[39]

4. We now observe the *manasic prāṇas* of animal-like, desirous propensity that come from the Stomach centre by the red dog-headed Ekacāriṇī Rākṣasī, who holds a *vajra* to try to convert ignorance of the true purpose of birth into *saṃsāra* to the rudiments of prescient awareness. Myriad are the desirous animal-like propensities generated by each personality that sustain people's ignorance as to the true nature of phenomena. This is because people strongly identify with all forms of transience, thinking them to be real. Those

39 Ibid., 229.

upon the path to enlightenment, however, utilise every opportunity to convert each impression derived from contact with transience and the effects of the sex impulse into enlightenment-attributes. These impressions become a base for the derivation of awareness as to the fundamental unreality of *saṃsāra*, so that eventually higher aspiration produces knowledge of the *saṃsāra-śūnyatā* nexus. One then inevitably realises that all attributes of the phenomena processed were just veils of awareness of the Void that is always present. All types of phenomena are modifications of the Void Elements, therefore are intrinsically Void.

The conventional and ultimate truths are inevitably one in the Void. One can consequently ride the conventional appearances of things to enlightenment when the mind is rightly orientated and can strip away animal-like propensities. Following this Dharmakāya Way then reveals the truth that phenomena exists simultaneously with the *dharmakāya* as one vehicle of expression.

Evans-Wentz states: 'Although the Wisdom of *Nirvāṇa* and the Ignorance of the *Sangsāra* illusorily appear to be two things, they cannot truly be differentiated. It is an error to conceive them otherwise than as one'.[40]

5. The theme that now confronts us is that of 'bewilderment and non-bewilderment' caused by the incessant nagging insect-like thoughts that beguile the average person. They are controlled by the activity of the red Hoopoe-headed Manohārikā. These fleeting *iḍā saṃskāras* generated via the left Gonad centre's activity are directed to the Stomach centre, which processes the *prāṇas* of one's conditioned views of the extraneous universe being real. These *prāṇas* are the most separative, assertive and mundane concepts possessed by the personal-I. They generate the 'eye doctrine' of the intellect, which thoroughly identifies with what it sees, perceiving what it sees as something separate to itself. Once generated, the thoughts can be processed by the *chakras* below the diaphragm or be refined as they flow to the higher centres where they are incorporated into analytical thought-streams that eliminate the bewildering perplexities.

40 Ibid.

Meditative calmness follows whereby refined thoughts are quietened, producing the percipient stillness of the Mind's natural state. Things can then be seen as they really are. All is but one unending mental continuum leading to *śūnyatā's* door. Within the continuum of the meditation-Mind no intrinsic dichotomy exists. The radiance of this Clear Mind pervades all space. Reality will then be found to not be the modifications of mind that came from having been born into a material universe that the 'self' thoroughly identifies with. Rather, that 'self' has merged into the all that is One Mind. That Mind's natural state is the Mind that is *dharmakāya*.

Evan-Wentz's version: 'Erring and non-erring are, intrinsically, also a unity. By not taking the mind to be naturally a duality, and allowing it, as the primordial consciousness, to abide in its own place, beings attain deliverance. The error of doing otherwise than this arises not from Ignorance in the mind itself, but from not having sought to know the Thatness'.[41] We know this duality to be the distinction between the concrete mind and abstract (enlightened) Mind.

6. The final petal (governed by the greenish-red deer-headed Siddhikarī) integrates *prāṇas* with the Base of Spine, Sacral, and right Gonad centres, where the mineral kingdom is utilised, to help build the form of the child of whatever is to be expressed. The 'child' evolves through a sequence that incorporates the philosophy of the three times earlier presented. This is viewed in terms of the *chakras* that process and consolidate the *prāṇas* obtained as one travels through time. In doing so the appearances of phenomena naturally originate and are resolved, though all is generated within one's own mind/Mind, of which the qualities of all *chakras* are expressions. The place where 'they abide in the interim' refers to any of the minor *chakras* of the Inner Round. The place to which they will finally be directed refers to the respective higher centre that forms a natural sink for the purified, transformed *prāṇas* of any minor *chakra*.

In time the aspirant to enlightenment learns that all things 'arise from the mind and subside into the mind of their own accord'. Such comprehension lays the foundation whereby *kuṇḍalinī* can rise to the Head lotus at the end of the cycle of meditative accomplishment. (Being the place 'to which they will finally go'.) The qualities of

41 Ibid.

all *chakras* find their resonance in the 1,000 petalled lotus. This is the 'one pond' to which the crow of perspicacious thoughts goes. The other *chakras* represent pools of minor habitation, with rivulets of thoughts leading from them to the main pond. Eventually these thoughts are transformed into the Mind's radiance.

Another interpretation of the symbolism is that the pond in the analogy has a direct reference to the Watery Element, and is therefore the Solar Plexus centre. It is the pond or lake for the entire psychic constitution of an individual. The Head lotus on the other hand is the domain of *manasic* Fire. The *nāḍīs* of all minor centres terminate in the Solar Plexus centre, which is the integrating centre for Sacral centre *prāṇas.* At this level of interpretation we see that the thoughts borne by this crow are Watery in nature. Note the strange mix of symbolism here in the 'pond-dwelling crow', as one would normally refer to such a dweller to be a duck, or other aquatic bird. The crow is used because its scavenging aspect (a more Earthy symbol) better suits the nature of the *kāma-manasic saṃskāras* generated by Base of Spine-Sacral-Solar Plexus centre interrelation than the very aquatic duck.

From this perspective the place where these thoughts originated is signified by the Base of Spine centre, which garners the *prāṇas* derived from material plane livingness. The place in the interim is the field of desire, governed by the Sacral centre, which produces attachment to the objects in *saṃsāra,* causing perpetual rebirths. The place 'to which they will finally go' then represents the Solar Plexus centre, wherein all emotional thoughts are stored. One therefore is asked to observe the interrelation between these three centres as a prelude to mastering *saṃskāras* derived from them. In this meditative process the fleeting phenomena will inevitably subside in the mind. Such observation is a major part of a *yogin's* focus during the initial stages of his practice. Later the centres above the diaphragm become the natural place of residence as Watery *saṃskāras* are no longer generated.

This section also relates to the way the five wisdoms of the Jinas are generated. First we have the generation of Amoghasiddhi's All-accomplishing Wisdom by means of a careful observation of the sum of *saṃsāra,* and of one's own psyche, to find the source 'from which these appearances initially originated'. We then have the generation of Ratnasambhava's Equalising Wisdom, in that the place where the *saṃskāras* 'abide in the interim' refers firstly to the mind itself, wherein all impressions derived from *saṃsāra* are processed. Next one can look to the integrated Watery disposition of the minor *chakras*, wherein most people's reactionary experiences are generated, and the Solar Plexus centre into which they also subside. Therein all emotions must be calmed, made placid, hence 'equalised', if the centres above the diaphragm are to be awakened and the higher Mind developed.

The place 'to which they will finally go' refers to the domain of the Mind of the meditating one, where the nature of the Sambhogakāya Flower and the entire *ālayavijñāna* environment can be analysed. Also, the nature of the Bardo states, the process of transition from one birth to the next, must be examined. Hence we have the generation of the Discriminating Inner Wisdom of Amitābha implied, wherein elements of mind are converted into attributes of Mind.

In the next sentence the reference to the pond implicates the calmness of Akṣobhya's Mirror-like Wisdom, thus to the art of meditation wherein the focus of thought ('a pond-dwelling crow') does not stray far from the meditation-Mind, even when flying away to observe the appearance of things in *saṃsāra.* The pond symbolises the stilled reflective pool of the Mind that allows the 'Mirror-like' attributes of Akṣobhya's wisdom to manifest. Finally we have the generation of Vairocana's Dharmadhātu Wisdom, wherein things arise and subside in the Mind by their own accord.

Evans-Wentz's version: 'Seek within thine own self-illuminated, self-originated mind whence, firstly, all such concepts arise, secondly, where they exist, and, lastly, whither they vanish. This realization is likened to that of a crow which, although already in possession of a pond, flies off elsewhere to quench its thirst, and finding no other drinking-place returns to the one pond. Similarly, the radiance which emanates from the One Mind, by emanating from one's own mind, emancipates the mind'.[42]

42 Ibid., 229-230.

Mind and the right Gonad centre

The final group of the twenty-eight Īśvarī relate to the functioning of the right Gonad centre, where the six 'Queens of yoga' projecting the 'rights of enrichment' find application. They control the Watery-Airy Life giving *prāṇas* of the five groups of Īśvarī. Being along the *piṅgalā* line we consequently have the symbolic reference to 'the sky' throughout the six related statements. Gyurme states:

1. This nature of mind, which is all-knowing, aware of everything, empty and radiant,

   Is established to be the manifestly radiant and self-originating pristine cognition,

   [Present] from the beginning, just like the sky,

2. As an indivisible [union] of emptiness and radiance.

   This itself is actual reality.

3. The indication that this is [the actual reality] is that all phenomenal existence is perceived in [the single nature of] one's own mind;

4. And this nature of mind is aware and radiant.

   Therefore, recognise [this nature] to be like the sky!

5. However, this example of the sky, though used to illustrate actual reality,

   Is merely a symbol, a partial and provisional illustration.

   For the nature of mind is aware, empty and radiant in all respects,

   While the sky is without awareness, empty, inanimate and void.

6. Therefore, the true understanding of the nature of mind is not illustrated by [the metaphor of] the sky.

   [To achieve this understanding], let the mind remain in its own state, without distraction![43]

With respect to the right Gonad centre, we saw in Volume 5A, chapter 5, that it helps generate the normally forceful and generally totally overriding passions of the emotions, strong desires and attachments to things material or sensual. Inevitably, the entire principle of desire becomes enriched through the development of various forms of social

43 Gyurme, 52-53.

mores, as well as refined through all types of human interrelationships. Desire is then converted into a loving disposition as people develop wisdom. Upon the path of yogic control it is transformed into right aspiration, where affectionate *saṃskāras* become enriched by all forms of compassionate undertakings. Finally, the attainment of the natural integration with the Heart centre's sublime awareness manifests as a consequence of it being the repository of the *piṇgalā* line. This sequence of expression can then be applied to all of the statements associated with the six 'Queens of yoga projecting the rights of enrichment'.

1. First we have that petal which regulates the Earthy flow of gonadic secretions via a minor *chakra* controlling the functions of either the testicles or ovaries, and the next minor level of *chakras*. The many little attributes of mind, symbolised by dark caves where the yellow bat-headed Vajrā resides (who controls the normal transformative expression of this petal), have been converted into the 'nature of mind, which is all-knowing, aware of everything, empty and radiant'. Once freed from the cave mentality of the desire-mind the bat of Mind is free to fly anywhere it wills in the sky of 'pristine cognition'. It has totally mastered the darkness of *saṃsāra.*

   Evans-Wentz's version: 'The One Mind, omniscient, vacuous, immaculate, eternally, the Unobscured Voidness, void of quality as the sky, self-originated Wisdom, shining clearly, imperishable, is Itself the Thatness'.[44] This 'One Mind' is the final attainment of the *piṇgalā nāḍī* stream, once it has found its repository in the Heart centre that manifests the expression of unobscured Voidness. To a normal waking consciousness, such Voidness can also be viewed in terms of a night sky skilfully navigated by the bat, which signifies the way enlightenment manifests. It is 'night' because unknown by mind, and 'radiant' in that it contains in its embrace the immaculate prescient presence of the sum of the starry cosmos. The best symbolism, however, relates to the deep blue of the dawn's early light. It represents 'radiant and self-originating pristine cognition' that is present 'from the beginning, just like the sky'.

2. This section concerns the accomplishment of the reddish-yellow crocodile-headed Śāntī holding a vase that contains the expression

44 Evans-Wentz, 230.

of the Watery Element associated with the *prāṇas* from the Left Gonad and a small *chakra* governing the activities of the sex organ. The most base, reptilian-like sexual *saṃskāras* that can manifest in a violent or unpleasant manner must now be transformed into the 'actual reality' of an indivisible sexual union of the masculine quality of emptiness (*śūnyatā*) and the feminine expression of radiance (wisdom). This nondual integration therefore becomes the highest expression of the sexual function. Long is the journey, however, from the level of incipient sexual desire to final enlightened consummation.

Evans-Wentz's version: 'The whole visible Universe also symbolizes the One Mind'.[45] The homogeneous whole of the universe manifests in a similar manner as an undivided singular Mind. It can be considered the expression of the meditation of a vastly ancient Ādi Buddha conjoined with his Consort, who embodies the entire expansion and growth of all sentience states and consciousness into the One Mind. The Base of Spine-Sacral-Gonadial interrelation is the foundation of the manifestation of the purposeful expansion of all phenomena, once the (mind's) sexual expression has produced the actual appearance (of the child of thought-desire) upon the phenomenal realms.

3. We now come to the transformed, transmogrified *prāṇas* of the *kāma-manasic* level of the Fiery Element evoked from the general *prāṇic* circulation of the minor *chakras*. These *prāṇas* have their genesis in a small centre governing the function of the sex act. The reddish-yellow scorpion-headed Amṛtā helps transform the many desire based attributes (emotional stings or impulses) and attachments associated with sexuality into generally loving *prāṇic* interrelationships. Inevitably the observation of the phenomena associated with one's desire body and sexuality causes one to realise that no matter what the senses perceive and the 'reality' of sexual experiences, all is actually an expression of 'one's own mind'. Utilising *dhāraṇīs,* one-pointed yogic concentration, the mind becomes singularly focussed upon the enlightenment-path. This meditation-Mind conquers the natural illusional attachment

45 Ibid.

to everything that causes the rebirthing process. Evans-Wentz's version: 'By knowing the All-Consciousness in one's mind, one knows it to be as void of quality as the sky'.[46]

4. We now consider the flow of energies coming from the Liver centre, that influence the general gonadic expression with the type of affectionate disposition found in all human relationships, and the loving attitudes between couples during courting rituals. The whitish hawk-headed Saumī, viewing from great heights, transforms the base, strongly desirous *prāṇas* generated through interrelation with the 'other' into those of love and veneration. The Liver centre is the receptor for *piṇgalā prāṇas* that inevitably lead to the Heart. It is thus the store of the general loving disposition of humanity, all of the *saṃskāras* of human affectionate interrelations. From a gonadial (sexual) perspective the store of all loving thoughts and images may be viewed as similar to the vastness of the sky. When the transcended, integrated minds and actions of mental-emotional humanity are taken into account, a far-sighted vista beyond the normal perception of a single mind is formed. The Heart centre is where the natural outward expansion of *piṇgalā* energies causes the *yogin* to recognise the true nature of the Heart's Mind, that all awareness is One Mind, where the dualities are integrated and radiantly comprehensive, similar to the sky.

   Evans-Wentz's version: 'Although the sky may be taken provisionally as an illustration of the unpredictable Thatness, it is only symbolically so'.[47] The sky symbolises the vastness of abstract space that is the natural primordial Mind wherein the entire panoply of universal activity (that is cosmos) unfolds its purpose. This is accomplished through the vivification of myriads of consciousness-streams and units of sentience that are incorporated as this panoply. It includes the entire population of liberated beings unfolding their united purpose in one immense *maṇḍala* of achievement.

5. The petal of the right Gonad centre now considered, channels the highest most abstracted *prāṇas* of the Watery Element developed by

46 Ibid., 231.

47 Ibid.

this centre to the Liver centre. The greenish white fox-headed Daṇḍī uses her cudgel to process all of the forces (symbols) pertaining to the sexual function and associated desirous yearnings of human interrelationships towards the spacious, empty, radiant, naturally aware 'nature of mind'. After this process begins, the *saṃskāras* to be transformed must undertake many provisional (sky-like) desire-forms before the true nature of Mind is realised. In these verses one's vision is focussed upon the petals of the minor *chakras,* and when gazing upwards, the centres above the diaphragm take the attributes of the sky. The nature of enlightenment, the Heart's Mind, however, transcends the limitations of symbolism. Though useful, the sky symbol is consequently no substitute for the direct experience of the nature of Mind.

Evans-Wentz's version: 'Inasmuch as the vacuity of all visible things is to be recognized as merely analogous to the apparent vacuity of the sky, devoid of mind, content, and form, the knowing of the mind does not depend on the sky-symbol'.[48] Similarly, the expansions of each individual consciousness-stream does not depend upon knowingness of the vastness of the panoply, but rather the process of enlightenment is inherent within each stream. All desire-impulses are vacuous (empty), the sky-like attribute gained through the transformations of the desire-principle therefore is a 'provisional illustration' of what is an intrinsic, inherently established function of Mind.

6. Finally we deal with the *nāḍī* which is integrated with the Base of Spine, Sacral and left Gonad centres, which normally channels well hidden, strong passions in the jungles of desires that can spring out at any moment to overwhelm the individual. These are converted by means of the blackish tiger-headed Rākṣasī drinking from a blood filled skull. Her purpose is to help produce the natural state of Mind that remains free and unobstructed (like a cloudless sky) 'in its own state' from all of the distractions that are the outcome of people's desire bodies. The ambrosial *bodhicitta* can then be drunk from this skull cup. Through yogic meditation the Base of

48 Ibid.

Spine centre and the 1,000 petalled lotus have become aligned and activated in such a way that the septenary *kuṇḍalinī* will rise up the spinal column. The 'sky' represents the complete awakening that the Head centre produces. However, because the *dharmakāya* is now the objective view, such awakening is beyond mere analogy with 'the metaphor of the sky'. To achieve this the *yogin* must become exceedingly one-pointed, totally undistracted by the attractions and sensations of the lower bodily nature.

Evans-Wentz's version: 'Therefore, not straying from the Path, remain in that very state of the Voidness'.[49] Following each consciousness-stream to its eventual conclusion, by not straying from their paths, the natural substance of Mind will unveil the Voidness that is the base of all that is.

If we project the information regarding the Gonads and minor *chakras* associated with the sexual function and their relation to the Base of Spine, Sacral, and Solar Plexus centres accurately upon the large scale activities of human affairs, then much that governs the *karma* of the present inhuman wars of aggression between nations would be revealed. Some nations and geographical areas upon the planet, as in Africa, South America, and the Middle East represent areas of cleansing of such amassed *saṃskāras* of humanity. People are born into cultural situations and nation states because of the collective *karma* they possess and must work out. Most nations represent small *chakras* in the body of the earth, whilst the regions within them and the adjacent areas are the petals of these *chakras* wherein collective transformations and psychic cleansing must occur. Groups of people coming into and out of incarnation and their social interactions, the commerce, exchange of ideas and trade between nations represent the moving *prāṇas* between the *chakras*. Most nations are controlled by self-interest, some form friendly partnerships, and others manifest forms of belligerence. There is much competitiveness for resources, and often major nations establish dominant political spheres of influence over others as a base for financial and aggressive (military) expansionism. Eventually such motives must be superseded by friendly cooperativeness.

49 Ibid.

Inevitably, a new era of resource sharing and uplifting universally spiritual and scientific activity, where nations work towards establishing a collectively beneficent civilisation, shall replace aggressive competition. They shall be freed from the vested interests of a rapacious elite utilising the power of money, numerous forms of wealth extraction, unjust laws, and malicious propaganda (all generating malignant *saṃskāras*) to deny the common wealth of humanity to the masses of people. This process is similar to what has been depicted above concerning the gradual transformation of the gross *saṃskāras* of desire-mind of an individual into the attributes of Mind.

This interesting theme could be vastly elaborated. Indeed, what is hinted at occupies the meditations of Bodhisattvas. The theme of widespread planetary transformation over a vast time scale, taking all of humanity into account, is complicated also by the continuous generation of new *karma* by human units. This necessitates further rearrangement of social and national groups with view of later cleansing the associated group *saṃskāras* in a positive way. Peaceful and 'wrathful' forces are involved that emanate from Shambhala to produce the necessary transformations and changes. Such activity has been the subjects of the world's myths, veiled in the symbolism of the stories they tell. They were created at a time when many more human units were more psychically awakened than today. Psychic perception was widespread, as is consistent with the developed powers *(siddhis)* associated with the lower centres, but intellectual faculties were mostly in abeyance. The development of the mind and its union with the emotions is the main cause of problems today. Hence the intelligent ones need to consider these teachings concerning the natural state of Mind so as to overcome the present problems in our societies.

4

Culmination of the Awakening of Mind

The natural liberation of mind.

Having analysed the twenty-eight Īśvarī and the centres below the diaphragm we come to the final section of this yoga, titled 'The Nature of Appearances'[1] in Gyurme's book, and 'The Yogic Science of Mental Concepts'[2] in Evans-Wentz's. As Vajrakīla Heruka and Consort and the five Jñāna Ḍākinīs still need to be accounted for we would expect their qualities to relate to this section. However, no direct symbolism relating to the liberation of *kuṇḍalinī* exists. Instead, liberation is implied to have already happened from converting the *saṃskāras* from the petals of the centres below the diaphragm. The technicalities concerning the awakening of the liberating Fires differs for each *yogin* because of the differing Ray lines governing them and because of the intrinsic differences of spiritual ages.

At the beginning of this 'Yoga of Knowing the Mind' the concern was with the descent of the energies of Mind from the Throat and Heart centres to the lower centres. This involved a process of invocation of the forces of Mind by the *yogin*. Prior to raising *kuṇḍalinī* the *prāṇas* of Mind evoked from the centres below the diaphragm must be sent upwards to the Throat and Heart centres and then to the Head centre. The remainder of this yoga concerns the upwards movement of *prāṇas* to fully awaken the Heart and Throat tiers of the Head centre, thus

1 Gyurme, 53.

2 Evans-Wentz, 231.

anchoring the fount of Mind. For this all dissonant attributes of the minor centres have to be transformed and the gain sent upwards.

When numbering the statements presented in this section we find there are 12 + 16 + 12 statements, making 40 altogether, with the last being inherently triune, producing the number 42 of the Peaceful Deities. This final section presents the genesis of the types of realisations that produce the attributes of these Deities. This implies the way that the petals of the three main tiers of the Head lotus are awakened.

The first group of twelve relate to the synthesis of the *prāṇas* developed below the diaphragm, and which are integrated into the twelve main petals of the Solar Plexus in the Head centre. They are effectively extensions of the *prāṇas* collectivised by the twelve petals of Splenic centre I. Again, zodiacal attributes become the main keys to analysing the lay of the land with respect to the unfoldment of the petals of the associated *chakras*. The second group consists of sixteen statements that relate to developing the attributes of the Throat centre and hence the Throat tier of the Head lotus. The final group of twelve statements relate to the qualities developed by the Heart centre plus the Heart in the Head centre.

There are no direct correlations between the statements and the attributes of the Deities, owing to the complexities of the awakening petals of the Head centre. Instead we have the development of the attributes of the mind that produce the fully awakened Mind, being the natural liberation through naked perception of the appearance of things.

Gyurme states under the heading 'The Nature of Appearances':

1. Now, with regard to the diversity of relative appearances:
   They are all perishable; not one of them is genuinely existent.
2. All phenomenal existence, all the things of cyclic existence and nirvāṇa,
   Are the discernible manifestations of the unique essential nature of one's own mind.
3. [This is known because] whenever one's own mental continuum undergoes change,
   There will arise the discernible manifestations of an external change.
4. Therefore, all things are the discernible manifestations of mind.
5. For example, the six classes of living beings discern phenomenal

appearances in their differing ways:

6. Eternalistic extremists [and others] who are remote [from the Buddhist perspective],
Perceive [appearances] in terms of a dichotomy of eternalism and nihilism;
7. And [followers of] the nine sequences of the vehicle perceive [appearances] in terms of their respective views, [and so forth].
8. For as long as this diversity [of appearances] is being perceived and diversely elucidated,
Differences [as to the nature of appearances] are apprehended,
9. And consequently, bewilderment comes about through attachment to those respective [views].
10. Yet, even though all those appearances, of which one is aware in one's own mind,
Do arise as discernible manifestations,
Buddhahood is present [simply] when they are not subjectively apprehended or grasped.
11. Bewilderment does not come about on account of these appearances—
But it does come about through their subjective apprehension.
12. [Thus], if the subjectively apprehending thoughts are known to be [of the single nature of] mind, they will be liberated of their own accord.[3]

Here it can be implied that the energies of Vajrakīla Heruka and entourage help awaken the seven *chakras,* hence the seven levels of mind/Mind manifesting via the planes of perception governing *saṃsāra.* This is in terms of their rulership of the centres of procreation and of desire, as well as of the associated interrelation between the Base of Spine centre and the Head lotus.

It was earlier stated in Volume 5A, chapter 4, that there is a correlation between Mahottara Heruka and Krodeśvarī, and Vajrakīla Heruka (Vajrakumāra) and Consort (Samayatārā), as the Base of Spine/Sacral centre represents the foundation for that which later appears fully blown in the Head lotus. In fact, the entire *maṇḍala* of Peaceful and Wrathful Deities that can be found contained in the lower centres is established in the Head lotus, as the mind/Mind is the real and all phenomena is born

3 Gyurme, 53-54. As per usual I have added the numbers.

in it and is carried by it. All attributes of *dharmakāya* are expressions of the primordial Mind of the Ādi Buddha from which emanates the Mind, and then the *manasic* attributes of *saṃsāra*. All levels of the natural expression of Mind are therefore expressed, including everything associated with the world of phenomena external to our sense-perceptors.

The twelve petals of the Head lotus

As the *saṃskāras* that concern us here are the consequences of activities from below the diaphragm, so the associated zodiac follows the way of the reversed wheel, of the procession of the equinoxes. Hence we start with Aries and then Pisces to Aquarius etc. This motion mirrors the real, of the universe existing above the diaphragm, representing the domains of enlightened being, where the zodiac travels to Capricorn via Aries and Taurus. In the reversed wheel the base *saṃskāras* are generated and the entire process of their conversion into the attributes of Mind effected. (Causing the turning about in the seat of consciousness.) As the *saṃskāras* become refined and established in the Head lotus they are differentiated into the twelve broad categories governed by the attributes of the zodiac. The attributes of both orientations of the zodiac can be accommodated by the petals (wheels) within larger petals (wheels) of that lotus. The overall motion of the various tiers of the Head lotus is either from right to left or from left to right, depending upon the attributes of the *saṃskāras* generated, of whether the individual is directly upon the Initiation path or ensconced in *saṃsāra*.

As one is born into each of the signs of the zodiac so the overriding characteristics of activity conditioned by their qualities are built into the perspective of the associated major petal of the Head lotus. The major sweeps of the unfoldment of mind and its transference into Mind are thereby accomplished.

1. The first of the signs concerning us is *Aries the ram,* governing the initial beginning of every new thought-form. First we have the establishment of 'the diversity of relative appearances', of the entire construct of phenomena developed from the Base of Spine centre right to the Head lotus. The corresponding statement is: 'Now, with regard to the diversity of relative appearances: They are all perishable; not one of them is genuinely existent'. Thus the transitory

nature of phenomena in *saṃsāra* is defined. All phenomenon must be thoroughly experienced, analysed and transformed by means of the developing will associated with the driving impetus of the ram. From the broader perspective Vajrakīla-Heruka anchors the appearances of Mind. They are originally emanated from the Consort of the Ādi Buddha,[4] via those of the Dhyāni Buddhas in the form of the phenomenal constructs we interrelate with by means of the five senses. From the copulative embrace of the Consort with the Ādi Buddha comes the phenomenal world wherein is found every action-reaction interplay of *saṃsāric* activity that humans take to be real. The domain of Ādi Buddha and Consort, however, is the *dharmakāya* and various intermediaries bring the originating concepts of Mind into the realms wherein mind can be found. Spiritual Power must be utilised to project the results of the interplay into the realms of manifestation in forms that all subsequent lives can experience and evolve by.

The strongest Will must be utilised by the meditation-Mind to hold all manifestation, 'the diversity of relative appearances', in complete control. The enlightened therefore know such phenomena to be the emanations of Mind, as all share expressions of the One Mind. They must develop a similar Will to overcome the bonds to formed existence before the fruits of *dharmakāya* are theirs.

The foundation of this entire striving is the Base of Spine centre, which governs the emanations of the kingdoms of Nature. This represents the womb of Samayatārā,[5] Vajrakīla's Consort, from which comes all perishable things that are not 'genuinely existent'. From here emanates the *kuṇḍalinī śakti* that turns the entire wheel of the Zodiac (or Head centre) and which the Ādi Buddha utilises to establish the basis of all that is. The entire action-reaction interrelation between these 'things' and the lives embodied by them is conditioned (nurtured) by the embrace of the active compassion

---

4 Also, Samatabhadra or Vajradhāra, depending upon the view of the Buddhist sect concerned.

5 Tārā is literally an emanation of a tear of compassion from the eyes of Avalokiteśvara, whilst *samaya* is a sacred pledge. Hence this Consort embodies a sacred pledge to relieve the suffering of the perishable ones. The pledge therefore exists for the untold aeons that incarnate lives undergo evolutionary experience.

of the Jina wisdoms that drives the entire karmic interplay to the envisaged fruition. The enlightenment of the evolving human units is the natural outcome. This process progresses via the *nirmalā* and *samalā tathatā*[6] attributes of the *tathāgatagarbha* aspect of each human. This Buddha-germ can be considered 'real', whilst the human form or vehicle needed to evolve wisdom is not. The appearances of mind become the battleground of what is finally established in consciousness and taken to be real, valid cognition. This entire process and evolutionary history of mind is expressed in the portals of the Head lotus as they unfold.

2. Next we have the characteristics of *Pisces the fishes* to develop and experience. They are summarised by the statement 'All phenomenal existence, all the things of cyclic existence and nirvāṇa, Are the discernible manifestations of the unique essential nature of one's own mind'. The individual must learn to travel up the *antaḥkaraṇa* (consciousness link) that unites *saṃsāra* to *śūnyatā* and thereby attain the point of stability known as the *saṃsāra-śūnyatā* nexus.

The attributes of the five Jñāna Ḍākinīs come into perspective here. They oversee the process of the transference of consciousness from attachment to 'all the things of cyclic existence' into *nirvāṇa*. The overall governance of everything is the natural expression of the white Buddha Ḍākinī situated at the centre of the *maṇḍala* of the Jñāna Ḍākinīs, which exists at the nexus between *śūnyatā* and *saṃsāra*. (Found at the subtlest level of the abstract Mind.) Here she utilises the Dharmadhātu Wisdom of Vairocana, from which all *karma* related to the development of Mind emanates and is also finally resolved into.

Note that the functions of the Heruka Ḍākinīs (Krodheśvarī) overlap somewhat with those of the Wisdom (Jñāna) Ḍākinīs. Thus the Heruka Ḍākinīs are specifically concerned with the evolution of the human condition, of the movement of *prāṇas* in the Head lotus before being directed to the various petals of the Sambhogakāya Flowers, as explained in part A. The five Jñāna Ḍākinīs on the

6 *Nirmalā* and *samalā tathatā* refer to the defiled and undefiled attributes of the *tathāgatagarbha*, which must transform the defiled attributes as it undergoes its evolutionary process to liberation. See Volume 3 for further detail.

other hand preside over the evolutionary status of all of Nature's kingdoms, with *saṃsāra* as a whole. They can be considered the reflex of the Consorts of the five Jinas, and work with *prāṇas* flowing from the Base of Spine and Sacral centres below the diaphragm of the established Logos (Ādi Buddha). Their purpose is to assist in the evolution of mind in Nature's kingdoms and of their higher correlations in the human unit.

The Heruka Consorts manifest a similar function above the diaphragm within the Throat centre with respect to the development of mind in humans. From this perspective the Jina Consorts are the directive agents of the associated *karma* of Mind working from the Head lotus of a Logos.

The Vidyādhara Consorts are the integrating mediators of the sum of this movement of mind into Mind. They work centrally as aspects of the Logoic Heart centre to integrate the transformed aspects of mind into the Mind that represents the floral whorls of the petals of the Sambhogakāya Flowers of humanity.[7] They embody the gain of the arduous evolutionary journey to develop mind by humanity.

At the eastern gate resides the blue Vajra Ḍākinī governing the natural reflection of Mind into manifestation. All of the discernments of mind thereby come into phenomenal existence from out of the Void of being/non-being. At this stage the *nāḍī* system that vivifies or impregnates Nature's kingdom with Mind is established by means of the power of the *vajra*. The reflex of this Mind then manifests as the development of the normal human mind, allowing it to convey the immutable power of the Jinas in its five-fold energy qualification via the five sense-consciousnesses. This process of the reflection of Mind into mind is a natural expression of the Mirror-like Wisdom of Akṣobhya. The mode of expression comes under the auspices of the fourth Ray to produce harmony and beauteous order from out of the strife and conflict found throughout *saṃsāra's* domain.

The entire wheel of the zodiac is thereby established, and also the procession of cycle after cycle of activity in the swamp of *saṃsāra*. Here swims the bonded fish, the incarnate personality, who is linked to the subjective form of the Sambhogakāya Flower, as symbolised by Pisces, a Water sign.

---

7 Each manifests a similar form as that of the Logoic Heart centre.

3. The sign *Aquarius the water bearer* follows, whose symbol is two wavy bands of flowing energy that is freely dispensed to all in need. The associated statements are: '[This is known because] whenever one's own mental continuum undergoes change, There will arise the discernible manifestations of an external change'. Change is all that is known in *saṃsāra* and the attributes of mind evolve by means of it as the motivating, flowing energy of consciousness moves from one effect to the next. Inevitably the Bodhisattva virtues are developed upon the liberation path whereby the processes of change are mastered in a continuum of clear-mindedness.

The attributes of the western gate of the *maṇḍala* of the Jinas are now developed, where we have the red Padma Ḍākinī. She helps awaken the petals of the kingdom of the Sambhogakāya Flower and the *chakras* found throughout Nature. They set the background panorama and field of interrelations that govern the awakening of the 'mental-continuum' of each individual and of groupings of people. The minds then evolve to produce enlightenment by developing the ability to reflect the complete expression of a Jina-Mind. This is effected through undergoing continuous changes by first creating and then transforming base *saṃskāras.* The mind then evolves total power over its own domain under the auspices of the fifth Ray of Scientific Reasoning. As a consequence, the Discriminating Inner Wisdom of Amitābha is developed.

The 'discernible manifestations of an external change' refers to the fluid images that are an expression of the Watery environment people reside in. Desire (emotional)-mind *(kāma-manas)* evolves and plays its role to produce major changes in consciousness. When the entire (astral) Watery domain is established by humanity as an illusional field of human interrelationships, the complete *maṇḍala* of *saṃsāra* appears. The integral Life embodying each group (species) of sentience manifests as a jewel-like portion of this *maṇḍala*, glistening in the evolutionary sun. The focus is upon the active expression of all types of phenomena into which units of consciousness have incarnated. The emotional Watery environment naturally receives the onus of attention, inevitably producing the forms of devotion people have in normal human interrelations. The work then concerns cleansing the resultant mental-emotional defilements, which happens via the activity of the southern Ratna Ḍākinī. (Under the auspices of

Ratnasambhava's Equalising Wisdom and the sixth Ray of Devotion.) The worship of images of deity and devotion to high ideals upon the upward arc of evolution is a natural outcome. Deity yoga performs its duty, and later the higher yogas, where the aspirant's devotion to instructions from a guru generates the path of liberation from enthrallment to Watery images and associated attachment.

Much concerning the evolutionary development of humanity therefore happens under the auspices of Amitābha's and Ratnasambhava's energies. The focus at first is upon the southern direction governed by Ratnasambhava's Equalising Wisdom, because significant *karma* concerning the immersion of mind in *saṃsāra* is Watery in nature. The resultant desire-mind must be thoroughly cleansed of defilements and the Watery qualities evaporated before one can naturally reside in the *saṃsāra-śūnyatā* nexus and embody *bodhicitta*. Such purpose must manifest with mathematically enlightened precision to rightly wield karmic law in Nature's kingdom in such a way that liberation from *saṃsāra* can be gained. Amoghasiddhi's energies thereby come to the fore and the mount of mind begins to be thoroughly mastered by drying up the Waters. Akṣobhya's energies fan the flames of mind to their highest intensity and refinement, so that the remaining attributes of Mind are Void of *saṃsāric* attachment.

4. The significance of the next petal represented by *Capricorn the goat,* which governs the entire empire of mind and its transformation into Mind, is implied by the next statement 'Therefore, all things are discernible manifestations of mind'. *Karma* manifests through whatever mind attaches itself to in order to change the state of what is. This mind interrelates with the phenomena of things via the five sense-perceptors (integrating them into its mind-space) and therein must later be experienced the resultant pleasure or pain that is the *karmic* ramification for the individual concerned. Over a significant time period a vast number of perceptions are accumulated by mind, with myriad interrelated *saṃskāric* pathways fused into one mass of mind substance garnered from the three worlds of human livingness. The mount of mind thereby evolves to govern perception of the entire physical domain. The complete panoply of such activity in *saṃsāra* is regulated by the wisdom of the green Karma Ḍākinī.

She embodies the demonstrable function of all aspects of *karma* that must be wisely expressed, directing the things that are a discerned manifestation of mind to produce right conclusions. Because external phenomena has been integrated into the consciousness-stream, so it must eventually return back to the originating source, allowing Nature's equilibrium to be maintained. Otherwise, we would have chaos governing the expression of the universe, not the ordered manifestation that actually is. Having become an integral unity of the expression of the mind of the conscious beholder the internal and external become 'discernible manifestations of mind'. All is mind/Mind caused, and thereby creates *karma*.

The cycles and rhythmic expression of the *karma* of all phenomena comes under the sway of the seventh Ray of Ritualistic or Ceremonial Ordering, and as part of the meditation demonstrating Amoghasiddhi's All-accomplishing Wisdom.

The above lays the background to the nature of appearances of the phenomena that we all experience. Consequently, the conditionings concerning human consciousness, the various attributes of mind that cause bewilderment, must now be analysed. This requires analysis of individual *karma*[8], the main concern, rather than the forms of universal *karma* associated with the universe external to the individual.

Evans-Wentz presents four statements under the heading of 'The Yogic Science of Mental Concepts'.

1 The various concepts, too, being illusory, and none of them real, fade away accordingly.

2 Thus, for example, everything postulated of the Whole, the *Sangsāra* and *Nirvāṇa,* arises from nothing more than mental concepts.

3 Changes in one's train of thought [or in one's association of ideas] produce corresponding changes in one's conception of the external world.

4 Therefore, the various views concerning things are due merely to different mental concepts.[9]

---

8 Mastery of this law consequently comes under the auspices of Capricorn when the mountain of mind must be overcome.

9 Evans-Wentz, 231.

Because these statements are self-evident nothing further need be added.

5. Though Gyurme's text starts with the statement 'the six classes of living beings discern phenomenal appearances in their differing ways', there is no further reference to these classes of beings. Our presumption is that they appear as a consequence of possessing human consciousness, as consistent with the philosophy associated with the Six Realms. *Sagittarius the archer* projects the attributes of consciousness into manifestation by firing arrows of perception to whichever of these realms is the appropriate target. The personality is then born therein to experience the *karma* of former activities.

Next follow six statements related to the manifestation of mind and the nature of appearances, plus a concluding statement. At first the six statements do not seem to relate to the Six Realms, nevertheless, upon close inspection one can obtain a correlation. Here we must take into account the view that all is mind/Mind, thus the statements must be interpreted from the different aspects of the human mindscape. *Pretas, asuras,* animals, etc., are therefore but permutations of mind and exist thus as part of the conditioning of the human psyche, of the qualities of the *chakras* below the diaphragm wherein the rebirthing principle is generated. The attributes garnered by the twelve major petals of the Head centre are obtained by perpetually incarnating into these realms. Then by undergoing the process of obtaining wisdom through transformation of the resultant *saṃskāras,* liberating attributes can be gained instead that awaken the powers of the petals concerned.

From this perspective, these statements summarise the section of the Wrathful Deities, indicating the propensity for cyclic rebirth, if one does not follow the instructions of the *Bardo Thödol* on the way of knowing the Mind. From another perspective, we also come to the beginning of the summary of the qualities of the Peaceful Deities, as the six Buddhas that administer to these realms are aspects of Avalokiteśvara and counted amongst them.

6. The eternalists are those (Hindus) that possess viewpoints of a perpetual unchanging soul/*ātman*, where the intensity of attachment to such a subtle concept of an ego is considered an extremism that perpetuates *saṃsāra* indefinitely. Many conflicting views are

espoused in the battlefield of opinions. They relate to the tests of discipleship that produce control of the mental-emotions governed by *Scorpio the scorpion* and its sting. This 'sting' represents the major points of the different philosophical speculations that exponents assail their opponents with.

Nihilists principally refer to agnostics that believe in nothing outside of what the five senses teach them. Those that are remote from the perspective of Buddhism, however, relate to the exponents of the Dark Brotherhood, practitioners of necromancy and sorcery, that produce a form of nihilism. They espouse a black version of the *dharma* that directly opposes the white *dharma* of Buddhism. In contradistinction, the Hindu viewpoints (the main Buddhist doctrinal adversaries) manifest kindred doctrines, as Buddhism evolved from this religion. A patient exposé of truth, eloquently and wisely delivered, is needed to overcome domineering assertive beliefs. Inevitably such believers will comprehend the relationship concerning the diversity of opinions with respect to the truth of *śūnyatā*. All factors or opinions concerning an 'ens' (an existing real thing or entity), if logically examined to conclusion, inevitably produces comprehension of one divine purpose, and that is the liberation of consciousness from all self-limiting concepts.

The consequences of black magical practices, on the other hand, leads one to the *hell realms,* to which consequently this first section refers. This is facilitated by the effects of the anger, jealousy, etc., associated with the Sacral centre's activity.

Evans-Wentz's version: 'The six classes of beings respectively conceive ideas in different ways. The unenlightened externally see the externally-transitory dually.'[10] The unenlightened are incapable of seeing the transcendent at-onement of all dualities, therefore they cloud their perception with the *manasic* substance and desire impulses that constitute the nature of their minds. This perpetuates the various forms of ignorance that are the causes of their wandering through the Six Realms.

7. The nine vehicles in the Nyingma tradition are the pious attendants, the *pratekyabuddhas*, Bodhisattvas, then the followers of the Tantras:

10 Evans-Wentz, 232.

Kriyātantra, Ubbhayatantra, Yogatantra, Mahāyoga, Anuyoga, and Atiyoga (the Great Perfection). All of these Buddhist vehicles have forms of meditation techniques in common, as signified by the sign *Libra the balances*. It is the mediator between extremes, able to express the qualities of the interlude between forms of activity that pertain to the experience of *śūnyatā*. The implication here is that the followers of these different paths view things differently, therefore doctrinal disputes and forms of jealousy can arise between them, similar to that attributed to the *asuras*.

As the wheel of the law (governed by Libra) cycles through time, so inevitably these disputes become resolved and the Bodhisattva path is followed. Inevitably the attributes of the wheels that are the *chakras* must be mastered by means of following the Tantras to conclusion. Thus the nine vehicles produce their fruit, according to the adjudication of the law of *karma* and the practice of the *dharma* that manifests under the auspices of Libra.

Evans-Wentz's version simply describes the nature of human perception: 'The various doctrines are seen in accordance with one's own mental concepts. As a thing is viewed, so it appears'.[11]

8. Next we have the petal governed by the qualities of *Virgo the virgin* that rules the entire material domain. The vicissitudes of everything people are attached to now come into view. *Humans* are firmly ensconced in this domain that incorporates all of the others, and from which they derive their major experiences via sense contact. Here people take to be real forms of *saṃsāric* allurements and transience within the diversity of appearances. Such illusional objects govern the continuous stream of perceptions obtained. The resultant bewilderments produce wrong views. Inevitably the process of pain and suffering cause people to seek the way of release from suffering by following the Eightfold Path. The individual can then travel the Bodhisattva way of the Heart. Eventually the nexus between cyclic existence and *nirvāṇa* will be found. Because this is the only domain where all dimensions of perception, including this most concreted domain, can be experienced, and must accordingly be mastered, a prospective Buddha must appear here to demonstrate such accomplishment.

11 Ibid.

The pride attributed to the human realm is technically a major attribute of the next sign, *Leo the lion*. Consequently, statements eight and nine are directly interlinked, where the diversity of appearances inevitably produces the bewilderment of the gods. This bewilderment is symbolised in the union of Virgo and Leo as the sphinx, possessing a lion's body and a woman's head .

Evans-Wentz's version introduces a description of a major erroneous mode of thinking of the human mind: 'To see things as a multiplicity, and so to cleave unto separateness, is to err'.[12] The entire multidimensional universe that is an emanation of the One Mind will be the superior view obtained by the liberated one.

9. The next petal is ruled by *Leo the lion*, thus the attributes of the self-conscious individual come to the fore. This story is well known and needs no explanation. In terms of the doctrine of the Six Realms, the denizens of the *god realms* are implicated, who are said to suffer from delusion gained through continuous pleasurable experiences. Such experiences are the objective of most personalities.

   The god realms are literally the domains of mind/Mind. Bewilderment ensues because of intoxication with all 'those appearances', which are natural expressions of mind. Inevitably people will realise that each experience is the unique essential nature of 'one's own mind'. This is a consequence of the yoga of knowing Mind,[13] as is presented in Evans-Wentz's version: 'Now follows the *yoga* of knowing all mental concepts'.[14]

   In this yogic path however one must not be bewildered by discernable (god-like) manifestations, of reverie in enticing visions, and the demonstration of *siddhis*. Once the Mind comes to rest in its own natural state then Buddhahood will be found to be present. The practice of the 'yoga of knowing Mind' thus first necessitates relaxation of all mental perturbations until no images pertaining to the 'self concept' remain. All *saṃskāras* that arise must be transformed to reflect the corresponding attributes of the wisdoms

---

12 Ibid.

13 A translation of the Tibetan text of this form of yoga is found in Evans-Wentz's *Tibetan Yoga and Secret Doctrines* (Oxford University Press, 1967).

14 Evans-Wentz, 233.

of the Dhyāni Buddhas. This process of transformation necessitates many years to accomplish. All petals of the Head lotus (the domain of the 'gods') must be awakened. Once mundane *saṃskāras* no longer condition the mind ('not subjectively apprehended or grasped') the result is enlightenment. The expressed wisdoms of the Jinas manifest as radiance. Transformed and transmuted *manasic* substance produces a luminous, radiant, natural state of Mind. A natural state manifests because Mind is no longer susceptible to being conditioned by *saṃsāra's* illusions, and because it spontaneously expresses the sublime discernments of the Jinas. Luminosity and radiance is the way its energy field is discerned by other minds.

10. The concept of appearances that arise in the mind has a relation to the qualities of *Cancer the crab*, which is the sign of incarnation, the mass movement of sentient life and of consciousness. Hence it lives at the shoreline, the juncture between the watery (astral) world and the dry land (the dense physical plane). As a consequence of such birthing all 'discernible manifestations' come into being. The crab carries its house of mind with it wherever it goes.

The concept of 'bewilderment' from the previous statement can be likened to the dumb delusion of the animal kingdom, however, we will see that this term carries through to statement eleven. Birth into the *animal form* (emotional *saṃskāras* associated with the Solar plexus centre) is therefore hinted at. These *saṃskāras* are the energies processed by the theriomorphic deities (Īśvarī) earlier dealt with. The term 'appearances', that 'one is aware in one's own mind', refers to the many types of thoughts that are accommodated by the mind. Such appearances can also be the animal bodies into which one incarnates (including that of the human form). They 'arise as discernable manifestations' because these forms represent the dense vehicle through which we experience things.

One must not fall into the trap of subtle apprehensiveness, of creating images that distort the true view. Instead one must accept things as they truly are, of the way they appear in the mind, without the mind adding its own qualifications. Buddhahood manifests when all forms of birthing (of mental concepts) are 'not subjectively apprehended or grasped'.

Evans-Wentz's version states: 'The seeing of the Radiance [of this Wisdom or Mind], which shines without being perceived, is Buddhahood'.[15] Thus people need to carefully observe the nature of mind to comprehend the way that 'discernible manifestations' correlate to the phenomena of the appearances of external changes. Once comprehended then it can be controlled. This radiance of wisdom becomes the 'house' carried by the individual.

11. The attributes of the petal of the Head lotus qualified by *Gemini the twins* (of whom one twin is considered mortal and the other immortal) are indicated in the distinction between 'appearances' (of 'things', the mortal brother), and 'subjective apprehension', when this phrase is interpreted in terms of enlightened discernments (the immortal brother) rather than emotional or psychic input. Bewilderment comes from one's emotional and desirous interrelation and attachments to the appearance of transient phenomena. The way that these appearances arise in consciousness depends upon what it identifies with and its interpretation of the nature of things. Bewilderment arises by taking that which is phenomenal to be real. The antidote necessitates a proper comprehension of the way the emotions affect consciousness. Such comprehension happens in the inner sanctum of the Temples of Life. The *iḍā* and *piṅgalā* attributes (the pillars of the temple governed by Gemini) of one's entire *nāḍī* system must be subjectively apprehended if mastery is to be achieved. If the Waters cannot be mastered, then sojourn in the domain of the *pretas* becomes a distinct possibility because of unrequited attachment to all desirous things. All defilements of mind (*kliṣṭamanas*) need to be thoroughly analysed in the yoga of knowing the Mind, if *saṃskāras* pertaining to bewilderment are to be transformed into enlightened discernments. In such analysis the forces of the Īśvarī and the other theriomorphic deities then become one's friends.

Evans-Wentz's version is: 'Mistake not, by not controlling one's thoughts, one errs'.[16]

15 Ibid.

16 Ibid.

12. The ability to discern the illusionality of 'appearances' observed with the eye is easy enough for most. However, to discern the differences between forms of 'subjective apprehension', implying here the subjectivity of the emotions, imaginings and feeling-perceptions, psychic phenomena, visions, as well as the subtle discernments of Mind, necessitates the use of an awakening Mind. Here the attributes of the *Taurean* petal of the Head lotus are implied, which governs the awakening of the Eye of vision and the development of wisdom. The procession of all twelve petals of the Head lotus generates Taurean attributes. Its influence (the desire to know) turns the wheel and the product is 'the single nature' of Mind. Through mastery of 'subjectively apprehending thoughts' via the revelation that 'all things are the discernible manifestations of mind', people will gain liberation from *saṃsāra.* The constructs of mind will have been removed to reveal the radiance of Mind and its intrinsic wisdom. The nature of the wheel of cyclic rebirth will consequently be comprehended and people will no longer manifest the forms of activity necessitating incarnation into the Six Realms.

    Evans-Wentz's version: 'By controlling and understanding the thought-process in one's mind, emancipation is attained automatically'.[17] The complete comprehension of such 'concepts of mind', from the minutiae to the universal, produces its control and liberation.

Summary of the petals of the Throat centre

The section related to the effects of the manifestation of the Peaceful and Wrathful Deities is now concluded. This is followed by twenty-eight brief statements that act as a *summary* as to the nature of the manifestation of Mind. They are divided into two parts, one of sixteen statements, related to the Throat centre and to perceptions pertaining to the *iḍā nāḍī* flow, and the other with twelve statements, related to the Heart centre and the *piṅgalā nāḍī's* flow. I shall only briefly elucidate them here, by relating the statements to their corresponding astrological sign, leaving the reader to make further correlations if so desired. The

17 Ibid.

statements relating to the *prāṇas* that would inevitably be absorbed into the Throat tier of the Head centre all describe the attributes of mind, thus are terminated with variants of the phrase 'they too are mind'. The meanings of the associated descriptions should by now be well known by the reader. The statements concerning the *prāṇas* that would inevitably be absorbed into the twelve petals of the Heart tier relate to the attributes of enlightenment. All of the twenty-eight statements appear as summaries of the entire philosophy so far presented and therefore need no in-depth analysis. Also, sufficient grounding has been provided to place them correctly with respect to the petals of the associated *chakras*.

1. The first of the twenty-eight statements presented by Gyurme[18] is: 'All things that appear are manifestations of mind'. The term 'mind' in this section should be conceived as mind/Mind, thereby taking the dual aspect of mind into account. The associated sign is *Cancer the crab,* signifying the birthing of every thought that manifests as the aspects of mind/Mind. With the appearance of each thought the entire *maṇḍala* of the mind-continuum representing the truth of phenomena is established. The southernmost petal of the Throat centre is thereby indicated. From the point of view of the evolution of mind, the links of Dependent Origination (*pratītyasamutpāda*) are generated by such thoughts. They are ferried into expression as the boatman crosses the river from the banks of one Bardo to the next. (The first three links signify the stages of generation of mind.) Evans-Wentz's version is: 'In general, all things mentally perceived are concepts'.[19]
2. The next sign of the zodiac is *Leo the lion,* which governs the attributes of the self-conscious individual, who observes the 'surrounding environment which appears to be inanimate'.[20] At first such appearances are taken to be real, but inevitably it is found that all is mind because only in the mind can the phenomena contacted

18 Gyurme, 54.

19 Evans-Wentz's statements are from pages 233-234 of *The Tibetan Book of the Great Liberation.*

20 Gyurme, 54.

be experienced, catalogued and interpreted. Evans-Wentz's version is: 'The bodily forms in which the world of appearances is contained are also concepts of the mind'.

3. *Virgo the virgin,* the feminine principle, denoted as 'the great Mother' (even though astrologically depicted as a 'virgin') governs the evolution of the sum of the kingdoms of Nature. All therefore that evolves in *saṃsāra* manifest from out of her 'womb', a subject that was explained in part A with respect to the Consorts of the various deities, who embody this principle. The next phrase: 'The sentient life-forms which appear as the six classes of living beings'[21] therefore refers to her governance of these 'life-forms'. They too are seen as apparitions of mind by those that develop the perception to perceive life in the various Bardo realms. Evans-Wentz's version is: '"The quintessence of the six classes of beings" is also a mental concept'.
4. The next phrase is: 'The joys of both gods and humans of the higher existences which appear, they too are mind'.[22] Here we have the attributes of *Libra the balances* implicated, that rules the cycles of the manifestation of time and of *karma.* The *karma* reaped is joyous, because of the gain of the seeds sown earlier, of philanthropic deeds and altruistic actions, as a consequence of following the *dharma* and undertaking meditative pursuits. The western petal of the Throat centre (of outwards service to humanity) is thereby implied. Evans-Wentz's version is: '"The happiness of gods in heaven-worlds and of men" is another mental concept'.
5. *Scorpio the scorpion* rules the trials and tribulations of the testings in the field of Life. They concern eventual mastery of the energies of sex, money, material comforts, fear, ambition, hatred, pride, separativeness and cruelty. Those that have no control over such attributes generate the 'sorrows of the three lower existences which appear'.[23] Those with insight will see that 'they too are mind'. Evans-Wentz's version is: '"The three unhappy states of suffering", too, are concepts of mind'.
6. Next we have the *kleśas,* the 'five poisons, representing the dissonant

21 Ibid.

22 Ibid.

23 Ibid.

mental states of ignorance, which appear'.[24] They are delusion, attachment, aversion, pride and envy. These aspects of mind are projected into manifest activity by means of the selfish or self-centred personal will, as governed by the attributes of *Sagittarius the archer.* Evans-Wentz's version is: '"Ignorance, miseries, and the Five Poisons" are, likewise, mental concepts'.

7. *Capricorn the goat* now appears upon the wheel, who governs the entire mountain of mind/Mind, and of one's aspiration to climb, therefore to master it. Upon this northern petal of upwards to divinity, we have the appearance of the 'awareness, that is self-originating pristine cognition'.[25] We see that 'it too is mind'. Evans-Wentz's version is: '"Self-Originated Divine Wisdom" is also a concept of the mind'.
8. The attributes of *Aquarius the water bearer* now manifest. Aquarius dispenses the free-flowing compassionate energies embodied by the liberated Mind, and which governs the Bodhisattva path. The pitcher carrying this energy is generally depicted as being carried upon the shoulders, but is best depicted upon the Head, signifying the accumulative gain of wisdom, and enlightenment. The *bodhicitta* it bears is, however, poured from the Heart. This path is distinguished by the 'beneficial thoughts conducive to attainment of nirvāṇa'.[26] Evans-Wentz's version is: '"The full realization of the passing away into *Nirvāṇa"* is also a concept of mind'.
9. *Pisces the fishes* governs the stagnant swamp of *saṃsāra,* wherein exist the unsavory Watery, psychic, mediumistic and emotional *saṃskāras* generated. Here we find the 'obstacles of malevolent forces and spirits, which appear'[27] in consciousness. These psychic delusions and mischievous entities (elementals), the denizens of the entire astral swamp, as well as the projections by the dark brotherhood, need to be mastered by one on the path to liberation. Evans-Wentz's version is: '"Misfortune caused by demons and evil spirits" is also a concept of mind'.

---

24 Ibid.

25 Ibid.

26 Gyurme, 54.

27 Ibid.

10. *Aries the ram* governs the eastern petal of inwards to the Heart of Life. The Arian impetus awakens the Heart centre, producing the beginnings of things, of all that is impregnated with vital Life. Contemplation upon the way the Heart centre unfolds produces experience of the 'deities and [spiritual] accomplishments which manifest exquisitely'.[28] The practitioner knows that 'they too are mind'. The sublime spacious experiences producing the Heart centre's awakening also manifest as emanations of Mind. Evans-Wentz's version is: '"Gods and good fortune" are also concepts of mind'.
11. *Taurus the bull* governs the awakening of the all-seeing Eye and the wisdom that is embodied by the sweep of its vision. Here, therefore, we have the 'diverse kinds of pure [vision] which appear'.[29] Evans-Wentz's version is: 'Likewise, the various "perfections" are mental concepts.' In his commentary Evans-Wentz states that these perfections are those of the six *pāramitās,* which he describes as 'transcendent virtues'. They are: 'Charity, Morality, Patience, Industry, Meditation, Wisdom. Four others are sometimes added: Method, Prayer, Fortitude, Foreknowledge'.[30] Taurus governs the gain from the entire movement of the zodiacal wheel, whereby such virtues are developed. The development of wisdom from the desire to incarnate, through overcoming of the entire field of the desire principle, of thought-form building of what one wants in *saṃsāra,* is the major characteristic of this sign.
12. The final sign to be discussed, *Gemini the twins,* governs the temple of Initiation and the Holy of Holies veiled in the adytum of its sacred precincts. The associated phrase is ''The non-conceptual' one-pointed abiding [in meditation] which appears, it too is mind'.[31] This sign interrelates all of the dualities of the zodiac and governs the entire *nāḍī* system, where the *iḍā* and *piṇgalā nāḍīs* represent the pillars supporting this temple. The remaining four statements represent the north-south (the *iḍā* stream) and east-west (the *piṇgalā* stream) orientations of these two *nāḍīs.* They then embody the

---

28 Ibid.

29 Ibid.

30 Evans-Wentz, 234, footnote 3.

31 Gyurme, 54.

qualities of the four outermost petals of the Throat centre. These four petals were earlier related from a higher perspective (therefore needing a different zodiacal assignment) to the four bodies of a Buddha. The ultimate attainment of their qualities therefore rest in the *dharmakāya*. Evans-Wentz's version is: '"Unconscious one-pointedness" is also a mental concept'.

13. The statement 'The colours characteristic of objects which appear, they too are mind'[32] refers to the seven Rays and their sub-Rays. (They are the characteristics of divinity manifesting.) The western, outermost petal of the Throat centre is here implicated, wherein the radiance of the enlightened Mind shines outwards to flood humanity with wisdom. This direction was equated with the appearance of a *nirmāṇakāya* in the earlier account. Such an appearance emanates the Rays of light to convey the attributes of Mind into manifestation so that humanity can be appropriately educated. The Rays of light are but the vehicles for the emanation of Mind. As a great one speaks, so light is conveyed through space to help produce enlightenment to those that listen. The effect is to increase the quality and intensity of light that is the substance of their minds. Evans-Wentz's version is: 'The colour of any objective thing is also a mental concept'.

14. 'The state without characteristics and without conceptual elaboration which appears'[33] refers to *śūnyatā,* and therefore to the main characteristic associated with the major eastern petal of the Throat centre, which directs and receives *prāṇas* from the Heart centre. The text informs us, therefore, that even *śūnyatā* is an emanation of Mind. This is specifically so when accessed via this petal of the Throat centre, which also allows it to be the medium for the expression of *dharmakāya*. This is the attribute of the Buddha-body assigned to this direction in the earlier account. Evans-Wentz's version is: '"The Qualityness and Formless" is also a mental concept'.

15. 'The non-duality of the single and the multiple which appears'[34] refers to the integration of the multiple aspects of *saṃsāra* into the single nature of Mind. The gain is the non-duality of the *mahāmudrā,*

32 Ibid.

33 Ibid.

34 Ibid., 55.

of the integration between wisdom and compassion. This relates to the southern direction of the *maṇḍala* of the major petals of the Throat centre, where such integration must be accomplished, and was earlier relegated to the *sambhogakāya* of a Buddha. Evans-Wentz's version is: '"The One and the Many in at-one-ment" is also a mental concept'. The *sambhogakāya* aspect integrates 'the One' (the Sambhogakāya Flower) with 'the Many', the myriad petals of the Head lotus, and consequently the entire body's *nāḍī* system. All exists within the domain of mind/Mind.

16. The characteristics of the northern petal of the Throat centre is here given in terms of the phrase 'The unproveability of existence and non-existence which appears'.[35] This refers to the attributes of the *saṃsāra-śūnyatā* nexus, wherein an enlightened one resides if *saṃsāra* is to be liberated. The concept of 'unproveability' relates to the fact that the concrete mind cannot properly comprehend the nature of this nexus (the fount of the *dharmakāya),* as it can really only be known by actual residence there, however, it is an expression of the embrace of Mind. Existence, non-existence, both existence and non-existence and neither are the four arms of Nāgārjuna's *catuṣkoṭi,*[36] all of which can be conceived to be integrated at this nexus embodied by Mind. This then represents the supreme integrated Body of a Buddha *(svābhāvikakāya)* described in the earlier account. Evans-Wentz's version is: '"Existence and non-existence", as well as "the Non-Created", are concepts of the mind'. The gain of the appearances of phenomena (conceived as 'existence', but effectively is 'non-existence') must inevitably be abstracted into *dharmakāya* (conceived as 'non-existence', but effectively is 'Existence') as the proceeds of Mind.

Summary of the petals of the Heart centre

We now proceed to a brief exposé of the twelve petals of the Heart centre, indicating the way of appropriation of their qualities into the

35 Ibid.

36 The fourfold system of dialectical negation utilised by Nāgārjuna: the positive is negated, the negative, both, as well as neither. Also the four categories of existence: being, non-being, both being and non-being, neither being and non-being.

Heart tier of the Head lotus. They shall also be cursorily treated, mainly noting the signs of the zodiac the qualities can be attributed to. Because we are dealing with the attributes of the Heart centre, to which Nāgārjuna's *catuṣkoṭi* can be applied with respect to mind/ Mind, the text drops the qualifier that they or 'it too is mind', because the Heart centre naturally expresses the qualities of *śūnyatā* viewed in terms of it being the heart of what is conceived as Mind. The following statements of this analysis of Mind must therefore be interpreted in this light. The rectified wheel of the zodiac is now empowered, signifying the normal way of progression of evolutionary space, as governed by the energy of Life provided by the Heart centre.

1. We start with an iteration of the standard Yogācāra—Vijñānavādin assertion that 'There are no appearances at all apart from [those that originate in] the mind'.[37] Detailed explanation of this concept was provided in Volume 2 of this series. Its comprehension literally represents the beginning of our quest for comprehending what is and what is not, as signified by the first sign of the zodiac, the Fiery *Aries the ram*, who embodies the functions of the abstract Mind and whose energy impels the entire wheel of the zodiac onwards. One gains access to the appearance of *śūnyatā* by way of Mind. Under the heading 'The Realization of the Great Liberation' for this section Evans-Wentz's rendering is: 'Nothing save mind is conceivable'.[38]
2. *Taurus the bull* (an Earthy sign) clothes the originating Thought of the Logoic Mind (or the empirical mind of a human unit) with the substance of what is to be expressed. The body of substance of the *maṇḍala* to be projected into objectivity thus manifests. Our concern here, however, relates to the process that unclothes the substance of mind so that 'the appearance' of *śūnyatā* can be found. This process is indicated in the second line of the text: 'The unimpeded nature of mind assumes all manner of appearances'. Evans-Wentz's rendering is: 'Mind when uninhibited, conceives all that comes into existence'.
3. The third statement is governed by the attributes of the (Airy) sign *Gemini the twins* that prepares the thought-construct to enter into

37 This and the subsequent quotes from Gyurme appear on page 55 of his book.

38 This and the subsequent statements appear from pages 234 to 237 of Evans-Wentz's text.

objective manifestation. The entire expression of etheric space, containing the *nāḍīs* and *chakras,* to propel the *maṇḍala* of Thought into manifestation is thereby vivified. Here an objective duality is implied; of the thinker (the immortal brother) and the thought construct (the mortal brother); of mind and that which it perceives; *iḍā* and *piṅgalā nāḍīs;* male and female forces coming into view. This is a correct assumption for as long as *saṃsāra* exists. The corresponding statement of the text hints at this understanding, but brings our thoughts to the resolution of all these dualities into Oneness in the Mind that represents the *saṃsāra-śūnyatā* nexus: 'Yet though these [appearances] arise, they are without duality'. Evans-Wentz's statement for Gemini is: 'The state of mind transcendent over all dualities brings Liberation'.

4. Next we have the Watery sign, *Cancer the crab*, that produces the birthing of the *maṇḍala* from out of the Waters of astral space. Everything that appears is an expression of the (Logoic) Mind and is conditioned to evolve by means of the laws of thought-incentives built into the *maṇḍala* whilst formulating it. The ten stages of evolution, as previously explained, are the consequence. The corresponding statement is: 'And they [naturally] subside into the modality of mind, Like waves in the waters of an ocean'. This phrase refers to the return sequence of this evolutionary process when the attributes of *saṃsāra* are resolved into Mind as the *saṃskāras* are processed and transmuted. The objective is to calm the waves and ripples of the ocean of mind so that it reflects images of the Real, *śūnyatā*, leaving the Mind in its natural state. Evans-Wentz's rendering is: 'That which comes into existence is like the wave of an ocean'.

5. The next (Fiery) sign is that of *Leo the lion* that is concerned with the appearance of self-consciousness in Nature. Human units bearing minds thus appear that give names (implying all forms of intellectual discursions) to every aspect of phenomena. The entire gamut of human evolution (the pains, tribulations and triumphs) is therefore implied. All, however, is an expression of the One originating Mind and will inevitably be resolved back into it. The associated phrases of this sign allude to this process. Gyurme's rendering: 'Whatever names are given to these increasingly [arising] objects of designation,

In actuality, there is but one [single nature of] mind'. Evans-Wentz's rendering is: 'It matters not what name may carelessly be applied to mind; truly mind is one, and apart from mind there is naught else'.

6. We can now analyse the (Earthy) qualities of *Virgo the virgin* and the sum of the vicissitudes of Nature's kingdoms she embodies, which human minds must comprehend and master. In observing the sum of *saṃsāra* and the bewildering plethora of objects and lives therein, it is easy to be confused by the seeming separative nature of all that is perceived. Though the empirical mind has its foundations therein and evolves by means of the experiences derived from it, the expression of Mind has no attachment to *saṃsāra*. It is not based upon its illusions. The statement for this sign assures us that though all this is but the expression of mind/Mind, yet Mind has 'no foundation' or 'root' in *saṃsāra*. Its roots lie in the unimaginably vast duration of *dharmakāya,* which in turn is conceived to have no foundation or source. The statement given is: 'And that single [nature of mind] is without foundation and without root'. Evans-Wentz's rendering is: 'That Unique One Mind is foundationless and rootless'.
7. Next we have the Airy sign *Libra the balances*, which embodies the meditative interlude between any new cycle of expression. In meditating upon the phenomenon of *saṃsāra* and all its events and upon attaining *śūnyatā*, one sees that phenomena 'is not perceptible at all, in any direction whatsoever'. Accordingly, the meditating one then resides in the Void of the meditation-Mind. Therein four of the following five statements then signify the products of this meditation.[39] They are perceived in terms of the transmuted correspondences of the sense-consciousnesses, being the five Void Elements, as governed by the Rays of Mind. This verse relates to the third Ray of Mathematical Exactitude, which conditions the process of gaining enlightenment through meditation. As Amoghasiddhi's All-accomplishing Wisdom is the gain of the meditation, so Evans-Wentz's rendering is: 'There is nothing else to be realized'.
8. Now the Watery sign, *Scorpio the scorpion* can be considered, which concerns the mastery of the field of the desires and emotions. Here,

39 Statements 2-6 represent the non-sacred petals of the Heart centre, the others the sacred petals bearing the Ray qualities.

however, our focus is upon the material domain that is 'perceptible as substance'. The scorpion lives in the symbolic deserts of the material world bearing the stings and barbs signifying people's nasty, envious loquacious, petty and often spiteful conversations. Thus we have the *kāma-manasic* propensity of people. (Another symbol of this Watery sign is the murky swamp of emotions wherein resides the hydra of people's normal interactions.) All of this represented the field of testings that had been mastered by the meditating one. No matter in which direction the meditator views such emotional interactions he/she sees that they are 'not perceptible as substance', for they lack 'inherent existence in all respects'.[40] Ratnasambhava's Equalising Wisdom is the outcome of such meditation, producing the accompanying mastery of the Watery substance concerned (hence governed by Ray six of Devotion). Evans-Wentz's rendering is: 'The Non-Created is the Non-Visible'. This statement has a direct reference to the fact that the emotions are normally not visible (but can be felt). The sense of touch is implied.

9. The attributes of *Sagittarius the archer* (a Fire sign) are now evoked to project the meditation to its conclusion. Having purveyed the sum of *saṃsāra* the meditating Mind fires the arrows of realisation to experience *śūnyatā*. The related sense-consciousness is taste, involving the refinement of perception so that the subtlest of discernments can be experienced. The conclusion is that the manifestation of mind/Mind is 'not perceptible as emptiness, for it is the resonance of awareness and radiance'. Emptiness by definition is empty of mind, therefore it is not perceptible by mind. When Mind however rests in its natural state it is empty, thus cannot be perceived, but what resonates from it is the awareness and radiance that are the natural attributes of Mind. The qualities of the Mirror-like Wisdom of Akṣobhya (here implying the fourth Ray of Harmony overcoming Conflict) are developed at this stage of the meditation. Evans-Wentz's rendering is: 'By knowing the invisible Voidness and the Clear Light through not seeing them separately—there being no multiplicity in the Voidness—one's own clear mind may be known,

---

40 The actual statement from Gyurme is 'It is not perceptible as substance, for it lacks inherent existence in all respects'.

yet the Thatness itself is not knowable'. Thatness *(dharmakāya)* can only be directly experienced, then it can be embodied by Mind, but not known by mind. The mind has been supplanted by Mind.

10. We now come to the totality of the domain of mind/Mind, which perceives diversity in all things, and collates them into systems of knowledge. This totality is ruled by *Capricorn the goat* (an Earth sign). It incorporates the mount of mind/Mind that is responsible for the effects seen as *saṃsāra* as well as the vastness of *dharmakāya.* What is emphasised here is the Mind that is attained at the pinnacle of the mountaintop of experience by means of the Initiation process, that demonstrates 'the indivisibility of emptiness and radiance'. The smell sense-perceptor, that which perceives the subtlest impressions, is here transmuted into its Void Element. Thus here Vairocana, as the embodier of the entire meditation-field via his Dharmadhātu Wisdom is implied. It fuses radiance with emptiness. The Ray expressed is the fifth of Scientific Reason. Evans-Wentz's rendering is: 'Mind is beyond nature, but is experienced in bodily forms'.

11. The next (Airy) sign of the zodiac, *Aquarius the water bearer,* dispenses the energies that vitalises Life in all of its expressions. This energy is the highest possible to be experienced through the abstract Mind and manifests as the 'intrinsic awareness' of the enlightened. The associated phrase is 'This present intrinsic awareness is manifestly radiant and clear'. The sense-perceptor transmuted is that of sight, and the inevitable gain is Amitābha's Discriminating Inner Wisdom. Evans-Wentz's rendering is: 'The realization of the One Mind constitutes the All-Deliverance'. The concept of 'All-Deliverance' signifies the Bodhisattva path ruled by Aquarius. Here the various Ray permutations via Mind are conveyed via the seventh Ray of Ceremonial Activity.

12. The remainder of the section concerns the attributes of (the Watery) *Pisces the fishes*, and the termination of one cycle of expression, followed by the beginning of a new one. The phrases provided are: 'And even though there exists no known means by which it can be fabricated, And even though [this awareness] is without inherent existence, It can be experienced. [Thus], if it is experientially cultivated, all [beings] will be liberated'. The last sentence of the

passage refers in part to this recycling, rebirthing process and that it has to be 'experientially cultivated' whereby the zodiacal wheel is again experienced. Similarly, the Bodhisattvic activity of the enlightened manifests through various cycles of activity, whereby the qualities expressed by coursing through the zodiacal qualities associated with the petals of the Heart centre are utilised to help liberate all beings. The focus is the 'intrinsic awareness' of the previous phrase, which is the *bodhicitta* impelling the Bodhisattva. Here the compassionate stance of the many hands of Avalokiteśvara (whose guise the Bodhisattva assumes) touches the hearts of all beings via the second Ray of Love-Wisdom. That which is 'not fabricated' and 'without inherent existence' relates to the wisdom part of this Ray, and that which causes all beings to be liberated through its experiential cultivation refers to the compassionate part. This Ray becomes the universal pool of energy that is activated for expression during every new cycle of incarnation.

The overwhelming need is to transform the Watery emotional domain of others, whereby the selfish desire-mind is generated causing cyclic rebirth, into compassionate considerations productive of liberation.

There are five aspects to the 'intrinsic awareness' that define the five main attributes or planes of perception associated with the expression of Mind here. Two are provided in the earlier phrase (radiance and clarity) and three are provided above: 'it cannot be fabricated', 'without inherent existence' and it 'can be experienced'. Arranging them in their correct order, and in terms of the associated planes of perception, we have:

- *Not fabricated,* which refers to the *dharmakāya,* which is not fabricated by means of the attributes gained from *saṃsāric* activity. It is the Logoic Mind in expression, part of a cosmic ocean of Mind projected via the *sūtrātmā* (Life line) that joins the Monadic or Buddha-aspect of the bonded fishes to the meditating *nirmāṇakāya.* The plane of perception associated is termed *ātma* (the third cosmic ether, or greater).[41]

41 These planes of perception are explained in Volume 6 of this treatise.

- *Void (śūnyatā),* as it has no inherent existence (as far as manifesting phenomena is concerned, though it intrinsically exists), via which the intrinsic non-fabricated Mind expresses itself. The plane associated is the fourth cosmic ether, *buddhi.*
- *Radiance,* the energy of the Clear Light of Mind, an emanation of the highest (first) sub-plane of the mental.
- *Clarity,* or clarified Mind, the attribute of the second mental sub-plane, wherein mainly reside the Sambhogakāya Flowers. This clarity is the result of transformed *saṃskāras,* and manifests as the fusion between compassion and wisdom.
- *Experienceable,* the substance of the third mental sub-plane. It represents the abstract Mind, which overshadows the four concreted mental sub-planes associated with the process of gaining discursive information and experiences via *saṃsāric* wandering. A bridge (the *antaḥkaraṇa)* must be built between the lower and higher minds via the use of the will in meditation if enlightenment is to occur. Building such a rainbow bridge (sometimes depicted as coming from the minds of great ones in Buddhist art) is an important facet of the early meditative process, as there is a 'gap' in consciousness between the empirical and abstract portions of mind. This is one major reason why so many find higher metaphysical thought near impossible to comprehend.

Conclusion

The following concluding statements sum up the main points related to obtaining an enlightened Mind. The teachings are simplified, aiming to inspire those with perceptive intellects to gain enlightened propensities. The statements are arranged in terms of the seven sacred plus five non-sacred petals of the Heart centre, as they veil the attributes of the development of Love-Wisdom *(bodhicitta)* and the natural state of Mind. After quoting the statements from Gyurme's text I shall briefly note how the passages relate to the specific Ray aspects (the sacred petals), or to the development of the five attributes of Mind (the non-sacred petals).

First the seven Rays:

7. All those of all [differing] potential, regardless of their acumen or dullness,

   May realise [this intrinsic awareness].

6. However, for example, even though sesame is the source of oil, and milk of butter,

   But there will be no extract if these are unpressed or unchurned,

5. Similarly, even though all beings actually possess the seed of buddhahood,

   Sentient beings will not attain buddhahood without experiential cultivation.

4. Nonetheless, even a cowherd will attain liberation if he or she engages in experiential cultivation.

   For, even though one may not know how to elucidate [this state] intellectually,

   One will [through experiential cultivation] become manifestly established in it.

3. One whose mouth has actually tasted molasses,

   Does not need others to explain its taste.

   But, even learned scholars who have not realised [this single nature of mind] will remain the victims of bewilderment.

2. For, however learned and knowledgeable in explaining the nine vehicles they may be,

   They will be like those who spread fabulous tales of remote [places] they have never seen,

1. And as far as the attainment of buddhahood is concerned,

   They will not approach it, even for an instant.[42]

The numbers to these phrases are reversed according to the Ray qualifications that govern their expression.

7. First we have the seventh Ray of Ceremonial or Cyclic Activity that governs the material domain and the constant ceaseless toil associated with those that garner information from it. No matter

42 Gyurme, 56. I have added the numbers.

their acumen, as all have different potential, everyone who learns the lessons that *saṃsāra* has to teach has the capacity to know Mind.

6. The sixth Ray of Devotion governs all forms of emotional and desirous activity, as signified by the Watery domain. The key phrase in the corresponding passage is 'there will be no extract if these are unpressed or unchurned', which refers to the way that the emotions act. The extract refers to the *saṃskāras* that are developed and which must eventually be rightly processed by consciousness if the attributes of Mind are to evolve.
5. Next we have the fifth Ray of Scientific Reason governing the attributes of the mind. The mind is the 'seed of buddhahood' gained through continuous 'experiential cultivation', where impressions are evolved, analysed, regurgitated on a higher cycle, and asserted to be truthful, false or useful. A huge morass of thoughts thus pass by before the individual realises the need to tread the path to enlightenment, based upon the development of pure logical thought.
4. The fourth Ray of Beautifying Harmony overcoming Conflict is veiled in the process needed to experientially cultivate intellectuality so that liberation is gained. Such cultivation necessitates the overcoming of base *saṃskāras* of mind, hence the harmonising of consciousness. Beautifying harmony amongst humanity is the energetic effect of such an accomplishment. 'A cowherd' refers to average humanity (who are ruled by this Ray) that has the capacity to develop such wisdom.
3. Next we have the perspicacious intellectuality of the third Ray of enlightening, Mathematically Exact Activity of one who has tasted the essence of scholarly knowledge and intrinsically comprehended the single nature of Mind. Having gained from the entire gamut of experiences that *saṃsāra* (the strong taste of molasses) offers, and consequently having developed astute comprehension of its problems and their solutions, one need not to be taught the basics by others. Indeed, many of the prospective teachers will still be bewildered by *saṃsāra*.
2. The attributes of the second Ray of Love-Wisdom are veiled by the 'nine vehicles' of Buddhism, which represent the sum of the wisdom

developed by all of their philosophers. The revelations pertaining to such wisdom and its compassionate basis will travel far and wide, even though many of the more esoteric doctrines concerning the single nature of Mind will evade most people. The way such esotericism is veiled should by now be apparent to the readers of this Treatise on Mind.

1. The first Ray of Will or Power that produces the highest enlightenment is depicted in 'the attainment of buddhahood', which necessitates the use of the strongest Will to overcome *saṃsāra*. However, those who do not comprehend the esoteric doctrines 'will not approach' buddhahood. Evans-Wentz's rendering is:

> Without mastery of the mental processes there can be no realization.
>
> Similarly, although sesamum seed is the source of oil, and milk the source of butter, not until the seed be pressed and the milk churned do the oil and butter appear.
>
> Although sentient beings are of the Buddha essence itself, not until they realize this can they attain *Nirvāṇa.*
>
> Even a cowherd [or an illiterate person] may by realization attain liberation.[43]

This quote veils the development of the attributes of the five Jina wisdoms which are gained as a consequence of cyclic rebirth, implied by the symbolism of Pisces. Every new cycle of evolutionary expression represents one further step of developing the attributes of these wisdoms. Inevitably, every needed characteristic will be obtained. It should be restated here that the lowest five Rays are known as the Rays of Mind, and incorporate the general attributes of the Jina wisdoms.

The realisation gained through mastery of the 'mental processes' refers to the development of Amoghasiddhi's All-accomplishing Wisdom. The process or objective of such mastery is the metric by means of which the remaining passages of the quote are to be interpreted. It is the purpose for the continuous cyclic turning of the wheel of Life.

The oil derived from pressing the sesame seed refers to the development of the Equalising Wisdom of Ratnasambhava. It manifests

43 Evans-Wentz, 236-237. This extract is tacked on to the end of the section that dealt with the Heart centre in Evans-Wentz's version. After this he presents his general conclusion.

the driving energy that produces the quest for liberation. The churning of milk to produce butter represents the development of Amitābha's Discriminating Inner Wisdom. The milk is already a nutritious food, symbolising the activity of the mind, and through its churning the valuable butter, the abstract Mind is extracted. Similarly, the mind must be worked upon to produce enlightened perceptions. The development of Ratnasambhava's and Amitābha's Wisdoms are treated together because they deal with processing *kāma-manas* (desire-mind) into wisdom. (Transforming the desire portion being the focus of developing Ratnasambhava's attributes and the mind part represents developing those of Amitābha.)

The reference to the Buddha essence (*tathāgatagarbha*) and to the fact that all possess such a germ, plus the ability to attain *nirvāṇa,* implicates the development of Akṣobhya's Mirror-like Wisdom. The attributes of first the *tathāgatagarbha* and then *śūnyatā* are reflected into the Mind of one striving for liberation.

The attainment of liberation hints at the gaining of the Dharmadhātu Wisdom of Vairocana. Even an illiterate person can attain liberation if he/she sufficiently strives and develops the compassionate Will to do so. However, ahead of such a person lies the development of the mental assertions needed to generate and transform the necessary *saṃskāras,* and to obtain the meditative revelations that awaken Mind. As Evans-Wentz states: 'If, as assumed and as the colophon states, Padma-Sambhava composed this aphorism, he very probably had in mind as he formulated it his own cowherd pupil, Hūṃ-kāra, who attained such mastery of the occult sciences that he became a *guru* in his own right'.[44]

The statement below is from the beginning of Evans-Wentz's conclusion. It parallels the last three points of Gyurme's quotation above.

> Though lacking in power of expression, the author has here made a faithful record [of his own *yogic* experiences].
>
> To one who has tasted honey, it is superfluous for those who have not tasted it to offer an explanation of its taste.
>
> Not knowing the One Mind, even *pandits* go astray, despite their cleverness in expounding the many different doctrinal systems.

---

44 Ibid., 237, footnote 2.

> To give ear to the reports of one who has neither approached or seen the Buddha even for a moment is like harkening to flying rumours concerning a distant place one has never visited.
>
> Simultaneously with the knowing of the Mind comes release from good and evil.[45]

There are some noted differences here to Gyurme's account. First we have the statement relating to the author having made 'a faithful record [of his own *yogic* experiences]'. Next, instead of molasses to be tasted we have honey, which is sweet, and refers to gaining exalted experiences. Gyurme's account refers to the nine different doctrinal systems explained in chapter 8, whereas Evans-Wentz's version simply states that there are many that are expounded by *pandits* (learned ones); the concept of approaching or seeing the Buddha (within), even momentarily (signifying the nature of awakening intuition), etc.

The final part of this treatise is now presented, consisting of five statements wherein the development of the wisdoms of the Jinas is implicated. Together they embody the attributes of the 'single nature of Mind', as embodied by the Ādi Buddha, from whose wisdom theirs stems. Gyurme's translation states:

1. If this nature [of intrinsic awareness] is understood,
   Virtuous and negative acts will be liberated, right where they are.
2. But if this [single nature] is not understood,
   One will amass nothing but [future lives within] cyclic existence, with its higher and lower realms,
   Regardless of whether one has engaged in virtuous or non-virtuous actions.
3. Yet, if one's own mind is simply understood to be pristine cognition, [utterly] empty [of inherent existence],
   The consequences of virtuous and negative actions will never come to fruition—
4. For just as a spring cannot materialise in empty space,
   Within [the realisation of] emptiness, virtuous and negative actions do not objectively exist.
5. So it is that, for the purpose of nakedly perceiving the manifestly present intrinsic awareness,

45 Ibid., 237.

> This *Natural Liberation through Naked Perception* is most profound. Thus, [by following this instruction], one should familiarise oneself with this intrinsic awarensss.
>
> Profoundly Sealed![46]

1. The first statement relates to the development of the All-accomplishing Wisdom of Amoghasiddhi that comprehends the nature of intrinsic awareness, and thereby spontaneously eliminates all hindrances to liberation.
2. Next we have the process of those that need to continuously reincarnate, experiencing cycles of pleasure and pain (because of 'virtuous or non-virtuous actions'), mostly via emotional intensities. Inevitably Ratnasambhava's Equalising Wisdom is developed wherein all such experiences become equilibrated. In the developing wisdom *saṃskāras* are cleansed of impurities, refined and transmuted, whilst karmic propensities for good and bad are eliminated through the awakening intrinsic awareness.
3. Amitābha's Discriminating Inner Wisdom is then evoked as all attributes of mind are explored and 'understood to be pristine cognition' and empty of inherent existence. To do so the concretising tendencies of the empirical mind must be overcome and the bridges built to the higher abstract domains of Mind, to finally rest at the *śūnyatā-saṃsāra* nexus.
4. Akṣobhya's Mirror-like Wisdom, wherein *śūnyatā* acts as a mirror to reflect *dharmakāya* into *saṃsāra,* is now evolved. The imagery of the spring is utilised to symbolise the turbulence of the emotions. Once these emotions are eliminated then the obstacles to the spaciousness of Mind cease. The natural continuity of the mind follows. With emptiness 'virtuous and negative actions' are non-existent, as no actions manifest. Both virtuous and non-virtuous actions are *karma* forming, and the *karma* of earthly activities must inevitably cease if Buddhahood is to be the gain. Compassionate action, however, is the driving force productive of liberation, when coupled with proper Tantric practices. The compassion rides out

46 Gyurme, 56-7.

the fruits of past actions, reaping the rewards of former good deeds and annulling the negative ones. All people are consequently taught the way to liberation whilst the enlightened one acts out the path.

5. The Dharmadhātu Wisdom of Vairocana is experienced as the naked perception of intrinsic awareness. The entire text of *Natural Liberation through Naked Perception* (the Ati Yoga of the *Bardo Thödol*) then provides the answer of how to achieve this.

Note that even though these five stages appear consecutively, often a number are taken simultaneously. The affirmation 'Profoundly Sealed!' signifies the completion of the Initiation process associated with unfolding the path of meditation producing the resultant realisations of the wisdoms of these Jinas. The 'seal' is that of accomplishment, which closes the doors of the respective *chakras* that lead to lower cognitive states, and the fields of *saṃsāra*. Only that pertaining to liberated states then remains.

Instead of the phrase 'Profoundly Sealed!' Evans-Wentz's version presents 'It is the Vast Deep', which he states in his footnote that it is a translation of the Tibetan Zab-rgya, and states that this expression 'may be rendered in its fuller form as, "Deep and vast is Divine Wisdom [or this doctrine]"'.[47]

The conclusion is followed by a pithy invocation which is a worthy ending to a profound treatise on Mind.

> E-MA!
> This *Introduction to Awarenesss: Natural Liberation through Naked Perception*
> Has been composed for the sake of future generations, the sentient beings of a degenerate age.
> [It integrates] in a purposeful concise abridgement,
> All my preferred tantras, transmissions and esoteric instructions.
> Though I have disseminated it at this present time,
> It will be concealed as a precious treasure.
> May it be encountered by those of the future,
> Who have a [positive] inheritance of past actions.
> SAMAYA *rgya rgya rgya!*[48]

---

47 Evans-Wentz, 238, footnote 5.

48 Ibid., 57. See chapter 1 for the meaning of this mantra. There is also a final

That which was once concealed is now revealed,[49] the *maṇḍala* of perfection related to the yoga of knowing the nature of Mind is thus available to a far vaster audience than hitherto possible. The Dharmakāya Way can then be trodden to reveal the nature of the immaculate prescience of the Jinas. The various deities that play their roles will be comprehended as *saṃskāras* are transformed upon the journey to knowing Mind. Transformed, the mind becomes Mind, and the *tathāgatagarbha* stands revealed as a Buddha. What is revealed only such a Mind can say, as words then are no mind's play.

This is the fifth Volume of the series, wherein the teachings on the nature of mind/Mind come to an apogee. The remaining two volumes deal with various esoteric subjects that have their foundation in the teachings presented so far. Accordingly, they diverge somewhat from considerations phrased in terms of the Buddhist philosophy, nevertheless, by extension they are but definitions of the same philosophy manifesting via other religious terminology.

Oṁ Maṇi Padme Hūṁ! Hrih!

Oṁ is the nature of the revelation of what must be accomplished via consciousness. Yogically it evokes the middle way, the path that controls the manifestation of *suṣumṇā,* who's liberation awakens the complete potential of the Head Lotus.

Maṇi is the attainment of the purified *nāḍīs* enabling the radiance of Mind to purify space. The syllables *ma* and *ṇi* awaken the full potential of the *iḍā* and *piṇgalā nāḍīs,* which manifest as the radiant jewel (in the heart of each lotus). The integrated, fully cleansed, vibrant *nāḍī* system constitutes the diamond-Mind, the wish fulfilling gem (*cintāmaṇī*) of all enlightened ones.

Padme further awakens the petals of the *chakras* encompassing all sentient beings via the transforming effect of the radiance that

---

colophon stating that Padmākara (Padmasambhava), 'the preceptor of Oḍḍiyāna' is the author of this text.

49 The reference here is to Terma (gTer ma), a hidden spiritual treasure or text. We can see, therefore, that spiritual treasures can be hidden even in texts that are well known, such as the *Bardo Thödol*, and can only be revealed (by a Terton, a Tantric treasure revealer), who knows the hidden codes to their unveiling at the appropriate time.

purifies their habitation. The seed syllables *pa* and *(d)me* produce the unfoldment of all petals of the *chakras* in the body to the total boundaries of their potential.

Hūṁ is the resultant expansion of Mind in its natural state as the *vajra* of the Heart expands to exert its power over all of Nature. The Will-of-Love extends Nature's space as the *mahāmudrā* that is the union between the feminine substance and the masculine purpose when properly resonated from the deep reservoir of the Mind that is the Heart. The *vajra* is the diamond-Mind embodying the Rays of the combined wisdoms of the Jinas. Interrelated *vajras* produce the lines of escape from our planetary system. They also enable fully awakened Ones to encapsulate *dharmakāyic* spaces containing lesser Minds still attached to forms and direct them to cosmic shores. Many fleets of *vajra*-crafts built by great Bodhisattvas and Buddhas will eventually leave the confines of the sacred space of this earth to serve the 'Boundless All'[50] of cosmos. Divine Will then will resonate its purpose.

Hrih! Is the consequent emanative Sound summarising all that has been accomplished. It manifests as a penetrative and a protective agent. All tendencies to the perturbations of the mind have been sealed and can no longer influence the individual. Every attribute of *saṃsāra* has consequently been mastered and the lower four below the diaphragm can no longer manifest an enticing pull. Consequently, Hrih completes the mantra by resonating the expression of the great Seal throughout *saṃsāra,* to fully demonstrate mastery over all its attributes.

Oṁ Svāhā!

---

50 The phrase is taken from H.P. Blavatsky's, *The Secret Doctrine,* The Adyar Edition, (The Theosophical Publishing House, 1971), Vol. 1, 113-114.

Bibliography

Bailey, Alice A. *Esoteric Astrology.* London: Lucis Press, 1968.

Balsys, Bodo. *A Treatise on Mind, Volume 4.* Sydney: Universal Dharma Publishing, 2014.

——. *A Treatise on Mind, Volume 5A.* Sydney: Universal Dharma Publishing, 2015.

——. *A Treatise on Mind, Volume 6.* Sydney: Universal Dharma Publishing, 2014.

Blavatsky, H.P. *The Secret Doctrine. Vol. 1.* Adyar: Theosophical Publishing House, 1971.

Dorje, Gyurme. Trans., *The Tibetan Book of the Dead: The Great Liberation by Hearing in the Intermediate States.* London: Penguin Books, 2005.

Dudjom Rinpoche, *The Nyingma School of Tibetan Buddhism.* Translated by Gyurme Dorje and Matthew Kapstein. Boston: Wisdom, 1991.

Evans-Wentz, W.Y. *The Tibetan Book of the Dead.* London: Oxford University Press, 1960.

——. *The Tibetan Book of the Great Liberation.* London: Oxford University Press, 1954.

——. *Tibetan Yoga and Secret Doctrines.* London: Oxford University Press, 1967.

Govinda, Lama Anagarika. *Foundations of Tibetan Mysticism.* London: Century Paperbacks, 1987.

Lauf, Detlef Ingo. *Secret Doctrines of the Tibetan Books of the Dead.* Boston: Shambhala, 1989.

Thurman, Robert. *The Tibetan Book of the Dead.* New York: Bantam Books, 1994.

Index

A

Abstract Mind, 45, 70, 76–77, 135, 144, 177, 181
Ādi Buddha, 46, 149, 157, 158
  role in evolution, 30
Ādi Buddha Consort, 47, 149, 158
  role in evolution, 30
Ālayavijñāna, 14, 19
  enlightenment, 16–17, 135
  environment, 21, 94, 119, 146
Antaḥkaraṇa, 88, 159, 183
Arhat, 16–17
Arūpadhātu, 9, 11
Ati yoga, 10–13
Ātman, 16, 164
Avalokiteśvara, 49, 164, 182

B

Bījas, 18
Birth (four types), 105
Bodhicitta, 6, 64, 72, 78, 80, 106–107, 112, 124, 151, 162, 173, 182
  expression of, 21, 29–30, 45, 136
  generation of, 18, 32
Bodhisattva path, 18, 30, 45, 88, 95, 96–97, 166, 173, 181
Bodhisattvas (council of), 29–30
Buddhadharma, 10
Buddha/s
  of the three times, 5–6
  three bodies of, 2, 126–127, 128

C

Chakra
  Ājña, 46, 108
    in relation to Throat and Heart, 47–48
    in relation to Throat centre, 25, 38, 51
    petals of, 50
    symbiosis with Throat centre, 22–23, 35
  Base of Spine, 47, 56, 128, 137, 145, 152, 158
    in relation to four female gatekeepers, 99–102
    in relation to Throat centre, 38
  Diaphragm, 47
    eight petals, 71–75
    in relation to Mind, 70–75
  Gonad left / right, 125–126
    in relation to Īśvari of enrichment, 104, 147–153
    in relation to Īśvarī of subjugation, 104, 138–146
    in relation to Mind, 138–153

Head lotus, 56, 102, 120, 145, 152
in relation to full awakening, 128
in relation to Throat centre, 38
major tiers, 51–52, 155
petals and the zodiac, 157–170
Heart, 46, 56, 65, 71, 89, 99, 102, 106–108, 110, 120, 126, 127–128, 131, 148, 150, 174, 182
in relation to Mind, 39–45, 68, 176–182
in relation to Throat centre, 38
in the Head, 35, 51, 155
main petals, 53
Liver centre, 72–73, 117–118, 150–151
Lung centres, 74
Maṇipūra. *See* Solar Plexus centre
Mūlādhāra. *See* Base of Spine centre
Sacral, 56, 108, 127–128, 137, 145, 152, 165
in relation to Īśvarī of wrath, 104, 121–129
Solar Plexus, 47, 75, 84, 124, 145, 152
in relation to Gatekeepers of emanational rites, 103
in relation to Īśvarī of pacification, 113–121
in relation to Throat centre, 38
in the Head, 36, 51, 155
Splenic centre I, 47, 155
in relation to Mind, 86–98
in relation to Throat centre, 38
Splenic centre II, 47, 72, 123
Stomach centre, 72–73, 74–75, 115, 116, 142–143
Svādiṣṭhāna. *See* Sacral centre
Throat, 46, 56, 74, 89, 95
four major petals, 31–39
in relation to Mind, 19–30, 31–39, 50, 58
in the Head, 34, 51, 155
main petals, 53–54, 170–176
symbiosis with Ājñā, 22–23
Viśuddha. *See* Throat centre
Chakras
above the diaphragm, 1–61, 48–55
below the diaphragm, 54
awakened, 62–68
in relation to seven Rays, 129–138
in relation to number 12, 106–107
Cittavṛtti, 27, 70
Clear Light, 7, 85
of Mind, 19, 23, 28, 76–79, 79
Consciousnesses, eight, 16, 23, 49, 51
Cross
cardinal, 37, 89, 97
fixed, 34, 37–38, 86, 88, 115, 123
mutable, 37, 39, 88, 108

D

Ḍākinīs, five Jñāna, 159–163
Buddha Ḍākinī, 159
Karma Ḍākinī, 162
Padma Ḍākinī, 161
Ratna Ḍākinī, 161
role in evolution, 159
Vajra Ḍākinī, 160
Ḍākinīs, Wisdom. *See* Ḍākinīs, five Jñāna
Dark brotherhood, 165, 173
Dependent Origination, 15, 171
Deva/s, 52
kingdom, 18, 27
Dhāraṇī, 23, 28, 33, 61, 149
Dharmadhātu, 18, 56, 107, 111
Dharmakāya, 27–28, 30–31, 94, 98, 110, 144, 152, 157, 175–176, 179

enlightenment, 18
environment, 21, 44, 74, 79, 121, 158
in relation to Throat centre, 33
karma, 42
space of the Dhyāni Buddhas, 14
Dharmakāya Way, 10, 48, 98, 110, 112, 143, 191
Dhyāni Buddha Consorts, 69
Samayatārā, 59
Dhyāni Buddhas, 46
Akṣobhya, 12, 14, 33–34, 56–57, 68, 70, 89, 91–93, 104, 107, 116, 137, 146, 160, 162, 180, 187, 189
Amitābha, 12, 15, 36, 58, 69, 89, 90–92, 95–96, 104, 107, 115, 137, 146, 161, 162, 181, 186, 187
Amoghasiddhi, 12, 14–15, 37, 59, 70, 89, 91–92, 94–95, 104, 107, 111, 116, 138, 145–146, 162, 163, 186–187, 189
as sources of Mind, 13–15
colours of, 56–57
developing attrubutes of, 186–190
in relation to Ati yoga, 12–13
in relation to five poisons, 137–138
in relation to Īśvarī, 103–104
in relation to Mind, 67–70
in relation to Solar Plexus centre, 115–121
in relation to Splenic centre I, 89–98
in relation to Throat centre, 31–37
mudras, 91–92
Ratnasambhava, 12, 15, 35, 57–58, 69, 89, 91–92, 96–97, 104, 107, 111, 115, 138, 146, 162, 186, 189
Vairocana, 13, 14, 33, 55–56, 57, 68–69, 103, 106–107, 111, 137, 146, 159, 181–182, 189, 190
Directions of space, eight, 14–15, 16–19, 48, 49, 51
east, 5, 14, 17, 24, 33–34, 78
in relation to Mind, 4–7, 46
in relation to Sambhogakāya Flower, 76–86
north, 6–7, 14–15, 16–17, 36, 79
northeast, 4, 17, 81–82, 109
northwest, 6, 18, 82–83, 109
south, 5–6, 15, 18, 35, 83–84
southeast, 5, 17, 84, 110
southwest, 6, 19, 85–86, 108
west, 6, 15, 19, 35, 80–81

E

Eightfold Path, 8, 166
Elements
Aether, 51, 54, 56, 69, 102
Air, 59, 70, 89, 102
Earth, 36, 70, 89, 140–141, 148
Fire, 26, 58, 69, 89, 105, 149
Water, 57, 66, 69, 89, 101, 103–104, 121, 142, 149, 150–151

F

Five poisons, 137–138, 172
Four Noble Truths, 8

G

Gatekeepers, four female, 46, 99–102, 110–112
Aṅkuśā, 111
Ghaṇṭā, 111
in relation to Base of Spine, 105
Pāśā, 111
Sphoṭā, 111
Guardians of four gates, 46–47, 48, 51, 53–55
Guardians of four gates Consorts, 47, 51, 53–55
Guṇa/s, 38
three, 44, 90

H

Heruka Consorts

Krodheśvarī, 156
role in evolution, 159–160
Samayatārā, 156, 158
Herukas
Mahottara Heruka, 156
Vajrakīla Heruka, 156, 158

I

Initiation, 28, 29, 47
Initiation process, 190
Īśvarī, twenty-eight
four enacting emanational rites, 108–109
in relation to Solar Plexus, 103, 105–106
Vajrā Lambodarā, 108
Vajrā Mahāchāgalā, 110
Vajrā Mahākālī, 109
Vajrā Mahākumbhakarṇī, 109
in relation to Mind, 103–113
six demonstrating rites of pacification
Brahmāṇī, 121
Indrāṇī, 118
in relation to Solar Plexus, 103–104, 113–121
Kaumārī, 117
Manurākṣasī, 119
Raudrī, 115
Vaiṣṇāvī, 116
six enacting rites of subjugation
Bhakṣasī, 140
Ekacāriṇī Rākṣasī, 142–143
in relation to Gonad centre, 104, 139–147
Manohārikā, 143
Ratī, 141
Rudhiramadhī, 142
Siddhikarī, 144
six manifesting rites of wrath
Agnāyī, 127
Bhujanā, 128, 137
Cāmuṇḍī, 124
in relation to Sacral centre, 104, 121–129
Varāhī, 126
Varuṇānī, 123
Vāyudevī, 125
six projecting rites of enrichment
Amṛtā, 149
Daṇḍī, 151
in relation to Gonad centres, 104, 147–153
Rakṣasī, 151
Śāntī, 148–149
Saumī, 150
Vajrā, 148

J

Jinas. *See* Dhyāni Buddhas

K

Kāmadhātu, 9, 11
Karma
cleansing of, 28, 55, 83
expression of, 78, 172
universal, 4
Kliṣṭamanas, 18, 169
Kuṇḍalinī, 158
awakening of, 47, 105, 106–107, 128, 144
channeling of, 102, 152, 154
in relation to Throat centre, 31

M

Mādhyamika, 1, 15
Mahābodhisattvas, 47, 51, 54
consorts, 47, 51, 54
Mahāmudrā, 17, 134, 175
Mahāyāna, 15, 16, 86–87, 90
Manasic substance, 16–17, 165, 168
via throat petals, 19–31
Mantras, 50, 58
e-ma-ho, 4
kye ho, 7
Oṁ Maṇi Padme Hūṁ, 191–192
Mātaraḥ, the eight
in relation to diaphragm, 71

Mind
- abstract, 45, 70, 76–77, 144, 177, 181
- as radiant awareness, 24
- clear light of, 19, 23, 28, 76–79, 79
- concrete, 66, 70, 76, 136, 144, 179
- dharmakāyic, 4, 7, 35
- in relation to Diaphragm, 70–75
- in relation to Gonad centres, 138–153
- in relation to Heart centre, 39–45, 176–182
- in relation to Īśvarī, 103–113
- in relation to Jinas, 67–70
- in relation to Peaceful Deities, 46–55
- in relation to Sacral centre, 121–129
- in relation to Sambhogakāya Flower, 76–86
- in relation to seven Rays, 62–67, 129–138, 183–186
- in relation to Solar Plexus centre, 113–121
- in relation to Splenic centre I, 86–98
- in relation to Throat centre, 19–30, 31–39, 170–176
- natural state of, 11, 26, 40
- single nature of, 4–7
- synonyms for, 13–15

Monad, 111

N

Nāḍīs
- iḍā, 17, 21, 24, 26, 41, 46, 54, 72–73, 75, 88, 105, 114–115, 124, 132, 170
- piṇgalā, 18, 21, 26, 39, 41, 46, 54, 72–73, 105, 109, 117–118, 127, 131, 148, 170
- suṣumṇā, 21, 26, 44, 46, 73–74, 86–87, 89, 102, 128, 130

Nāḍī system, 26, 35, 57, 59, 111, 117, 120, 160, 169, 174

Nexus
- śūnyatā-saṃsāra (saṃsāra-śūnyatā), 4, 15, 24, 26–28, 34, 74, 77, 94, 98–99, 111, 112, 118, 126, 128, 132, 134, 143, 159, 162, 176, 189

Nirmāṇakāya, 2, 30, 112, 175, 182
- in relation to Throat centre, 35–36

Numerology
- of chakras above diaphragm, 49–52
- the number 7, 5
- the number 12, 106–107
- the number 24, 49–50
- the number 44, 53
- the number 84, 5

P

Peaceful Deities, (fourty-two)
- in relation to Mind, 46–55
- in relation to Throat centre, 53–54

Personal-I, 25, 42, 58, 73, 80–85, 88, 97, 116, 120, 124, 143

Planes of perception, 156, 182–183
- mental sub-planes, 129–138

Pond (symbolism), 145

Prajña (definition), 14

Prajñāpāramitā, 17

Pratītyasamutpāda. *See* Dependent Origination

R

Ray aspects, 5, 16, 22
- 1st ray, 64, 130–131, 186
- 2nd ray, 64–65, 109, 131, 181, 182
- 3rd ray, 59, 65, 132, 185
- 4th ray, 58, 65–66, 130–131, 132–133, 136, 160, 180, 185
- 5th ray, 58, 66, 132–133, 136, 161, 184, 185

6th ray, 60, 66–67, 134–135, 136, 185
7th ray, 61, 67, 133–134, 134–135, 163, 181, 184
in relation to chakras, 108
in relation to Mind, 62–68, 107, 129–138, 175, 183–186
rDzogs-Chen, 11, 117
Rūpadhātu, 9, 11

S

Sacral centre, 46
Śamatha, 39, 41, 67, 101, 126
Samaya, 69
definition of, 3
Sambhogakāya, 176
in relation to Throat centre, 35
Sambhogakāya Flower, 2, 17, 35, 111, 132, 146, 176
influences on, 60–61, 161
in relation to Dhyāni Buddhas, 70
in relation to Mind, 76–86
Knowledge petals, 78–80, 82–86, 86
Love-Wisdom petals, 78, 80–83, 84, 86
Sacrifice petals, 77–81, 86
Saṃsāra-śūnyatā nexus. *See* Nexus, Saṃsāra-śūnyatā
Saṃskāras
manasic, 73
transformation of, 43, 75, 101, 125, 132
Sense-consciousness
hearing, 17, 70, 104, 137
sight, 19, 69, 104, 136, 181
sixth sense (intellect), 19, 49
smell, 18, 69, 103, 135, 181
taste, 17, 70, 104, 136, 180
the five, 22, 38, 49, 52, 58, 160
touch, 17, 69, 104, 180
Shambhala, 47
Siddhis, 153
awakening of, 74, 107, 110
demonstration of, 167
premature development, 32
supramundane, 47
Six Realms, 8–9, 46, 49–51, 54, 165–170
animal, 168–169
asura, 59, 166
experience in Bardo, 55–61
god, 56, 59, 167–168
hell, 165–166
human, 166–167
preta, 59, 169
Skandha/s, 57–58, 99–102
definition of, 100
rūpa, 57, 100–101
samjñā, 58, 102
saṃskāra, 101
vedanā, 58, 101
vijñāna, 57, 106
Śūnyatā, 27, 74, 79, 85, 97, 144, 149, 166, 175, 177, 183, 187
enlightenment, 17
mirror, 12
Śūnyatā Eye, 61, 77, 82
Sūtrātmā, 18, 182
Svabhāvikakāya, 176
definition of, 31
in relation to Throat centre, 33, 36–37

T

Tathāgatagarbha, 2, 17, 30, 42, 52, 60, 76–86, 97, 132, 159, 187, 191. *See also* Sambhogakāya Flower
Thoughts, expression of, 79
Three times, the, 21, 98–102, 105
Two truths, 14, 34, 37, 110, 117, 143

V

Vajra, 31
Vidyādhara Consorts, 60
role in evolution, 47, 52, 54, 160
Vidyādharas, 60–61
role in evolution, 47, 52, 54
Vipassanā, 39, 42

Viśvavajra, 37
Void, the, 26, 27, 43, 64, 79, 101–102, 112, 116, 118–119, 126–127, 142–143, 179
  three, 44

W

Wrathful Deities, 67
  principal function, 32, 47, 61, 71

Y

Yogācāra, 1, 15, 16, 67, 120, 177–182

Z

Zodiac, 5, 51
  Aquarius the water bearer, 30, 34, 38, 45, 95, 161–162, 173, 181–182
  Aries the ram, 24, 30, 40, 93, 157–159, 174, 177–178
  Cancer the crab, 26, 41, 96–97, 168–169, 171–172, 178
  Capricorn the goat, 29, 44, 94, 162–163, 173, 181
  Gemini the twins, 25–26, 41, 97–98, 169–170, 174, 177
  in relation to Head centre, 157–170, 170–176
  in relation to Heart cemtre, 177–183
  in relation to Splenic centre I, 89–97
  in relation to Throat, 23–31, 31–38
  Leo the lion, 26–27, 34, 36, 38, 42, 97, 167–168, 171, 178
  Libra the balances, 28, 43, 95, 166, 172–173, 179
  Pisces the fishes, 30–31, 45, 94–95, 159–160, 173, 181, 186
  Sagittarius the archer, 29, 44, 95, 164–165, 173, 180
  Scorpio the scorpion, 28, 34–35, 35, 38, 43, 96, 165, 172, 179
  Taurus the bull, 25, 34, 37–38, 40–41, 93, 170, 174–175, 177
  Virgo the virgin, 27, 42, 96, 166–167, 172, 179

About the Author

BODO BALSYS is the founder of The School of Esoteric Sciences. He is an author of many books on subjects centred on Buddhism and the Esoteric Sciences, a meditation teacher, poet, artist, spiritual scientist and healer. He has studied extensively across multiple traditions including Esoteric Science, Buddhism, Christianity, Esoteric Healing, Western Science, Art, Politics and History. His advanced esoteric insights, gained through decades of meditative contemplation, enable him to provide a rich understanding of the spiritual pathway toward enlightenment, healing and service.

Bodo's teachings can be accessed via the School of Esoteric Science's website:
http://universaldharma.com

For any other enquiries, please email
sangha@universaldharma.com

About Universal Dharma Publishing

Universal Dharma Publishing is a not for profit publisher. Our aim is make innovative, original and esoteric spiritual teachings accessible to all who genuinely aspire to awaken and serve humanity. The books published aim in part to provide an esoteric interpretation of the meaning of Buddhist *dharma* with view of reformation of the way people perceive the meaning of the related teachings. Hopefully then Buddhism can more effectively serve its principal function as a vehicle for enlightenment, and further prosper into the future. A further aim is to provide the next level of exposition of the esoteric doctrines to be revealed to humanity following on the wisdom tradition pioneered by H.P. Blavatsky and A.A. Bailey.

Cover Design by
Angie O'Sullivan & Kylie Smith

www.ingramcontent.com/pod-product-compliance
Lightning Source LLC
Chambersburg PA
CBHW021841220426
43663CB00005B/342